MASCULINITIES
AND CULTURE

ISSUES in CULTURAL and MEDIA STUDIES

Series editor: Stuart Allan

Published titles

News Culture
Stuart Allan

Television, Globalization and Cultural Identities
Chris Barker

Cultures of Popular Music
Andy Bennett

Masculinities and Culture
John Beynon

Cinema and Cultural Modernity
Gill Branston

Ethnic Minorities and the Media
Edited by Simon Cottle

Modernity and Postmodern Culture
Jim McGuigan

Sport, Culture and the Media
David Rowe

Compassion, Morality and the Media
Keith Tester

MASCULINITIES AND CULTURE

John Beynon

OPEN UNIVERSITY PRESS
Buckingham · Philadelphia

Open University Press
Celtic Court
22 Ballmoor
Buckingham
MK18 1XW

email: enquiries@openup.co.uk
world wide web: www.openup.co.uk

and
325 Chestnut Street
Philadelphia, PA 19106, USA

First Published 2002

A catalogue record of this book is available from the British Library

ISBN 0 335 19988 7 (pb)   0 335 19989 5 (hb)

Library of Congress Cataloging-in-Publication Data
Beynon, John.
     Masculinities and culture/John Beynon
         p. cm. – (Issues in cultural and media studies)
     Includes bibliographical references and index.
     ISBN 0-335-19988-7 – ISBN 0-335-19989-5 (alk. paper)
         1. Masculinity–Philosophy.   2. Masculinity–Public opinion.
         3. Masculinity in popular culture.   4. Sex role.   I. Title.   II. Series.

HQ1090 B484 2001
305.31–dc21
                                                                                    2001036104

Typeset by Type Study, Scarborough
Printed in Great Britain by Biddles Limited, Guildford and Kings Lynn

CONTENTS

The urgent need to challenge the cultural construction of masculinity has long been an organizing imperative of feminist and gender-sensitive research in cultural and media studies. Frequently singled out for particular attention by researchers, amongst other concerns, is the extent to which media representations help to reproduce (and thereby reinforce as *normal*) cultural configurations of femininity and masculinity as being *naturally* determined by sexual difference. This kind of essentialist language and imagery typically works to privilege 'masculine' discourses about the world (deemed objective, rational and unitary) over and above 'feminine' ones (held to be subjective, irrational and fragmented) in ideological terms. For these researchers, then, seemingly *common sensical* media representations of masculinity need to be interrogated in ways which avoid tacitly reaffirming as *legitimate* or *appropriate* what are patriarchal assumptions about gendered and sexualized identities, subjectivities and experiences.

In seeking to further extend a critical understanding of the cultural politics of masculinity, John Beynon's *Masculinities and Culture* makes an exciting intervention into current debates. His dicussion centres from the outset on the tensions engendered between discourses of 'maleness', based on a conception of physiological difference, and those of 'masculinity' as a complex set of cultural constructions. At issue, in his view, is the need to examine masculinity as it is inflected in culturally specific ways so as to better account for how it is shaped by such factors as class, ethnicity, sexuality, age, nationality and so forth. Here Beynon makes key distinctions between 'masculinity-as-experienced', 'masculinity-as-enacted' and 'masculinity-as-represented', the latter referring primarily to depictions of *what it is to be a man* in media texts such as films, literature, men's magazines, advertisements, and television. This approach enables him to engage with media accounts of the so-called 'crisis in masculinity' in a way that demonstrates precisely why the concept of a single, fixed and unified masculinity is untenable. Accordingly, in documenting a wide array of socially constructed 'masculinities', ranging from 'Imperial Man' to the 'new lad' and beyond, Beynon elucidates their contradictory, fragmented and contingent enactment in a variety of everyday contexts. This book offers a timely and absorbing exploration of an acutely important area of inquiry, and will be warmly welcomed by readers prepared to recast familiar premises about what counts as masculinity today.

The Issues in Cultural and Media Studies series aims to facilitate a diverse range of critical investigations into pressing questions considered to be central to current thinking and research. In light of the remarkable speed at which the conceptual agendas of cultural and media studies are changing, the authors are committed to contributing to what is an ongoing process of re-evaluation and critique. Each of the books is intended to provide a lively, innovative and comprehensive introduction to a specific topical issue from a fresh perspective. The reader is offered a thorough grounding in the most salient debates indicative of this book's subject, as well as significant insights into how new modes of enquiry may be established for future explorations. Taken as a whole, then, the series is designed to cover the core components of cultural and media studies courses in an imaginatively distinctive and engaging manner.

Stuart Allan

INTRODUCTION AND ACKNOWLEDGEMENTS

The book is structured as follows. Chapter 1 raises general issues and debates about gender, masculinity and 'masculinities'. Chapter 2 introduces a historical dimension by examining the construction of masculinities in the Age of Empire. Chapter 3 reviews four interdisciplinary ways in which masculinities have been critically studied and theorized to date. Chapter 4 focuses on the assertion that contemporary men or masculinity, even both, are in a chronic state of 'crisis'. Chapter 5 investigates the origins of the so-called 'new man' and looks at the commercialization of masculinity, something that accelerated during the 1980s and 1990s. Chapter 6 examines the discursive construction of 'Millennium masculinity' in both the British broadsheet press and in popular books over the millennium. Finally, Chapter 7 details six 'research modes' by which masculinities might be studied in different ways and by drawing upon a wide variety of data. Throughout I have tried to write a book which is wide ranging and has intellectual breadth as well as depth. Accordingly I have drawn upon a range of sources, including literature, history, popular culture (in particular film and television), magazines and the broadsheet press, sociology, ethnography, anthropology, as well as cultural, media and literary studies. While the Glossary contains many terms with which readers will be familiar, it (nevertheless) makes an important contribution to the book and provides a summary of the main topics.

Writing is a solitary business at the best of times and one in which the author is constantly reminded of the immense debt owed to others. I want, therefore, to record my warm gratitude to the following, each of whom contributed, whether in large or small part, to this book's appearance:

- Members of the University of Glamorgan Policy Centre, who granted me teaching remission for part of 2000–01. Without this, *Masculinities and Culture* would never have seen the light of day.
- My immediate friends and colleagues in Media and Cultural Studies in the School of Humanities and Social Sciences (HASS), in particular Tom O'Malley and Philip Mitchell. Since succeeding me as Subject Head of Media-Culture Tom could not have done more to ensure that I completed the manuscript of this book on time. I am equally in debt to Gabrielle Vernon, who has now taken over as Co-ordinator of the European Media and Cultural Studies Network.
- Much-valued friends/colleagues (in alphabetical order) in HASS, namely Steve Blandford, Penny Byrne, Mike Connolly, David Dunkerley, Colin Gent, Peter Jachimiak, Gary Llewellyn, Maggie McNorton, Milena Morgan, Ieuan Morris, Chris Peters, Tony Powell, Adrian Price, Jane Prince, Erin Striff, Andy Thompson and Diana Wallace, along with many others too numerous to mention.
- Stuart Allan, for his gentle encouragement from the outset and helpful editorial comments in the latter stage of the project; and Justin Vaughan and Christine Firth at the Open University Press, Buckingham, both excellent professionals with whom to work.
- Carl Davis, the proprietor of Dolphin Books, not only for keeping me supplied with reading matter but also for his bibliographical endeavours on my behalf. Likewise, staff in the University of Glamorgan Learning Resources Centre (notably Bill Newman and Alan Cotton); Cardiff University Library; Senate House Library, London University; Central Missouri State University Library; and the British Film Institute, London, in particular the ever-helpful Ian O'Sullivan.
- The many authors on whose work I draw. I am particularly indebted to Michael A. Budd for his highly original study of Victorian bodybuilding (Chapter 2); and to Frank Mort, Sean Nixon and Tim Edwards for their charting of the commercialization of masculinity during the 1980s and 1990s (Chapter 5).
- This book is the product of teaching about masculinities over some years and is intended to feed back into teaching. I want to thank, therefore, the many past and present undergraduate students of the 'Men, Masculinities and Culture' module in HASS, particularly Adam Gerrish and Maggie Magor, to whose unpublished studies I make passing reference. I am, also, particularly appreciative of two current doctoral students, Peter Jachimiak and Richard Thurston. Both Peter and Richard are engaged in researching in the area of men and masculinities and I briefly refer to their ongoing work.

- The staff of 'Hilltop' Hospital; 'Victoria Road' Comprehensive; and 'Green Acres' Junior School for allowing me to carry out the field studies briefly referred to in Chapter 7.
- The organizers of conferences to which embryonic versions of this book were delivered from 1998 to date at Manchester University; Aberystwyth University; the University of Lodz British Studies Centre, Poland; Nottingham University; Warwick University; the London University Institute of Education; the University of Santiago de Compostela; the University of Wales Conference Centre at Gregynog Hall, Newtown, Powys; and to the HASS Staff Research Seminar, University of Glamorgan. I would particularly like to thank contributors to the 'Posting the Male' International Conference held at Liverpool John Moores University in August 2000, organized by Berthold Schoene-Harwood and Daniel Lea. This impressive gathering proved, if proof was needed, the variety and vitality of contemporary research into masculinities. 'Posting the Male' took place as I was writing Chapter 7, 'Researching Masculinities Today'. It is no coincidence, therefore, that many references to the excellent state-of-the-art papers delivered at Liverpool John Moores feature prominently therein.
- My family, Helen, Sarah and David. I am immensely grateful to Helen for conjuring the well-ordered references out of illegible scribbles on numerous scraps of paper.
- Finally, it is particularly appropriate that I should dedicate this book to the memory of my father, Walter Beynon (1903–74). He was brought up surrounded by the adventure stories of Empire and his childhood coincided with the long 'Edwardian summer' of Imperial ascendancy. At the age of 15 he did something straight out of the pages of *Treasure Island* and *Coral Island*: he cast aside his comfortable surroundings and ran away to sea, the words of a music hall song popular at the time no doubt ringing in his ears:

> Daring boys till the end of time
> In every age and clime
> Will run away to sea,
> Having little notion of the mighty ocean
> When it is in commotion
> Or how sick they'll be!
> Life on shore is such a bore
> Whilst on the deep they will surely reap
> Wealth and fame . . .

Thereafter he travelled to every far-flung corner of the then British Empire. Writing Chapter 2 helped me to understand him a little better.

John Beynon
University of Glamorgan
Trefforest, Wales, UK

1 | WHAT IS MASCULINITY?

Terry: 'When I was a lad, things weren't half as complicated as they are today. A man was a man and a woman was a woman. That was it, no argument! Now you don't know where you are! . . .'
(Background chorus of 'Yea, that's right, that is!', etc.)
   '. . . You've only got to look around at the people who come into this place to see what I mean. They look different and they behave differently from when I was their age. There's blokes that come in here who hug and kiss each other and there's women who weight train and kick box. One of them even applied for the Marines! There's no doubt about it: man-woman-wise, everything's gone arse over tit, if you don't mind my French!'
                     (Front bar of the Park Hotel, 'Seatown', South Wales, October 2000)

Introduction: 'masculinity' or 'masculinities'?

One thing has to be made crystal clear at the outset: 'masculinity' is composed of many **masculinities**, as this book will illustrate repeatedly and which is reflected in the title. Each chapter explores or points to the existence of a range of masculinities for, while all men have the male body in common (although even that comes in a variety of sizes, shapes and appearances), there are numerous forms and expressions of **gender**, of 'being masculine' and 'being feminine'. Masculinity is always interpolated by cultural, historical and geographical location and in our time the combined influence of feminism and the gay movement has exploded the conception of a uniform masculinity and even sexuality is no longer held to be fixed or innate. As a result it is becoming ever more fashionable to employ the term 'masculinities' (as do, for example, Buchbinder 1994; Connell 1995; Mac an Ghaill 1996) both to reflect our **new times** (Hebdige 1989) and to expose the cultural construction and expression of masculinity to closer and more exacting critical scrutiny. It is hardly surprising that when first encountered, the plural form surprises because it contradicts the widely held, commonsensical assumption that masculinity is a standardized container, fixed by biology, into which all 'normal' men are placed, something 'natural' that can even be measured in terms of psychological traits and physical attributes. But when we link masculinity to culture (itself, obviously, hugely varied) it immediately becomes evident that in terms of enactment masculinity is a diverse, mobile, even unstable, construction. So, let me emphasize this: whenever 'masculinity' appears it should not be read as implying uniformity but, on the contrary, variety and fragmentation. (In fact, it is best regarded as a 'singular-plural', much like 'data', that can take many different forms.) Indeed, readers are urged to list the range of masculinities they have encountered at the end of each chapter: by the end of the book that list will be considerable.

If 'maleness' is biological, then masculinity is cultural. Indeed, masculinity can never float free of culture: on the contrary, it is the child of culture, shaped and expressed differently at different times in different circumstances in different places by individuals and groups (Berger *et al.* 1995). Men are not born with masculinity as part of their genetic make-up; rather it is something into which they are acculturated and which is composed of social codes of behaviour which they learn to reproduce in culturally appropriate ways. It is indexical of class, subculture, age and ethnicity, among other factors. Furthermore, any easy generalizations like 'working class', 'middle class', 'gay' or **'black' masculinities** are greatly misleading because within each of these broad categories there is considerable variation in both experience and presentation. Indeed, men globally have never shared the same conception of masculinity: as anthropology demonstrates, it is interpreted, enacted and experienced in culturally specific ways (Franklin 1984; Gilmore 1990; Cornwall and Lindisfarne 1994). Also, very different versions of masculinity can coexist within the same setting as has been evident even in my own occasional excursions into field settings like schools (Beynon 1985, 1989, 1993), hospitals (Beynon 1987) and prisons (Thurston and Beynon 1995; Beynon, 1996, 2001). Likewise, Cornwall and Lindisfarne (1994) reject any notion of a fixed **masculine essence**, pointing instead to masculinity's multiple and ambiguous meanings, meanings which alter according to context and over time. They talk of **cultural borrowings** and comment that 'masculinities imported from elsewhere are conflated with local ideas to produce new configurations' (Cornwall and Lindisfarne 1994: 12). But not everyone, however, is happy with the term 'masculinities'. For MacInnes (1998) its ever-widening adoption is an irrelevance which solves nothing and may even create a whole new raft of confusions. He argues that masculinity exists in the first place only as a fantasy about what men should be like, a chimerical construction to help people order and make sense of their lives.

Shifting to the plural form makes absolutely no difference, therefore, since 'just as there is no such thing as masculinity, neither are there any such things as masculinities' (MacInnes 1998: 40).

Let us momentarily return to the front bar of 'Seatown's' Park Hotel where we started. Maybe the philosophical Terry, observing social change from his nightly vantage point in the corner with his group of elderly friends, is right. Maybe masculinity and femininity (both used in the 'singular-plural') have changed in substance and appearance out of all recognition over the past 70 or so years. Blissfully ignorant of what is currently being written on the subject, maybe he has, nevertheless, put his finger upon something essentially true, namely that masculinity and femininity have become far more amorphous and difficult to define in our society than even in the recent past. But is he right in his assumption that masculinity was once fixed and stable, or is this just part of his overall nostalgia for the world of his long-lost young manhood? What can be said with undeniable certainty is that as we embark upon the twenty-first century masculinity is being placed under the microscope as never before, magnifying the fissures of which we may not have previously been fully aware. This examination is, of course, itself a product of our times, in part a consequence of **feminism** and in part a reaction to it. In spite of the doubts cast upon the usefulness, even the existence, of 'masculinity' as a viable concept, interest in studying and teaching about it (or them!) has snowballed in British universities since 1990, a little later than in the United States. Now it is unusual for programmes in cultural, communication and media studies, along with sociology, literary and film studies, not to make extensive reference to contemporary debates centring on masculinities. Masculinity may be having a crisis (Chapter 4) out there on the streets, but in academe it has never been more in demand as a means of 'unlocking' texts and settings. The sudden spate of recent publications on **literary masculinities** (for example, Knights 1999; Schoene-Harwood 2000) alone testifies to this.

I want now to say something about how masculinity is culturally shaped and how, in all its diversity, it is both experienced and enacted. The concept of **hegemonic masculinity** is then introduced as a prelude to looking at masculinity, first, in a historical context and, second, through the lens of class. By the way, it will already be evident that I am adopting what is best termed a 'culturalist' approach to masculinity. In doing so I sideline perspectives associated with sociobiology and evolutionary psychology and which tend to 'naturalize' male behaviour. Sociobiology, for instance, maintains that there is a causal link between being genetically male and masculinity as a gender. In the most extreme versions men are viewed as puppets to raging hormones which render them innately competitive, aggressive and violent. Some readers may regard this omission as a gross limitation, so it is perhaps useful to note what Clare (2000), himself a scientist, has to say on biological differences:

> Such biological differences as exist between men and women are not of an order that casts in stone men as phallic supremacists, as sexual predators, or as violent killers.
>
> (Clare 2000: 217)

Questioning masculinity

Before moving back to the relationship between biology and gender, a number of questions can be usefully asked. My objective in doing this is to force readers to stand back from any monolithic 'take' on masculinity; re-examine their assumptions and render its 'commonsensical meaning' problematic; and, thereby, destabilize the notion that masculinity is fixed, unified and immutable or, indeed, ever has been. So here goes!

- What is masculinity and how is it 'normally' understood? Is there really something fundamentally masculine locked inside men and shared by them all? Is 'maleness' the same as 'masculinity'? Is there is a 'commonality' of male experience? What is the effect of masculinity upon men (and upon women and children)? Are we witnessing the birth of a **new masculinity**, of new ways of 'being a man'? In which case, of what does this 'new masculinity' consist?
- What is the relationship between biology, sex and gender? Do common sets of gender **ideologies** exist and, if so, what is their relationship to class, sexuality, age and ethnicity?
- What is specifically 'male' about masculinity and is it the case that only men can be 'masculine'? Are men less masculine than they were in the past? In what sense can a woman be 'masculine'? Conversely, is it possible for a man to be 'feminine' and, if so, is this either desirable or acceptable?
- Is a man always the upholder of the same definition of masculinity or does an individual's sense and expression of the masculine change as a man ages? Has masculinity changed throughout history and, if so, how? How is masculinity enacted differently in different settings? Why are boys in most societies first instructed and then tested before being accorded the status of men?
- Do men everywhere aspire to be 'manly' in the same way? Are there continuities of masculinity and femininity across cultural boundaries? Why is

the demand upon boys to grow into men held to be so important and does it take different forms in different cultures?
• How do people in different cultures construct an image of ideal masculinity (for example, through rituals, trials of skill, sports and endurance)? Does a **deep structure of masculinity** (Tolson 1977), a global archetype of manliness, exist across different cultures world-wide?

Masculinity under the microscope

As has already been made clear, masculinity has been placed under the spotlight during the 1990s as never before. In 1998 John MacInnes published his important book *The End of Masculinity* in which he argues that the old masculine privileges have now disappeared. This, he claims, is a thoroughly good thing and that, as a result, numerous new possibilities have opened up for men as fathers, husbands, partners, lovers, workers and so forth. Young men are no longer happy to be defined solely by their occupations, as were their fathers, certainly their grandfathers, before them. They are, instead (or so the rhetoric would have us understand), happy to swap domestic and other roles with their partners, while both heterosexual and homosexual men can now adopt an extended range of lifestyles (if, of course, they have the resources). There is now greater tolerance of homosexuality (although, especially outside London and the major cities, a strong, residual homophobia remains) and evidence of this comes in many forms. For example, as I write this (February 2001) the conservative British broadsheet *Daily Telegraph* concluded in one of its editorials that there is no reason why a gay man would not be acceptable as British prime minister. Such things mark a huge advance since until the second half of the twentieth century masculinity (defined here as the socially accepted way of 'being a man') and femininity ('being a woman') were commonly referred to as if they were stable, even innate, states directly linking biology and gender. Such a view appears to derive some support from the often-mentioned case of a little boy, 'John', who suffered a botched circumcision and was reassigned the gender of a girl in the belief that surgical reassignment, along with firm socialization, would yield a well-adjusted girl (most recently reported in K. Jackson (1999) and the subject of a BBC2 *Horizon* television programme in October 2000). However, in spite of the sex-change operation, plus twelve years of social and hormonal treatment, 'Joan' (as she was renamed) never felt like a girl and, as an adult, had an operation to change her back into a man.

Even in the recent past masculine and feminine roles were more clearly differentiated and a woman taking on a male role (or vice versa) was viewed with the utmost suspicion (vividly captured, for example, in the figure of the resolute Bathsheba Everdene, the farm-owning heroine of Thomas Hardy's novel *Far from the Madding Crowd*, 1874). The situation has now become far less clear cut as male and female roles and values have become more similar, so much so that men and women increasingly appear to be able to choose from a shared menu of attributes (although, as previously emphasized, the more privileged of both sexes are more able to choose than the less). Indeed, when people now refer to someone as 'masculine' it is far from clear, post-Thatcher, whether they are referring to a man or to a woman. Yet a little over a generation ago it was held that men were 'naturally' more powerful, competitive, successful, vigorous and successful in sport, as well as in business, far better equipped to operate in the 'real world' outside the home than women. There still remain powerful resonances of this in the west where a tough, heroic, mythic masculinity is deeply ingrained in the national psyche, ironically at a time when its limitations have been cruelly exposed by feminists and others. While western pop culture (whether films, records, television, videos or cyber games) continue to celebrate the 'he-man', certainly since the 1970s there has been a strong hint of parody, even dysfunction, in the portrayal. The outcome is that many men are now upholders of a **hybridized masculinity** that is experienced and displayed differently at different times in different situations. Perhaps what we are currently witnessing at the start of the twenty-first century is nothing less than the emergence of a more fluid, **bricolage masculinity**, the result of 'channel-hopping' across versions of 'the masculine'. Narrow stereotypes, based upon biological differences, have finally been laid to rest. Indeed, no less a figure than the eminent British historian David Starkey has argued that a sharp separation of 'the male' and 'the female' is unsustainable in the present day rich, consumerist west:

> We are in a supermarket and we are primarily consumers . . . we have unlimited freedom . . . we are in a world essentially without scarcity. That is why we can behave as we do and we can run two or three families and we can welcome gays and can have this wonderful world without definition . . . [today] there is a confusion between role and nature and we need to get back to a proper understanding of what it is to be a man, woman and human.
> (David Starkey in *The Moral Maze*, BBC Radio 4, June 1999)

It would appear that we live at a time when gender identity has less to do with biology than with economic and cultural circumstances. But (as we have seen in the case of the 'eyes-of-the-bar', Terry, quoted above) for many there remains a strong nostalgia for a time when gender differentiation was less ambiguous.

I now return to the connection between biology, on the one hand, and gender, on the other, which has already been touched upon. Although the physiological (the male body) and the cultural (the social relations of masculinity) are obviously linked, the nature of that link needs to be explored carefully because it is not as straightforward as it may, at first, appear. Accordingly, I examine briefly what a small number of leading writers have to say on these and related matters. The authors (some of whom we have encountered before and selected from an increasingly long line) are, in order of appearance, Morgan (1992), Sedgwick (1985), MacInnes (1998) and Cornwall and Lindisfarne (1994). All agree that masculinity is socially and historically, not biologically, constructed. A good point with which to start is Morgan's (1992) assertion that what is masculinity (and femininity) is best approached from the standpoint of what men and women *do* (that is, how they behave) rather than what they *are*. If gender is cultural, then it follows that women as well as men can step into and inhabit (whether permanently or temporarily) masculinity as a 'cultural space', one with its own sets of behaviours. In this view 'the masculine' and 'the feminine' signify a range of culturally defined characteristics assignable to *both* men and women. By also introducing sexuality Morgan raises the contentious issue of how far expressions of sexuality are also socially and culturally constructed (see also Simon 1996), thereby producing the 'gender map' shown in Figure 1.1.

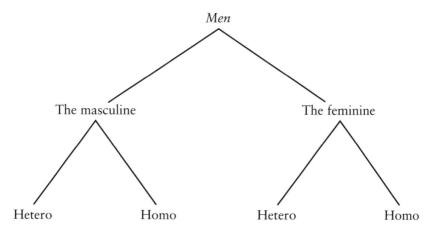

Figure 1.1   Morgan's 'gender map'

Factor in additional elements such as class, ethnicity, age, religion and geographical location, and the picture becomes even more complicated. A few obvious examples will serve to illustrate the point that the biological male and female can step into either male or female gender roles:

- *The tomboy*: this is a masculine identity temporarily adopted by young girls but which, if maintained for too long into young womanhood, raises doubts about their heterosexuality.
- *The transsexual*: 'he' or 'she' can be a 'man' or 'woman' as the situation demands or as they wish.
- *The high-flying female executive*: she heads a large company and has to demonstrate daily leadership, initiative, grit and aggression (traditional masculine attributes), but she is also a devoted wife or partner and a caring and gentle mother in her private life.
- *The male nurse*: he has to be gentle, nurturing and caring, attributes usually associated with the feminine.

Masculinity and femininity are habitually defined in terms of the difference between them, but Sedgwick (1985: 12) repudiates any automatic equating of masculinity with men, arguing that 'when something is about "masculinity", it isn't always "about men" '. She opposes the positioning of masculinity and femininity as a dichotomy, arguing that instead of being at opposite poles of the same axis, they are actually in different perpendicular dimensions and, therefore, what she terms 'independently variable'. Some people score high on both dimensions, others low in terms of stereotypical male and female traits, leading her to conclude that such research indicates only that 'some people are just plain more "gender-y" than others' (Sedgwick 1985: 15–16). One of the most comprehensive explorations of this (and related) issues to date is by MacInnes (1998) in an argument I have earlier touched upon. In his analysis, if 'being male' is largely anatomical, masculinity is most certainly social, cultural and historical, 'something for the girls as much as the boys and, over time, it must surely come to have no special connection to either biological sex' (MacInnes 1998: 45). Masculinity and femininity, as characteristic of men and women, exist only as sociocultural constructions and not as the property of persons. Indeed, they are no more than a set of assumptions which people hold about each other and themselves in certain contexts:

> gender, together with the terms of masculinity and femininity, is an ideology people use in modern societies to imagine the existence of differences between men and women on the basis of their sex where, in fact, there is none . . . [it is something] we imagine to exist and which is represented to us in material form through the existences of the two sexes, male and female.
>
> (MacInnes 1998: 1, 10)

He maintains that there can be no simple correspondence between sexed bodies and masculinity and femininity because 'genitals and biological capacities aside, men and women are not different . . . Being a biological male does not confer masculinity' (MacInnes 1998: 77). He forecasts that there will come a time when there will be no difference between men and women apart from the anatomical and, therefore, 'both in the real world and our analysis of it it is time for the end of masculinity' (MacInnes 1998: 47). By the **end of masculinity** he means the demise of the belief in masculinity as a gendered identity specific to men. Indeed, this 'end of masculinity' would, in his view, be a major step in the direction of global equal rights.

Perhaps even more challenging is Cornwall and Lindisfarne's (1994: 10) stance that the sexed body and the gendered individual should not be chained together since *both* are culturally constructed. They argue that 'biology is no more primary or "real" than any other aspect of lived experience'. They hold that (as shown in Figure 1.2) 'there are male and female versions of masculinity and, equally, female and male versions of femininity' (Cornwall and Lindisfarne 1998: 15). As a consequence 'male' and 'female' have no intrinsic biological reality and are better understood as metaphors through which identity is constructed, given that 'an essentialist "male–female" dichotomy cannot account for the ways people are gendered in different places at different times . . . the idea of "being a man" can no longer be treated as universal' (Cornwall and Lindisfarne 1998: 3).

Furthermore, they argue that the three most familiar descriptors (namely 'men', 'male' and 'masculinity') are not necessarily compatible (as, indeed, is the case with 'women', 'female' and 'femininity'). Each has multiple meanings and can even describe contradictory aspects. As a consequence, 'there is no "natural", nor necessary, connection between men and masculinity' (Cornwall and Lindisfarne 1998: 37).

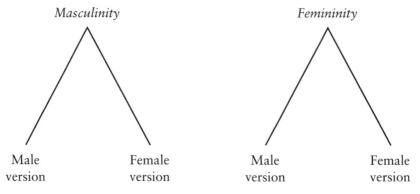

Figure 1.2   Versions of masculinity and femininity

Shaping and enacting masculinities

What are the social factors that impact upon and pattern masculinity? How is masculinity culturally constructed? In Figure 1.3 the principal factors that shape the form, experience and enactment of **masculinity-as-a-text** are itemized. These clearly overlap and, depending on the individual, some will be more influential and enduring than others. Masculinity is never to be set in concrete: rather, it always has the capacity for rapid modification. For instance, we have seen in the example of Terry that as a man ages, his sense and expression of the masculine inevitably change, just as the world evolves around him. Another obvious example of 'masculinity-on-the-move' would be a man who changes his class, status, culture and geographical location and becomes upwardly (or downwardly) mobile and, in the process, modifies his sense, experience and enactment of the masculine (or even the 'masculines').

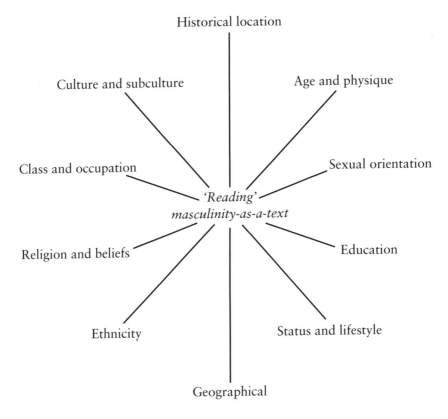

Figure 1.3 Key factors that shape masculinities

How is masculinity displayed? While some approach masculinity as the internalized product of structural features like class and ethnicity, writers like David Morgan (1992) and Judith Butler (1990) present it more as a **Goffmanesque presentation**, a 'dramaturgical accomplishment' (Coleman 1990). Rather than being made up of 'essences' or 'fundamentals', masculinity and femininity are sets of signs that are performed in what Kersten (1995) refers to as a 'situational accomplishment' and Butler (1990) as a 'performative act'. The 1980s (to which I return in Chapter 5) are a good example of this as a whole new range of commercially driven masculinities performed through fashion came into being, including Punk 'collage dressing'. Increasingly personality came as part of the fashion statement: as Edwards (1997) puts it, you were the clothes you wore. The emergence of this narcissistic masculinity mirrored the bigger, structural picture, namely the shift from production-led to consumption-led values, from **Fordism** to **post-Fordism**, from undifferentiated mass marketing to more flexible, niche marketing, in turn facilitated by new technologies of clothing production that could easily be 'retooled' for short runs.

In thinking of 'masculinity-as-enactment' it must be remembered that those who do not perform their masculinity in a culturally approved manner are liable to be ostracized, even punished. For example, in the nineteenth century avant-garde artists and bohemians like Oscar Wilde and Aubrey Beardsley contradicted biologistic, **eugenistic** definitions of masculinity. Similarly, the rock stars of the 1960s and 1970s (from the androgynous David Bowie to the butch Gary Glitter) repeatedly challenged accepted notions of 'the masculine', as did the men's magazines of the 1980s (Chapter 5). As Burt (1995, 1998) and others have demonstrated, in spite of its grace and athleticism, male dance is widely viewed as an invalid expression of the masculine, the antithesis of 'manly' activities and sports like rugby. Applause may be lavished upon the film *Billy Elliot* (2000), but for a young man to aspire to be a ballet dancer in Britain is still likely to occasion raised eyebrows and homophobic innuendoes, even outright censure. Most men are still culturally propelled to incorporate dominance, whether in terms of crude physical strength or displays of 'masculine' rationality and competence, into their presentation of self. Of course, by presenting gender as cultural and performative, the paradigm that holds that masculinity and femininity are straitjackets into which all biological males and females are automatically fitted, begins to be severely undermined. In this view 'the masculine' can be displayed in a variety of ways by both men and women in different places at different times. It also makes itself available as an analytical concept by means of which a variety of settings and behaviours therein can begin to be examined.

I have sought to establish the case for the development and expression of masculinity being shaped by such factors as culture, age, ethnicity, belief system, locality, disability, nationality and sexual orientation and so forth. The outcome of this is that it is open to debate which aspects of 'the masculine' the following might have in common: an unemployed former coal miner in his sixties living in the Rhondda, Wales; a successful City of London stockbroker in his fifties; a poor Indian ekeing out a meagre living off the land in the rural hinterland; a rich, young, gay fashion designer in New York; and a middle-aged, family-orientated schoolteacher in Bolton, Lancashire. Biologically the same, each is positioned to experience and display their masculinity very differently. Tillner (1997) concludes:

> the whole diversity of lived masculinities can be understood as specific realizations of a vague set of ideas and demands, images and stories that are defined as masculine, adapted to the concrete situation an individual or group has to cope with.
>
> (Tillner 1997: 2)

An interesting instance of a group having to cope with a particular situation is that of gay men, who still encounter considerable prejudice. When Forrest (1994), for example, talks of the 'butch shift' he is referring to how young, gay men sometimes choose to present themselves through body images, clothes, sporting activities and other signifiers previously associated exclusively with 'straight' men. Other gay men, on the other hand, have adopted **hyper-masculinity** as a presentational strategy, exaggerating signs previously exclusively associated with macho masculinity. So fashionable did this and other 'gay looks' based on a gay iconography heavily featured in the men's magazines and advertising of the 1980s become (Chapter 5) that many heterosexual men adopted it as they would any other fashion, much to the disgruntlement of sections of the gay community at the time.

It is often now asserted that masculinity and femininity are becoming more fluid and that men and women are increasingly occupying a shared middle place. The evidence for this assertion that men are becoming more like women and women more like men is somewhat tenuous and is usually based on isolated instances. For example:

- 'Housefathers' taking responsibility for home and hearth while the female partner goes out to work.
- Women breaking through the 'glass ceiling' and attaining high positions in the professions, running organizations and institutions and adopting a 'masculine' demeanour.

- Groups of young women drinking heavily and behaving in a 'laddish' manner in city 'nite spots'.
- Strong men breaking down and crying (especially in sport, as witness the English footballer Paul Gascoigne (Gazza) and the German world motor racing champion Michael Schumacher).

As far as fashion is concerned, men have certainly become more style and appearance-conscious and have stepped into a domain once almost exclusively associated with the feminine. Led by a gay subculture for whom clothing has long been a crucial identity marker, young men have increasingly come to value designer labels and are highly receptive to subtle, nuanced changes in dress codes, much as women have long been.

Experiencing masculinity

How masculinity is experienced is always on the move, sometimes gradually, sometimes rapidly. Men in the twentieth century witnessed enormous social and cultural changes during the course of their lives which impacted, both directly and indirectly (and differentially, depending on the social and geographical location of individuals), on how masculinity was experienced. Let us take a hypothetical example of a man born in the United Kingdom in the early 1900s and living until the millennium and highlight some of the socio-economic and cultural factors that moulded his experience of masculinity.

The rise of women

The **Suffragette** movement, from its origins in the 1860s, swept into the early decades of the twentieth century when women were finally granted the vote (in two stages, 1918 and 1928). Feminism gathered momentum throughout the 1960s and changed women's experience of the world. By the end of the century some claimed that the chains of patriarchy had finally been broken and that women were no longer 'owned' or controlled by men. Equal rights were, in theory at least, on the statute book and institutionalized. If women's lives had been transformed, so had men's.

Conflict in the twentieth century

Men in their millions died on the battlefields of Europe, most notably during 1914–18 and 1939–45. Any heroic and patriotic notion of it being glorious to die for king and country was forever severely compromised. The two world wars transformed the lives of both men and women. Men were placed in the combat role and toughness, endurance, courage and emotional reticence were demanded of them. Women had to cope on both the home front and (for many) in the battle zone. They entered into the industrial world in the absence of men, only to be banished back to the kitchen when hostilities ceased. Men returned from fighting one week and were searching for a job the next. It was only later that it was recognized how many had been traumatized by their experiences, but this was prior to the advent of counselling. It is not surprising, therefore, that many encountered immense problems in adjusting to civilian life (Turner and Rennell 1995).

Changes in the world of work

In 1929 the world of work spectacularly collapsed in the Great Depression and throughout the bleak 1930s millions of men were unemployed. In the process they were deprived of one of the great markers of traditional, patriarchal masculinity, namely the role of the **breadwinner**. Many blamed themselves rather than the economic system, devastated by their inability to provide for themselves, their families or aspire to their dreams. Later in the century new technology changed the nature, availability and nature of work. Men could no longer base a sense of masculinity upon heavy graft as the amount of manual labour required in, for example, farming was greatly reduced. The 1980s and 1990s witnessed the demise of traditional heavy industries (like mining, shipbuilding and docking). The shift from the mass production of Fordism to the short, flexible production and niche marketing of post-Fordism resulted in more women being employed than ever before, along with an increase in part-time and temporary work. In the process the whole nature of work for most men was utterly transformed.

The advent of the consumer society

The rise of **consumerism** and the **celebrity culture** that now permeates every area of western society had its roots in post-Second World War reconstruction, in particular the development and proliferation of the 'image industries', starting in the 1950s and advancing rapidly in the 1960s. 'Desires' replaced 'needs' and what people were became increasingly based upon what they owned. Goods such as houses, clothes, cars and other indicators of 'success' assumed enormous importance for people's self-images. Indeed, in line with the consumerist ethos a number of commodified masculinities are now on offer which men can 'buy into' if they have the resources (whether money, looks, age or location: see Chapter 5).

The rise of the gay movement

It is just over a century since Oscar Wilde was arrested, tried and subsequently imprisoned in Reading Gaol, a broken man. The **gay movement** has, in spite of the advent of AIDS, become an influential subculture in both Britain and the United States. Evidence is that people have become more tolerant of gay and lesbian rights, although a strong element of homophobia survives, especially outside centres of gay culture like Soho. The gay movement has, of course, thrown into question the previously largely taken-for-granted 'normality' of heterosexuality.

Changing views on masculinity

It is not only feminists who have attacked masculinity since the 1960s. In the 1970s some men themselves began to call it into question, particularly within the so-called **men's movement** in North America, with their call for **male liberation** (to parallel 'women's lib'). Traditional masculinity began to be regarded as a 'neuro-muscular armour' that forced them to suppress tenderness, emotion and any signs of vulnerability. Writers such as Pleck and Sawyer (1974: 4) argue that men learn too well to repress joy and tenderness, so much so that 'the eventual result of our not expressing emotion is not to experience it'. Masculinity is presented as damaging, driving men down the destructive path of addiction to achievement, power, prestige and profit-seeking. The outcome is that many men are racked by anxiety about the level of their achievement, inept at disclosure and seemingly unable to express their feelings. Indeed, traditional masculinity is seen to be based on a very fragile foundation and what is needed is 'male liberation'. This means a renunciation of the chasing after impossible masculine goals and Pleck and Sawyer (1974) call on men to pursue instead internal satisfaction that comes from fuller emotional involvement in (their) activities and relationships. They must no longer depend on women for love and emotional support, but need instead to employ their creative energies for their own purposes and not just for others' profit. Only by questioning masculinity themselves will men understand who they are, how they came to be that way and what they can now do about it.

It is a risky undertaking to generalize about the impact of these kinds of changes, but what can be said with some certainty is that both the enactment and experience of masculinity was very different at the end of the twentieth century from the beginning. Perhaps the biggest difference is the degree of fragmentation of the 'masculine text' in 2000 as compared to 1900. After three decades of 'deconstruction' it comes as no surprise that there are now numerous masculinities on offer, a point emphasized by Cornwall and Lindisfarne (1994: 1) when they write that 'from the "wounded male" to the "new man", images of reconstructed men appear on advertising bill-boards and television and in magazines and newspapers.'

Hegemonic masculinity

Besides masculinities, another term commonly in play is 'hegemonic masculinity', which defines successful ways of 'being a man' in particular places at a specific time (Kimmel 1994; Connell 1995). In the process other masculine styles are rendered inadequate and inferior, what Cornwall and Lindisfarne (1994) term **subordinate variants**. Hegemonic masculinity is established either through consensual negotiation or through power and achievement. At its most brutal it is predicated upon raw coercion. The tension between hegemonic and subordinate masculinities is readily observable in many workplaces and organizations. Many are saturated by hegemonic masculine values which are embedded in their structures and practices (Pringle 1989; Burton 1991; Cockburn 1991). Power (which, of course, can be variously defined and displayed) is the crucial factor in hegemonic masculinity and resistance ensures that many sites are ones of ideological struggle for contested senses of masculinity. Cornwall and Lindisfarne (1994) comment:

> Not only 'being a male', but 'being male' can be interpreted differently in different circumstances . . . masculinities are performed or enacted in specific settings . . . ethnographic descriptions of masculinity need to be located squarely with respect to contested interpretations of power.
>
> (Cornwall and Lindisfarne 1994: 37–8, 44)

Whereas middle class, professional men are more likely to exert power via emails and memos, men in manual, semi-skilled and skilled occupations are more likely to express power physically. It is a point underlined by Back (1994: 172) when he writes that 'where men are economically dependent on the sale of their labour, the expression of maleness provides a means to exert power'. However, the old working class based hegemonic masculinity, born of the Industrial Revolution and celebrating physical strength, male camaraderie and trade union solidarity, was decimated by Reagan-Thatcher 'free market' and 'trickle down' economic policies. These resulted in the demise of many heavy industries (like, for example, coal mining in South Wales), a 'downsizing' of the labour force, and the advent of a post-Fordism which witnessed an increase in part-time working and the employment of more (usually less well paid) female workers.

How does hegemonic masculinity, as a cultural expression of a pro-claimed male ascendancy, manage to attain and then retain its position? A variety of hegemonic representations win ideological consent and alternative constructions are either beaten down, ridiculed or absorbed. For example, many elements of a generalized **new man-ism** (men as more caring, sensitive, domesticated and expressive) now feature in contemporary versions of hegemonic masculinity. Hanke (1992) shows how television contributes to this through its images, plots and narratives. Similarly, Fiske (1987) looks at the construction of 'telemasculinity' by means of the 'engendering' devices of action, adventure, competition and aggression, along with an emphasis upon 'male toys' (whether cars, helicopters, tanks or guns). Furthermore, **masculinism** is celebrated through 'buddydom' and relationships between men (as in archetypal 'buddy films' like *Butch Cassidy and the Sundance Kid*, 1969). Versions of culturally praised hegemonic masculinities become part of general consciousness, even if they contrast with the more mundane everyday lives of most men. In any sociohistorical context there are a multi-tude of masculinities (Carrigan *et al.* 1983; Roper and Tosh 1991). Some are hegemonic and are constructed in relation to weaker and subordinated forms and thereby become legitimized as being 'normal' or 'natural'. These are continually shifting so that we can point to diverse masculinities, taking different forms, in different places both simultaneously and at different times. These differences may not be great (and there may be many com-monalities) but they are, nevertheless, significant. MacInnes (1998) asks a very interesting question, namely, what historical conditions encourage men (and women) to imagine such a thing as 'masculinity'? He goes on to argue that since masculinity cannot exist as the property of a person but only as a social ideology, what is best studied is

> the specific historical conditions under which men and women ever came to believe that such a thing as masculinity exists in the first place; the different forms and beliefs take; and the consequences that they have within such historical conditions.
>
> (MacInnes 1998: 77)

Masculinity in history

Masculinity is positioned in time in two senses: it changes *around* the individual man and *for him* as he ages. As will be discussed in Chapter 2, the mid-nineteenth century ideal of **Arnoldian masculinity** appears, in our post-Empire, postcolonial era, grossly antiquated (although, clearly, many echoes of it still survive). But change can occur very quickly: for example, the **discourses** surrounding the **new lad** of the 1990s differ considerably from those of the **new man** of just a few years before (Chapter 5). One thing a historical approach to masculinity reveals is that what have attained the status of 'facts' underpinning the 'true' nature of masculinity (and, of course, femininity) are really sociohistorical and cultural constructions. For example, as a result of the division of labour occasioned by the Industrial Revolution (that is, men into the factories, most women consigned to the home) and the resulting patriarchy (based on men's economic superiority), the idea that men were innately practical, rational and competitive, unlike women, was 'naturalized'. Also, in both Britain and the United States in the latter half of the nineteenth century (following the debacle of the Crimea and the trauma of the Civil War respectively) there was a determined effort to **re-masculinize** men through sports and outdoor activities and to reverse what was held to be a loss of manliness. Certainly since then manliness has been strongly associated with performance in sports.

I shall have more to say about historical approaches to masculinity later, but in the mean time I refer briefly to three writers, each of whom throws an insightful light on how masculinity has changed over time. I start with Laqueur (1990), who charts the development in Europe between the seventeenth and the nineteenth centuries of the model of sex-gender, based on biological difference, that is currently so familiar to us. Previously sexual difference was held to be a matter of degree, not kind: to be a man or a woman was to hold a place in society and not to be one or the other of two incommensurable sexes. The ideological distinction between sex and pre-gender did not apply and the move has, therefore, been from a single sex model of human sexual identity to a bipolar one. In discussing this Mangan (1997) comments that:

> Galen's anatomical model of the nature of the male and female reproductive organs, which dominated Western conceptions of sexual identity from its inception in the Second Century until the time of the Enlightenment, asserted that women were essentially imperfect men.
>
> (M. Mangan 1997: 8)

Meanwhile, Hoch (1979) identifies two recurring themes in the history of masculinity, namely:

- the 'puritan theme', which celebrates a masculinity based on duty, hard work and the meeting of laudable goals

- the 'playboy theme', the emphasis being upon enjoying life, leisure and pleasure.

Finally, for Connell (1995) the history of masculinity cannot be presented as linear: rather, 'dominant, subordinated and marginalised masculinities are in constant interaction, changing the conditions for each others' existence and transforming themselves as they do' (Connell 1995: 198). He points to three key events:

- the emergence of a domestic sphere for women and a public sphere for men
- the outlawing of homosexuality in medical terms and its criminalization in legal ones, accompanied by the equating of heterosexuality with acceptable (and respectable) manliness
- the expansion of industry in the nineteenth century and the development of a definition of masculinity based on manual labour, wage-earning capacity and 'breadwinning' capability.

Masculinity, class and work

Turning now to class, working class masculinity has been well documented by a succession of researchers in sociology and cultural studies. For example, Hargreaves (1967), Willis (1977) and Beynon (1985) document the development of subversive, working class male subcultures in the lower streams of secondary schools in Britain. This is accompanied by compliant behaviour in the upper streams, epitomized by Willis's (1977) portrayal of the subversive 'lads' and compliant 'earoles' respectively. The former did not perceive school achievement as an opportunity to attain qualification and a good job. Their disruptive counterculture, honed in school and then reproduced in the workplace, eventually proved not to be freedom but, ultimately, capitulation to a life of labour. While there is a tendency on behalf of some researchers to extol fighting and 'having a larf' as valorous 'resistance', others see it as feeding upon the subordination of other young men and young women. Moreover, Back's (1994) study of working class youth in South London reveals a variety of young masculinities rather than a single adolescent form. The young men he interviewed positioned themselves differently in relation to gender, ethnicity and race. He talks of 'estate kids', 'homebirds', young Vietnamese, **white negroes** (white kids who adopted a black identity) and 'apprentices', young men who, in the context of work, had to establish themselves not just as qualified workers, but as 'men'. Most revealing about the study, however, is how some white youths adopted elements of macho sexuality associated with black, heterosexual men. In doing this Back follows in the footsteps of Gilroy and Lawrence (1988), who look at the white adoption of black cultural forms, style, accent and dialect. Back (1994) demonstrates how the image of blackness appropriated was a stereotyped, essentially white artefact, a white image of 'being black' taken on without necessarily transforming the upholder's racist attitudes. Rather, black youth became the objects of young whites' fantasies about hyper-sexuality. In comparison young Vietnamese immigrants were viewed as feeble and feminine. Back (1994: 182) concludes that 'the white negro [*sic*] accepts the real negro not as a human being in his totality, but as the bringer of a highly specified and restricted cultural dowry'. Cornwall and Lindis-farne (1994: 7), commenting on this, point to a paradox in that 'the appropri-ation of these images can produce new, popular, anti-racist masculinities, yet simultaneously reinforce racist stereotypes in the wider society'.

The stereotypical picture that emerges is that whereas middle class men can wield institutional power, their working class counterparts employ physical power through fighting, sports (football especially), drinking, **machismo** and displays of sexual prowess. Young working class masculinity involves acts of collective bravado, with fighting, public rowdiness and drinking as key signifiers (Willis 1977; Corrigan 1979). Canaan (1996) notes how as they age, working class men sever the link between drinking, fighting and masculinity: no longer able to afford or inclined to drink heav-ily or exercise physical dominance over young men, they continue to assert dominance in the private domain of the family. Also, whereas young men actively seek out sex, older men come to accord greater value to compan-ionship in their personal relationships. Working class men experience little formal power in the workplace and, as a consequence of this, will frequently adopt macho identities to mask this powerlessness and compensate by domi-nating in the home. In the past, a working class man gained respect and dig-nity through being 'handy' and practical and being the breadwinner by providing a 'family wage' so that his wife did not have to seek employment. It is perhaps difficult to appreciate the ignominy that was formerly attached to a man's inability to provide adequately for his family. Along with being a breadwinner and having a housebound wife went a strict sexual division of labour in the household. The valorization of hard labour and the working man's pride in a masculinity based on strength, stamina and pride is beauti-fully caught by Willis (1977). Recorded in the early 1970s and still vivid, it is a voice from a bygone age of heavy industrial labour:

I work in a foundry . . . you know, drop forging . . . do you know anything about it? . . . no . . . well, you know the factory down in Bethnal

Street with the noise . . . you can hear it in the street . . . I work there on the big hammer . . . it's a six tonner. I've worked there twenty four years now. It's bloody noisy, but I've got used to it now . . . and it's hot . . . I don't get bored . . . there's always new lines coming and you have to work out the best way of doing it . . . You have to keep going . . . and it's heavy work, the managers couldn't do it, there's not many strong enough to keep lifting the metal . . . a group standing there watching you working, I like that.

(Willis 1977: 53)

Other notable studies of working class occupational culture are by Lippert (1977), on the aggressive masculinity of motor workers in Detroit, and Burgmann (1980), on Sydney's building workers. Meanwhile, Collinson (1988, 1992) and Collinson and Hearn (1994, 1996) look at the subcultural reproduction of masculine identities among male manual workers. These identities were expressed through macho acts and speech which demonstrated a mixture of compliance and resistance. Treated as second class citizens, working men were seen to redefine the setting (through jokes, swearing and the 'piss taking' of newcomers) and, thereby, better able to gain some control over their working environment. Shopfloor interaction was both playful and humorous, as well as sexist and degrading. Masculinity was enacted through, for example, the use of jokes and put-downs; sexual and physical threat and harassment; nude calendars and pin-ups; horseplay; and homophobic jokes and activities. The management was rejected as effeminate and incompetent and office staff as jumped-up 'pen-pushers'. Men often refused promotion because of the danger, as they perceived it, of becoming emasculated 'yes-men', unable to 'have a larf' and compelled to allow the bosses to impinge upon their private life by having to take work home.

Definitions of middle class masculinities are also heavily based on work, but in this case career and profession. For middle class men, employment is certainly not something they do just for remuneration: they are likely to be far less alienated from it and be prepared to invest more of themselves in it than their working class counterparts. Collinson and Hearn (1996) point to the fact that many middle class occupations have strongly masculine connotations: for example, a certain masculine mystique abounds in the 'dangerous' and 'sexy' worlds of technology, finance and advertising. Life in the corporate corridors of power and in the City is highly gendered, highly masculine (McDowell and Court 1994; McDowell 1997). Successful professional masculinity has come to be firmly associated with the business suit, the mobile phone, the flashy car, beautiful and compliant women and the large house or penthouse suite, all indicative of entrepreneurial masculine values (Podmore and Spencer 1987) which, as much as working class masculinity, excludes the feminine. Collinson and Hearn's (1994, 1996) study of managerial culture notes how management differentiates between managers and non-managers, as well as between different types of managers. Men-as-managers exerted their masculinity through absolute control over the men and women beneath them. Indeed, many were seen to have an unhealthy preoccupation with control and quite prepared to display inordinate managerialism and authoritarianism if need be. Still, of course, this may be equally true of women occupying a managerial role and acting in an analogous masculine way. Collinson and Hearn point to a whole raft of dominant 'management masculinities', often drawing upon aggressive sporting and militaristic metaphors. Built into it, too, is the assumption that 'real men' are leaders, can soak up unlimited pressure and, whatever the situation, remain cool, calm and collected. In spite of such work on the enactment of masculinity in the workplace, we still need to know much more about how men exhibit 'the masculine' in a variety of occupations and engage in a range of strategies of control, resistance and compliance.

Given the inescapable impact of globalization upon 'locals' and 'lives' everywhere (Beynon and Dunkerley 1999, 2000), its incorporation into the study of the formation of masculinities is clearly overdue. As Gee *et al.* (1996) note, the new generation of Gordon Gekko-like corporate capitalists operate on a global canvas and have no real commitment to anything or anyone except to the accumulation of capital, both corporate and personal. In a highly innovative paper, Connell (1998) points out that even to understand 'local masculinities' we are compelled to think in global terms. He talks of **global masculinities** (mostly, but not exclusively, associated with the North Atlantic countries) and documents the emergence of one, namely 'transnational business masculinity'. He defines this as 'a masculinity marked by increasing egocentrism, very conditional loyalties (even to the corporation) and a declining sense of responsibility for others (except for the purposes of image-making)' (Connell 1998: 16). Operating on a high octane, sexy mix of corporate power and endless first class travel, transnational business masculinity

differs from traditional bourgeois masculinity by its increasingly libertarian sexuality, with a growing tendency to commodify relations with women. Hotels catering for businessmen in most parts of the world now routinely offer pornographic videos and in some parts of the world there is a well-developed prostitution industry catering for international businessmen. Transnational business masculinity does not require bodily force since the patriarchal dividend on which it is based is accumulated by impersonal, institutional means.

(Connell 1998: 16)

Researching masculinities: a word of caution

In conclusion I want to turn to Kenneth Clatterbaugh, who is a professor of philosophy at the University of Washington and the author of the highly thought-provoking *Contemporary Perspectives on Masculinity* (1990). In 1998 he published a similarly challenging paper in which he raises a number of issues that might profitably be borne in mind by readers of this book. He starts by acknowledging the existence of many masculinities such as Black, Jewish, Chicano, gay, middle class and so forth, within which some versions are hegemonic. He broadly defines these 'adjectival masculinities' as 'complex sets of attitudes, behaviours and abilities possessed by distinct groups of individuals' (Clatterbaugh 1998: 25), before attempting to explicate what he terms the current 'conceptual tangle' surrounding masculinities. He argues that listing distinct characteristics such as age, race, wealth and so on is 'insufficient to demonstrate that those so catalogued do, in fact, display distinct masculinities' (Clatterbaugh 1998: 33). In his view,

> Masculinities are not like the number of shoes at a gathering . . . their kinds (pumps, loafers, etc.) are not apparent. There are no ready criteria that allow me to identify masculinities . . . It may well be the best kept secret of the literature on masculinity that we have an extremely ill-defined idea of what we are talking about.
>
> (Clatterbaugh 1998: 27)

This, of course, raises a major problem namely, how can masculinities be explored if they cannot be identified? This leads to another question, namely: are 'varieties of masculinity' the same as masculinities? The former would surely imply, as has been previously mentioned, that these varieties have something essentially masculine in common (but precisely what?), whereas the latter could enjoy a high degree of (if not complete) autonomy. Clatterbaugh, while advocating the continued exploration of the diversity and differences among men, nevertheless warns that

> talking about masculinities . . . imposes a layer (and a very confused layer) between ourselves and the social reality we want to discuss . . .

we [need to be] clear about what we are doing and about the limits of these enterprises in contributing to our understanding of men.

(Clatterbaugh 1998: 42).

He deplores, moreover, the too-easy equating of 'masculinity' and 'men', describing it as a 'subterfuge' which only goes to compound 'meanings that were intended to treat masculinity as something social and historical, whereas being a male adult was biological' (Clatterbaugh 1998: 39–40). If we are to avoid further confusion and mystification a distinction needs to be drawn at the outset between images and discourses on the one hand, and men and male behaviours on the other:

> We should be reasonably clear that we are not talking about men when we are talking about images, stereotypes or norms; and that we are not talking about images when we talk about men, male behaviours, privileges and attitudes.

(Clatterbaugh 1998: 42)

Finally, he finds many (if not most) approaches to studying masculinities unsatisfactory because, he argues, they do not actually throw much light on what 'masculinity/ies' actually is or are! He has reservations about two of the approaches I employ later, what he terms the 'postmodern option', or the ways in which masculinities are produced in and through discourse ('discursive masculinity': see Chapter 6) and masculinity-as-performance, as a 'dramaturgical accomplishment' (see Chapter 7).

A great deal more research is needed of men's actual lived experiences of masculinities before these difficult questions can be adequately addressed. At the risk of sounding evasive it is now time for this chapter to be brought to an end. Its purpose has been to stir things up, to compel readers to think critically about masculinity and the masculinities on offer, both in the world around us and in the past. And it is to the latter that we now turn, stepping back in time to look at how, in the nineteenth century and early twentieth century, 'Imperial masculinity' was the norm (both in its 'toff' and 'commoner' versions) and the sociohistorical factors that underpinned this.

Further reading

Butler, J. (1990) *Gender Trouble, Feminism and the Subversion of Identity*. New York: Routledge.

Clatterbaugh, K. (1990) *Contemporary Perspectives on Masculinity: Men, Women and Politics in Modern Society*. Boulder, CO: Westview.

Connell, R.W. (1985) *Masculinities*. Cambridge: Polity.

Cornwall, A. and Lindisfarne, N. (1994) *Dislocating Masculinity: Comparative Ethnographies*. London: Routledge.

MacInnes, J. (1998) *The End of Masculinity*. Buckingham: Open University Press.

Morgan, D.H.G. (1992) *Discovering Men*. London: Routledge.

Sedgwick, E.K. (1985) *Between Men: English Literature and Male Homosocial Desire*. New York: Columbia University Press.

Willis, P. (1977) *Learning to Labour*. Farnborough: Saxon House.

2 | MASCULINITIES AND THE IMPERIAL IMAGINARY

> In everything that makes a people great, in colonizing power, in trade and commerce, in all the higher arts of civilization, England not only excels all other nations of the modern world, but all nations in ancient history as well. The British are a breed apart, superior to all others on the face of the earth.
>
> (Sir Wilfrid Laurier 1898, cited in Howard 1967: 53)

Introduction: masculinity in the Age of Empire

In this chapter we escape momentarily from contemporary debates surrounding masculinity to look instead at how masculinity was viewed and shaped in the latter half of the nineteenth century up to the outbreak of the First World War in 1914. The British Empire had expanded steadily throughout the eighteenth century (although the American colonies were lost) and reached its greatest extent in the nineteenth century with the penetration and partition of Africa. Indeed, the generation that were, like my father, in school in the early years of the twentieth century were accustomed to a large proportion of the globe being coloured red to indicate British 'possessions'. The Empire generated a huge demand for manpower to serve its diverse needs, both abroad and at home, as leaders, administrators, clerks, soldiers, seafarers, merchants and so forth. There were also fortunes to be made. Accordingly, this chapter examines the emergence of **Imperial man** and some of the factors that patterned Imperial masculinity. How was Imperial masculinity (by which I mean a masculinity suitable to serve the Empire) constructed and represented in the second half of the nineteenth century, the Age of Empire?

In order to address this question the chapter is structured as follows. First, I examine the ways in which masculinity was shaped in the nineteenth and early twentieth centuries. Second, I look at how masculinity was 'imagined' and represented in some of the colonial adventure literature of the period, with specific reference to two popular novelists of Empire, namely R.M. Ballantyne and Henry Rider Haggard. Third, I turn to another aspect of the construction of Imperial man, namely the response to the fear that the national 'stock' of men was degenerating. I pick on two responses, the growth of sport and the popularity of **physical culture**. Fourth, I examine the charges that Imperial masculinity damaged its upholders. Fifth, I show how Imperial masculinity survived in stories for boys up to the Second World War. Finally, I argue that although Imperial man may be dead, elements of Imperial masculinity survive in, for example, modern day sport and bodybuilding.

'Fit for Empire': Imperial masculinity

In the mid-nineteenth century a huge emphasis began to be placed in the education of young men upon athleticism, stoicism, sexual purity and moral courage (Mason 1982; J. Mangan and Walvin 1987). This was evident in the works and deeds of eminent figures as diverse as Thomas Arnold, Thomas Carlyle, Charles Kingsley, Thomas Hughes and Robert Baden-Powell. Thomas Arnold, the influential headmaster of Rugby School, equated manliness with intellectual energy, moral purpose and sexual purity. Organized sport was important in training not only young men's bodies, but also their minds. Christianity was presented as a muscular and manly faith and Christ himself was represented in masculine terms. Arnold's contemporary, Thomas Carlyle, advocated a more aggressive version of manliness, expressing his admiration for men of rugged independence and action like Oliver Cromwell and Frederick the Great. Although Arnold's version of masculinity was taken up by the governing elite after 1832, Roper and Tosh (1991) conclude that by the 1880s Carlyle's version had triumphed since he had anticipated Imperial man's emphasis upon action, authority, the celebration of the will and (reflected in Sir Wilfred Laurier's sentiments) even the assertion of British racial superiority (which, of course, viewed from the twenty-first century, might be read as gratuitously racist).

Gilmore (1990) talks of an **obsessive moral masculinization** at work in the period when a 'hard masculinity' was promulgated through austere training to discipline and toughen boys in all-male organizations to counter what were seen as the damaging influence of the feminine. The gentry and the aspiring upper middle class dispatched their sons to the harsh environment of the boarding school to inculcate the qualities of self-reliance and determination needed to serve the Empire (Chandos 1984). Furthermore, MacKenzie (1987) has documented the late nineteenth century cult of the hunter when bushcraft and the wilderness became the basis for an ideology of phys-icality, which was picked up in both Britain and the United States with the foundation of the **Scout movement** (Hantover 1978). In his manual *Scouting for Boys* (1963 [1908]) Baden-Powell spoke of the 'softening' effect of home comforts. True manliness had to be taught to boys and its virtues (grit, self-reliance, determination, leadership and initiative) acquired in male com-pany from exposure to the 'great outdoors' far removed from the domestic and the feminine. This was paralleled by the Boys' Brigade, a quasi-religious foundation by which the Church of England reached out to working class boys.

Imperial masculinity was a product of time, place, power and class, along with firmly held and unquestioned conceptions of racial and national superi-ority. It was influential in shaping British male subjectivities in the latter half of the nineteenth century, certainly up to the First World War and even beyond. Not every man in Britain at the time strictly conformed to the par-ameters of Imperial masculinity. Rather it provided, from a variety of sources, a powerful set of influences towards a hegemonic masculinity to which all 'proper' men should, at least, aspire for the future well-being of the Empire and even the **British race**.

Late twentieth century accusations that the majority of men are estranged from their emotional selves, from women and the feminine, and are homo-phobic have their origins in the shaping of masculinity in the mid-nineteenth century. For example, Roper and Tosh (1991) demonstrate that it was defined in terms of a series of 'others', namely domination over women, homosexuals and native peoples. Let us take each of these in turn.

Women

The nineteenth century saw working women increasingly excluded from the industrial workplace and limited to the less skilled jobs. Meanwhile, work-ing men's masculinity came to be constructed around notions of craft and skill, waged labour and the support of a dependent wife and children, with the resulting pride in breadwinning.

Homosexuals

Gay historians have charted the institutionalization of heterosexuality in the Victorian family while, at the same time, a legal, medical and social onslaught was launched against homosexuality (Weeks 1995). Intense homo-phobia was a feature of the latter half of the nineteenth century, particularly following the Oscar Wilde scandal in the 1890s.

Native peoples

British (and, in particular, 'English') masculinity was generally held to be superior to other 'races' and a civilizing force at the heart of the Imperial mission. Subordinated native masculinity, on the other hand, was depicted as idle, lascivious and sexually decadent. This was not to say, however, that icons of Imperial masculinity did not sometimes incorporate aspects of the 'native other', but it was always tempered with English phlegm. The representation of Lawrence of Arabia, for example, combined the exoticism and fighting qualities of Arab men with the stereotypical elements of the brave, inspirational and superior English man-in-control (Dawson 1994). This representation, of course, was partly created and sustained by Lawrence himself in his account of the Arab war in his *Seven Pillars of Wisdom* (1926).

The new gentleman

Another aspect of Imperial masculinity was the emergence of a new, expanded definition of the 'gentleman'. The term was widened from class of origin to include behaviour so that it could incorporate the increasing numbers of intermediates required for service to Empire abroad and to the growth of business and industry at home. Throughout the nineteenth century, as Britain moved from an aristocratic society to an increasingly capitalist one, the bourgeoisie engaged in a process of gentrification of their occupations (for example, through the foundation of the Law Society in 1825 and the British Medical Association in 1856).

Girouard (1981) describes the new gentleman thus:

> He was brave and straightforward and honourable, loyal to his monarch, country and friends, unfailingly true to his word, ready to take issue with anyone he saw ill-treating a woman, child or animal. He was a natural leader of men and others unhesitatingly followed his lead. He was fearless in war and on the hunting field and excelled at all manly sports, but however tough with the tough, he was invariably gentle with the weak. Above all, he was always tender, respectful and courteous to women, regardless of their rank.
>
> (Girouard 1981: 260)

As Skovmand (1987) makes clear, the gentleman was 'a cultural configuration, a social ideal mediating between the values of the aristocracy ('gentlemen-born') and those of the new, aspiring, self-made Victorian middle class ('gentlemen-made'). He identifies four variations: the 'officer and gentleman', 'the scholar gentleman', 'the Christian gentleman' and 'the gentleman-sports-man'. Central to the construct was an 'Englishness' based on the country squire and the village, something to be protected at all costs against foreign invasion and contamination. Samuel Butler's novel *The Way of All Flesh* (1903) is a celebration of the **gentleman-bachelor** hero, as are Conan Doyle's Sherlock Holmes and Dr Watson. Perhaps he reached his apotheosis in the figure of John Buchan's Richard Hannay in *The Thirty Nine Steps* (1915), outwitting and thwarting the fiendish threat of dastardly 'foreigners'. Other examples might be Sapper's Bulldog Drummond or Sawyer's Lord Peter Wimsey, but the English gentleman-hero survives (in literature at least) up to Geoffrey Household's *Rogue Male* in 1939. In real life his demise had already taken place, on the muddy battlefields of France during 1914–18. He held sway through most of the later nineteenth century, but 'the Great War killed off the bachelor gentleman . . . after 1918 the ideal of the gentlemen had ceased to exist as a major social force' (Skovmand 1987: 57).

An additional perspective is thrown on the Victorian gentleman and his representation in literature by Brown's (1987) analysis of Dickens' *Great Expectations* (1861). Magwitch, the convict and Pip's hidden sponsor, returns from banishment in Australia and says of himself and Pip: 'If I ain't a gentleman, nor yet ain't got no learning, I'm the owner of such . . . a brought-up London gentleman!' (Dickens [1861] 1999: 302).

Pip's developing career itself reflects the inexorable rise of the Victorian petty bourgeoisie and of an expanding economy that demanded a seemingly unending supply of 'gentleman' clerks and administrators who will go abroad and make their fortune. Brown (1987) comments that

> this identity is located at the period of British ascendancy over the globe. It is constructed in a network of the movements of the growing legal system, the movements of expanding capitalism.
>
> (Brown 1987: 71)

'Masculine imaginings'

Victorian and Edwardian Britain was a period of unprecedented male achievement in engineering, the sciences, exploration and Imperial expansion, building, technological advances and medicine. Men were expected to be strong, authoritative, decisive, disciplined and resourceful. It is an ideal of masculinity which still echoes in the heads of men. The late Victorian era up to the First World War was the era of what Dawson (1994) terms **popular Imperialism**. At its heart was the image of the brave British soldier-hero serving the Empire in endless colonial conflicts, with the emphasis very much upon nationalist, racist and militaristic aspects of masculinity. It was an image that, in Dawson's words, coloured the 'psychic landscape' of a generation of British boys. Soldier-heroes like Sir Henry Havelock of Lucknow and the martyred General Gordon of Khartoum attained a Christ-like stature in terms of 'moral manhood', patriotism and bravery-unto-death.

For many of the writers of the period, the Empire was the site of 'masculinist imaginings' in which men could enjoy homosocial comradeship in physically challenging, arduous circumstances far from what they perceived to be the damaging influences of 'the feminine'. It is perhaps not surprising that – as Tosh (1991) points out – many of the most notable upholders of Imperial masculinity (like Gordon, Kitchener and Rhodes) never married, or did so late in life (like Baden-Powell). These novelists 'hero-ized' a distinctively British form of masculinity (Kestner 1995) and wrote these 'masculinist narratives' (Green 1991) with middle class readers primarily in mind but in the knowledge that sectors of the increasingly literate working class would also read them. This adventure literature, which dominated boys' reading in the period 1880 to 1914 (and well beyond, even into our own time) was strongly allied to the needs of the British Empire. As a result it was overtly masculinist, didactic and (in our eyes) racist, written by Imperial men for their heirs. The kind of warrior masculinity demanded for service in the Empire was 'mapped' into a 'geography of adventure' (R. Phillips 1997) by such authors (to name but a few) as George Alfred Henty, R.L. Stevenson, R.M. Ballantyne, Captain Marryat and, later, John Buchan, each of whom invoked their juvenile readers to grow into 'manly men'. Indeed, 'real masculinity' could be constituted only in and through colonial adventure. Notions of 'Englishness' in Imperial literature (well documented by, for example, Brooker and Widdowson 1986, and Collis and Dodd 1986) are overwhelmingly framed in terms of the valorious qualities of the 'Englishman', only rarely English women.

Before turning to two novelists of Empire (R.M. Ballantyne and Rider Haggard) I want to say something about 'masculinist imaginings'. David Jackson (1990) makes three helpful points:

• A distinction can be drawn between masculine and feminine narratives. The former are typically based on adventures and emphasize the physical and impersonal, whereas the latter usually emphasize personal relations and emotions (Fiske 1987). Boys' storybooks of the later nineteenth century and the first half of the twentieth century 'naturalized' the need to win at all costs and, Jackson (1990) argues, encouraged the goal-orientated, masculine attitudes necessary to sustain patriarchy. Commenting on the courage, grit and determination of the stereotypical British adventure hero, Jackson points out that 'he didn't seem to have an inner world: his whole focus was on public actions in the public domain' (Jackson 1990: 234).

- Rendering mute the potentially threatening voice of the feminine is a feature of boys' stories. Jackson comments that

> the ideological construction of masculinity, produced through all these competitive clashes, trials of strength and mental and physical conflicts, was achieved through the exclusion of those repressed 'feminine' elements . . . that it most feared.
>
> (Jackson 1990: 235)

Codes of acceptable masculine behaviour are established, whereas the unacceptable becomes synonymous with the feminine and the 'sissy'.

- British boys' stories contain epic warrior heroes who acquire and affirm their masculinity and honour by engaging in impossibly dangerous quests and undergoing a series of trials. The island becomes a kind of 'laboratory' (Hannabuss 1983) in which character is tried, tested and proved. Neither is it just a matter of acquiring and demonstrating manliness, but of 'being English'. To do this, boys and young men have to display not only physical strength and valour but also inner psychological toughness and self-discipline.

Undoubtedly the main agent for the shaping of Imperial masculinity was the prep and public school system. At the earliest age the upper middle class Victorian boy was separated from the home and the perceived dangers of the feminine and placed in the hands of school masters. Close behind in influence came the literature for boys with its emphasis upon loyalty, whether to school, regiment, college, nation or Empire. In her study Kanitkar (1994) concentrates on the 'ripping yarns' that appeared in *The Empire Annual for Boys, 1909–1919* and other Christmas annuals. These were read by prep and public school boys as well as their less fortunate counterparts, who would thus pick up something of the ethos of these schools at second hand. The stories and the masculinity they espoused are historically and culturally locatable in that they served a specific purpose at a particular time, namely the moral instruction of British boys as 'cadets of Empire'. In order to do this they emphasized sports, sportsmanship, team spirit and a 'strong' manliness defined against the 'fragile' feminine.

Kanitkar (1994) sees three kinds of 'British boys' emerge in these stories: the 'sporting boy', 'all-white boy' and 'Christian boy'.

The sporting boy

A direct link is made between all-male games and sport on the one hand and patriotism and Empire-building on the other. Sport (in particular rugby, cricket and boxing) is accorded the key role in training the boy into the ways of leadership, teamwork, loyalty to fellows and pride in his achievement. Arthur Mee (quoted in Kanitkar 1994: 187) writes that 'if we are loyal to our team, to our school, we shall be loyal to our village, to our town and to our country. The very beginnings of patriotism lie in the cap that the schoolboy wears'. Above all else the clean-living, clean-thinking sporting youth must avoid what was termed at the time 'love rot' and becoming one of those

> immature and weedy youths [who] are not true boys at all. Rather, they are the kind of youth that can be seen, with pale and pimply face, sucking a cigarette or cane top, loafing about and ogling the girls, instead of joining in the sports of his more manly fellows.
> (Williams 1911, quoted in Kanitkar 1994: 186)

The all-white boy

These 'cadets of Empire' were trained to regard themselves as superior to both the domestic working class and the colonial native peoples, presented as simple and inferior to the British. Indeed, it was the white man's duty to civilize and bring order and fair play to wild and exotic distant places. These sons of the British ruling class were educated into a belief that they had, as Kanitkar (1994: 195) puts it, 'the God-given right, as well as the duty, to govern and control those unable to do so for themselves'. Leadership and the judicious and fair use of authority was the path forward to a masculine nobility, something that Kipling (1910) captures in his poem *If*, which we examine later.

The Christian boy

These ripping yarns embraced the previously mentioned notion of **Muscular Christianity**, a bringing of both civilization and Christianity to the savage. Time and again the gap between, as Kanitkar (1994: 194) expresses it, the 'intelligent and reasoning white and the instinctual black' is stressed.

Literary discourses

Kanitkar (1994) identifies two sets of literary discourses coexisting in Victorian literature. First, the depiction of white men as chaste 'Imperial cadets' operating in a homosocial world in which heterosexual desire was deemed as unmanly (in comparison with sports and the serious work of Empire) and homosexual desire was simply not acknowledged. The sexuality of natives is never mentioned and women, both white and native, seldom appear, except in service roles or to occasion brave acts of rescue by men. Women did not enter the world of the boarding school, Oxbridge college, the regimental dinner or the gentleman's club. Rather, they were consigned to their 'natural' role as the 'gentler souls at the side of great men' (Arthur Mee, quoted in Kanitkar 1994: 185). Second, the representation of the black male, as sexually rampant and continually posing the threat of rape of white women, paralleled with black women's assumed easy sexual availability to white men.

It is not surprising that colonists looked upon many native men as both inferior and unmanly (in British India, for example, Bengali men were held to be effete and effeminate). Something of the dominant style of colonial masculinity was appropriated by native men themselves in subordinate positions of authority, thus becoming a trusted buffer between rulers and ruled (for example, the rise of the native 'clerk class' in British India and who exerted considerable bureaucratic power). Among the native populace that the British admired most were those who conformed to the ideal of loyalty, honour and service, namely the Sikhs (who were admired for their physical strength and warlike character), the tribesmen of the North West Frontier, and most of all (because they responded quickly to command and were brave and true) the Gurkhas.

Kanitkar's (1994) study is wide ranging and insightful. Her provocative conclusion is that in spite of what we now see as the obvious racism of these stories, their messages live on because they are deep rooted in the British psyche. In turning now to the novelists R.M. Ballantyne and Rider Haggard it is as well to remember that while they prescribe a form of masculinity, they simultaneously block off other possibilities. Rereading these novels well over a century since they were written is to be reminded that it is in the 'silences' of a text (that is, what is not said) that its ideology can be most readily detected (Macherey 1978). The text is not for passive consumption but is, rather, an object of work by the reader to negotiate and produce meaning (Belsey 1980).

Ballantyne: boy heroes en route to manhood

Tosh (1991) argues that there was a flight from the stifling effects of domesticity in the 1880s as significant numbers of young men uprooted themselves

from home and hearth for service in the Empire. Such journeys were meta-
phorical as well as actual, from (soft) boyhood to (hard) manhood, crucial
socializing rites of passage for white, Christian, middle class boys destined
for service in the cause of Queen and Empire. The Imperial adventurer's
manhood is constituted in a specific adventure setting far from civilized
society. In this setting he acquires, proves and displays his masculinity
through 'roughing it' and, thereby, hardens body and spirit. This is opposed
to the cancerous 'easy life' they have chosen to forsake. In perhaps the most
famous representative novel of the genre, Ballantyne's *Coral Island* (1858),
the three boy heroes are, in effect, on a colonial mission: overcoming the
obstacles they encounter on the Pacific island upon which they are ship-
wrecked is an exercise in being British and an apprenticeship in Imperial
masculinity. They are middle class, superior, confident, adventurous, ethno-
centric, religious, racist and overtly nationalist. They map the island, con-
vert the natives to Christianity and triumph over nature (for example, in the
celebrated encounter with a killer shark). Phillips (1997) illustrates how
Ballantyne plays on his reader's geographical fantasies, locating the action in
a generalized, generic landscape (a space rather than a place), a *terra incog-
nita* in which the boys run wild (without ever once becoming savages) and
build the muscles and spirit associated with Muscular Christianity (a requi-
site, it seems, for Imperial service).

A number of elements characterize this 'island space' in which hegemonic
masculinity (Donaldson 1993) is physically, spiritually, nationally and
racially constituted:

- There is a celebration of strong masculine bonding in an all-male context
  of homogeneous masculinity. In these exotic settings (of Pacific islands or
  the great outdoors of Canada or the Americas) where they conquer the
  terrain and control nature, boys are rendered manly through adversity.
  There is an open intolerance of 'unmanly males' and a reification of
  trusted **voyageurs**, older and wiser men, experienced in the ways of the
  world, who act as mentors.
- There is a marked absence of women and the feminine: where women
  appear they do so as passive vehicles through which men define themselves. Masculinity is associated with mobility, toughness and adventurousness, femininity with immobility and the softness of faraway home.
- Valorous white, Christian masculinity is defined in relation to the threat
  of the savage, primitive 'otherness' of the non-white savages that sur-
  round them. In these circumstances white, Christian and British boys
  invariably triumph and come out on top. In these adventure stories
  masculinity and race are, as Phillips (1997) puts it, 'mutually constitutive'.

Imperial masculinity is naturalized as boys are 'mapped' (we may now say 'trapped'?) into a narrowly defined, simplified masculinity that blocks any alternatives. Meanwhile, the black masculinity of the natives, while they are admired as 'noble savages', is caricatured.

If Ballantyne's *Coral Island* maps imperial masculinity, then William Golding's (1954) *The Lord of the Flies* subverts and 'unmaps' it. By then belief in Imperial masculinity (as the very existence of the Empire itself) had been eroded by the horrors of two world wars. Golding's boys find darkness and savagery not outside (in the form of the cannibals), but inside themselves. Two very different versions of masculinity emerge, separated by 70 years, namely Ballantyne's heroic boy en route to Imperial man and Golding's twentieth century counterpart, British boys en route to savagery. In Golding's 1950's Britain, Ballantyne's confidence in the decency of Christian men and the civilized behaviour of white, European masculinity could no longer be sustained and Imperial masculinity held less and less relevance.

Rider Haggard: masculinity-in-action

Crang (1998: 73) argues that another popular novelist, Rider Haggard, a leading member of the Right in turn-of-the-century Britain, responded to the degeneracy fears by treating the Empire as 'a cure for alienation associated with a domestic and, crucially, urban working class'. Meanwhile Low (1993) comments:

> Haggard's texts fed into and were sustained by a cultural map of epics, travel narratives, exploration and the 'boy's adventure', set within a contemporary history of new imperialism abroad and a growing pedagogic militarism in Public Schools at home.
>
> (Low 1993: 191)

Low demonstrates how Haggard joined literati like Andrew Lang (who castigated literature that was unmanly) and George Saintsbury (who called for a literary equivalent of 'healthy beefiness and beeriness') in demanding adventure stories celebrating British male vitality. Haggard set out to rebuff what he held to be the increasing feminization of English literature (and the corrupting influence of French and Russian realism) and hoped that his stories would help his young male readers attain the 'state of dignity of English gentlemen'. He aimed to give expression to Muscular Christianity with its emphasis upon character-building through courage, fortitude, patriotism and self-discipline as markers of an Imperial masculinity rooted in reason, not emotion, and forged in the (necessary) absence of women: indeed, repeatedly in the Haggardian landscape women are forces for instability and chaos, desire and fear (Crang 1998).

Low (1993) argues that to read Haggard against-the-grain is to lay bare underlying anxieties concerning 'Englishness' (as opposed to 'Britishness': writers of the period often equated being British with being English, as if the Welsh, Scottish and Irish did not exist). Similarly, there are anxieties about Empire, masculinity and patriotism, along with Imperialist ideologies colouring colonial representation and cultural difference. She rereads Haggard in the light of Theweleit's (1987) study of masculinity and Fascism. He focuses on the **Freikorps**, who were instrumental in the rise of the Third Reich and for whom the years from 1914 to 1945 was continuous war. The masculine identity of these officers was, Theweleit argues, shaped by the desire for adventure, a distrust of the feminine, racism and anti-communism. Masculinity could be achieved apart from the feminine only through a strict regime of discipline and overt militarism. War is the only outlet for these 'men of steel' as it allows the expression of order, precision, strength and bravery in battle. Ehrenreich (1987) quotes a former member of the Freikorps:

> People told us [in 1918] that the War was over. That made us laugh. We ourselves are the War. Its flame burns strongly in us. It envelops our whole being and fascinates us with the enticing urge to destroy. We obeyed . . . and marched into the battlefields of the post-war world just as we had gone into battle on the Western Front: singing, reckless and filled with the joy of adventure as we marched to the attack, silent, deadly, remorseless in battle.
>
> (Ehrenreich 1987: x)

Although careful not to equate Fascism and British Imperialism, Low (1993: 212) nevertheless discerns similar male fantasies at the heart of Empire, putting the case that 'the male fantasies evoked by Haggard share with Theweleit's Freikorps' narratives their evocation of the seduction of war and death and their dreams of masculine power'. British Imperialism had a strong paramilitary aspect that wallowed in masculinity-as-action, with warfare valorized and the feminine held at bay. The feminine is viewed as a threat to the wholeness and hardness of the soldier and so women are marginalized as a threat to masculinity and forces for chaos and instability. She comments:

> The radical polarization of the sexes and obsession with a male militaristic culture which deliberately marginalizes women are formed

within the Haggardian adventure genre and are echoed in the culture of the Right.

(Low 1993: 189)

A central tenet of Imperial imagining is that men, removed from the influence of women and placed in the great outdoors, bond and become leaders. A hero like Rider Haggard's *Allan Quartermain* (1887) longs to escape nineteenth century Britain and its decadence and 'cultural feminization' and return to Mother Nature. Haggard paints a mythopoetic pastoral idyll of masculinity through nature. The romance and grandeur of the great open spaces as the true home of men is celebrated, along with an imperialistic nostalgia for the lost tribes of Natal, the Transvaal and Zululand. Low (1993) argues that this mythopoetic yearning for an innocence lost on the coming of 'civilization' is, in fact, a gloss obscuring the brutal geographical, political and economic exploitation and greed of British colonists and the systematic destruction of the indigenous inhabitants and their way of life. Behind the front of nostalgia for a lost innocence (both of landscape and boyhood), these are really narratives about ownership, power, masculinity, ownership and exploitation.

In these (in our eyes) highly racist texts, the Zulus are depicted as 'black beasts' and 'blood-thirsty savages', yet their muscular bodies are admired (in the eyes of asexual, white voyeurism), as is their courage (they are described as a 'man-slaying human military machine'). Other 'savages' are dismissed as 'effeminate' in comparison. Zulu courage is admired in a chivalric way (Frye 1976) and their suicidal charging into British gunfire is held to be magnificent. Being English equates with being honourable and so there can be no indiscriminate revenge: in war, justice and notions of fair play are as much the order of the day as in play and sport.

'Rotting from within': fears of degeneracy

Understandably, there was enormous pride in the British Empire in Victorian Britain. The major concern was that it, like the Roman Empire, would rot from within, so much so that the so-called golden age was, in reality, an age of deep anxiety about the security, administration and future of the Empire. These insecurities and degeneracy fears were fuelled by a number of factors, among these being the following.

- A series of invasion threats from 1859 on, coupled with a string of humiliating colonial defeats, from the Indian Rebellion and the Crimean debacle to the death of General Gordon at Khartoum in 1885. The Boer

War (1899–1902) was a particular shock to the British public as a series of setbacks that demonstrated that British soldiers were neither as fit nor as well led as the enemy.

- Increased economic competition globally and the growing military strength of the United States, Germany and Russia.
- Accelerating urbanization, with an all-too-visible attendant social misery and the resulting belief that contemporary life was spiritually debilitating (in 1869 the poet Matthew Arnold talked of the 'disease of modern life'); this was accompanied by claims that there was a marked physical decline in the nation's men (as measured, for example, by the weight and height of military recruits). There was also a fear that young men (feminine 'muffs') were being rendered soft and effeminate by desk-bound occupations in banks and offices. Such anxieties were frequently expressed in terms of racial superiority. Lord Brabazon, for example, demanded the improvement of health and fitness to offset what he foresaw as the wholesale degeneration of the British 'breed' and Viscount Garnet Wolseley called for urgent measures to maintain the Anglo-Saxon's 'virile energy':

> It is the nature of the Anglo-Saxon race to love those manly sports which entail violent exercise . . . This craving for the constant practice and employment of our muscles is in our blood and the result is a development of bodily strength unknown in most nations and unsurpassed by any other breed of men.
>
> (quoted in Low 1993: 190)

Similarly, Benjamin Disraeli maintained in *Tancred* (1847) that the 'Saxon race . . . has stamped its diligence and methodical character on the century . . . a superior race with a superior idea to work and order . . . All is race, there is no other truth' (Disraeli 1971 [1847]: 18).

- A growing awareness of the importance of bodily health. For example, there was considerable concern throughout the Victorian period about the spread of venereal disease, particularly among enlisted men, resulting in the Contagious Diseases Acts of 1864, 1866 and 1867, later repealed following the campaign orchestrated by the remarkable Josephine Butler. In the 1880s Koch and Pasteur identified the agents responsible for a number of major diseases and thus set in motion the development of what subsequently became known as 'germ theory'. Thereafter the nation began to be talked about in terms of a body vulnerable to infection, with the consequent need for healthy bodies if the Empire was to prosper.
- Concerns clustering around the collective power and growing political demands of the working class. In the latter decades of the nineteenth

century the aspiring working class was seen to be threatening the stability of the nation through increasingly organized labour, growing union power, strikes and vociferous demands for the vote (at least for men, if not at first for women). The working class, as a force to be both controlled and harnessed, was becoming increasingly problematical and there was, among the middle class, a genuine fear of burgeoning, out-of-control socialism enveloping the nation.

• Concerns, too, about the growing aspirations of women, culminated in the Suffragette movement in the early decades of the twentieth century.

By the 1880s links had been made between bodily health, fitness for work and voting ability. The **Fabian Society**, founded in 1884, joined in the call for an able-bodied citizenry as the best antidote to the moral and physical virus held to be devouring Britain's martial and economic sinews. The health of the nation was equated with the state of the male body, in particular an 'athletic soldier-citizenry' (Budd 1997). More than ever the bodies and minds of both workers and soldiers were, it was felt, in urgent need of control and rationalization if the cycle of threatened instability at home and regular humiliation abroad was to be averted. But while an empowered and disciplined physique was the source of productivity and wealth creation, there was the other side of the coin, namely the accompanying fear that the masses would rise up and the nation succumb to anarchy, insurrection and chaos. Out of a mixture of genuine philanthropy and hard-nosed protection of their own interests, the middle class addressed these fears in a number of ways, among them being:

• The building of libraries, art galleries, museums, swimming baths and gymnasiums and the donation of land for the creation of parks for public recreation.
• A determined attempt to introduce 'dangerous' working men to Christianity, temperance and a healthier lifestyle (for example, the founding of the Young Men's Christian Association in the 1840s and the Working Men's Club movement in the 1860s).
• Attempts to improve working class housing, diet and hygiene allied to a growing discourse of bodily health correlated with national and Imperial well-being, eventually culminating in the provision of school meals and medicals in the first decade of the twentieth century.

The middle class response was to control both the minds and bodies of the working class and, at the same time, ensure that its own sons were rendered fit for leadership and service to both nation and Empire. What was required was the right 'medicine' for the good of both the body and the mind. We shall look at the role of juvenile literature to inculcate boys and young men into the right set of values and attitudes and, in the next chapter, the promotion of exercise and weight training to build the physique and toughen the body.

Sport, Muscular Christianity and masculinity

The Victorian public school is aptly termed by Mason (1982) as nothing less than a 'factory for gentlemen'. With its rites of passage based upon intimidation and violence – admirably captured in Hughes' novel *Tom Brown's Schooldays* (1856) – it was held to facilitate the development in boys of both the mental and physical toughness which were the hallmarks of Victorian masculinity. Meanwhile, at home, fathers were emotionally and physically aloof. This was the value system into which large numbers of upper and upper middle class young men were acculturated, one characterized by 'self-reliance, independence, emotional control and the deep suspicion of intimacy' (Clare 2000: 88). Meanwhile, late nineteenth century organizations like Baden-Powell's Boy Scouts and the Boys' Brigade, while being heavily informed by the public school ethos of a healthy mind and body and the repression of sexuality, were aimed at 'rescuing' lower middle class boys, even reaching working class boys (Macdonald 1993).

One of the key influences in the promotion of Muscular Christianity was Dr Thomas Arnold, the charismatic headmaster of Rugby School from 1828 to 1842. He both caught and helped to shape the mood of the time with his emphasis upon the inculcation of character strengthening through sport. The 1864 **Clarendon Commission** Report on public schools not only accorded status to cricket and football, but also linked them directly to 'manly virtues':

> The cricket and football fields are not merely places of amusement, they help to form some of the most valuable social qualities and manly virtues, and they hold – like the classroom and boarding house – a distinct and important place in Public School education.
>
> (Money 1997: 123)

No less a person than the Duke of Wellington, who regarded sport as essential to Britain's military prowess ('The battle of Waterloo was won on the playing fields of Eton') had directed in the 1840s that every military barracks, home and overseas, should have its own cricket ground.

Public school teachers were the principal promoters of Muscular Christianity. George Cotton went from Rugby to head (1851–8) the newly opened

Marlborough School, where he immediately introduced organized sport, in particular promoting rugby football (a 'game for ruffians played by gentlemen'). Rugby and cricket (famously described as 'Britain's gift to the world') marked out the contours of Empire. Sport became increasingly seen as essential preparation both for character and service in Empire: a 'blue' at Oxbridge opened the career door (a 'blue' being someone who has represented Oxford or Cambridge University at a particular sport) and, as Money points out, 'the Anglo-Sudan was known as "a country of blacks ruled by blues"' (Money 1997: 173). Cricket was directly linked with the development of skills for Empire service. Dr Ridding, the head of Winchester from 1866 to 1884, advocated it as an essential training for discipline and teamwork, while Robert Singleton, the warden of Radley School, argued that while the teaching of music may be important, it was only so provided that it did not 'interfere with cricket and other manly and muscular diversions' (Money 1997: 67).

In the middle of the nineteenth century ancient folk games were given rules and, as the century wore on, sport-as-spectatorship gradually developed. Much of this codification and regulation was undertaken by the upper middle class in the context of the public schools. In the latter half of the century sport became the main nurturing ground for what were regarded as 'typical' British values of never-say-die competition and fair play. Indeed, young men's engagement in healthy, sporting activities at all levels of society was held to be necessary for the perpetuation and well-being of the Empire (J. Mangan 1981; Mangan and Walvin 1987; Holt 1989). It became a marker of the health of the nation and of masculinity. Indeed, masculinity was both attained and displayed through athleticism, strength, speed, fitness and muscularity. Men dominated nineteenth century sport and women participants were ridiculed, being regarded as too weak to play games, whereas for men it was 'natural'.

The development of sport as mass entertainment was well advanced by the start of the twentieth century. Seaman (1973: 423) attributes this to shorter working hours, improvements in transport and communication, and 'the missionary activities in the industrial towns of muscular young Christians from the Public Schools and Universities'. At the heart of sporting Muscular Christianity (characterized by Money as a throwback to medieval chivalry) was 'the spirit' in which the game was played. Indeed, this version of sport was as much, if not more, about character training than physical prowess. This was symbolized by the Corinthian football club, founded in 1882 for former public school men and whose motto was that 'this club shall not compete for any challenge cup or any prizes of any description whatsoever'. The game was played for the game's sake, not to win: it was, in other words, about the character behind the physical skills and display. Marvellous examples of the ethic in action are of goalkeepers standing clear of their goal to allow the opposition to score, or of batsmen 'walking' at cricket (that is, voluntarily relinquishing their wicket). 'It's not cricket' (meaning 'it's not fair') came to stand for (English) gentlemanly behaviour both in sport and in life. Even the most brutal of sports, boxing, reflected the same ethic. The move away from bare-knuckle fighting was finally achieved with the Marquis of Queensberry's rules in 1869, resulting in the foundation of the Amateur Boxing Association. Many public schools took up the 'noble art' and some founded missions in slum areas (as part of the Victorian rescue movement) and introduced boxing to inculcate not only skill in self-defence, but also respect for the opponent, inner control and learning to 'act like a gentleman'. Reports on public school missions regularly appeared in the Christmas annuals for boys (for example, see 'What old boys have done and are still doing for less fortunate brothers in poor districts', by A.B. Cooper, *Boys Own Annual*, 1915–16: 463–6).

Team games were promoted in Victorian times by both social reformers and the Muscular Christians. Whereas rugby remained a predominantly middle class game (perhaps the greatest exception being its growth in popularity in the working class industrial belt of South Wales, from Llanelly in the west to Newport in the east), football took its place along with the workplace, pub and hobbies at the centre of male working class socialization (Holt 1989). Local capitalists founded and invested in clubs as part of municipal pride and they thrived through a process which Cohen (1988) has termed 'neighbourhood nationalism', especially in the growing urban centres where it provided a rite of passage between juvenile street play, gangs and the adult world of week-long hard labour and weekend leisure. It was not surprising that aggressive and hard players came to be admired over the 'fancy dans' (Holt 1989), players who exhibited on the pitch on a Saturday afternoon the kind of masculine attributes admired in the industrial settings of mill, mine and docks.

Physical culture and 're-masculinization'

In pre-industrial times physical strength and material rewards were closely linked. The effects of the Industrial Revolution diminished the importance of physical strength (a process which has been accelerated by the technological revolution of our own time) and this no doubt contributed to the idea that men were getting soft and weak. A major response to the degeneracy myths was undoubtedly the spectacular rise in popularity of a particular aspect of sport, namely physical training or 'physical culture'. There had been previous calls for mass exercise for the working class to tackle the perceived physical and moral decline and, thereby, 'improve the stock'. Eugene Sandow, whose amazing physique resulted in his becoming a celebrity, was the key figure behind the huge popularity of physical culture as the nineteenth century moved to an end. An East Prussian émigré, he began to publish books on physical training which attracted a considerable readership (see for example Sandow 1894, 1904). In particular, in 1898, he started his hugely popular *Magazine of Physical Culture* through which readers could purchase fitness schedules and equipment and submit photographs of themselves for cash prizes. The typical images were of young men, statuesque and sculptural, bare chested, muscles flexed, with short, military haircuts. The magazine organized regional heats for its *Empire and Muscle* competition, a weekly window on Empire with the masculine form presented as the nation's physical property. The photographs were presented not as 'a mere indulgence of male vanity, but as necessary tools for the preservation of family, nation and Empire' (Budd 1997: 61).

Sandow (1894; 1904) argued that neglect of the body was a sin against nature and that all men, irrespective of class, must take possession of their bodies through organized physical training schedules. He played strongly on the degeneracy fears and provided a pseudo-scientific culture of physical 'self-help' and development which would produce men capable of fathering children 'free from hereditary taint'. He aimed at nothing less than to reform British society and equated the muscular physical form with individual strength and success, national resurgence and Imperial well-being. Indeed, Budd regards the healthy male body, exhibited in energetic service to nation and people, as one of the most pervasive and powerful symbols of the time. Sandow's masculinity was in sharp contrast to that of his contemporary, Oscar Wilde. Whereas Sandow stood for 'normal' masculinity and the improvement of the national and racial 'stock', Wilde represented the 'abnormal' and was the living embodiment of the debauched, the fear of 'rotting from within'. The strongman, with his neo-classical, man-of-action aesthetic stood in sharp contrast with the effeminate, literary dandy. The concept of homosexuality was largely a nineteenth century invention and Wilde's humiliation was seen in many quarters as a victory for Imperial masculinity and, by implication, for national and Imperial health. Budd concludes that 'a large part of the success of physical culture was its assertion of the male body as heroic rather than erotic, in the body's depiction as "under control" rather than "out of control"' (Budd 1997: 77).

The physical culture rhetoric connected with a number of late nineteenth century **self-help discourses** and I now comment on three of particular interest: the self-reliance ethic, 'racial' superiority and the growing demand for spectacle.

The self-reliance ethic

This was popularized by Samuel Smiles in his influential *Self-Help* (1859), which had its origins in sixteenth century chivalric texts, notably Castiglione's *The Book of the Courtier* (1528) and Sir Thomas Elyot's *The Governor* (1531). Smiles, for example, writes:

> Riches and rank have no necessary connection with genuine gentlemanly qualities. The poor man may be a true gentleman, in spirit and in daily life. He may be honest, truthful, upright, polite, temperate, courageous, self-respecting and self-helping: that is, be a true gentleman. The poor man with a rich spirit is in all ways superior to the rich man with a poor spirit.
>
> (Smiles 1996 [1859]: 245)

Sandow, too, was promising self-improvement of body and empowerment for self, work, family, community and Empire to all, cheaply. At little cost, ordinary men could acquire the strength and shape of the strongman as an escape route from poverty and anonymity, as in the case of numerous Jewish and black boxers, wrestlers and strongmen (like Sandow himself). This connected with mid-century Muscular Christianity and Thomas Arnold's radical view for the time that elites were made, not born. Even class differences could be bridged by sportsmanship, teamwork and a shared, common purpose through sport.

'Racial' superiority

This took the form of the reaffirmation of the belief in the innate superiority, in mind and body, of the English gentleman, in scientific racism and in eugenicists' call to improve genes. The term eugenics was first used by Francis Galton in 1885 to describe the study of agencies which may improve (or impair) the racial qualities of future generations, either physically or mentally. It focused on the role played by inborn qualities and the raising of the level of 'racial qualities' by, for example, preventing the reproduction of 'defective types' and encouraging congress between 'sound stock'. Galton saw in Sandow a valid anthropometric model, namely the perfect white, European male physique. There is no evidence, however, that Sandow ever subscribed to Galton's notion of this 'ideal' male physique and its racial superiority: his emphasis was, rather, upon empowerment for all prepared to invest the time and effort. As Budd (1997) notes:

> The genetic elitism of Eugenics was never reconciled with physical culture's persistent utopian promises of bodily empowerment for all.
>
> (Budd 1997: 82)

Similarly, one of the most revered figures of his time, Robert Baden-Powell, turned to Empire for a model of aggressive, hardy manhood which, he believed, would save boys from the debilitating routine of domestic and urban life (Macdonald 1993). As founder of the Scout movement, the ideology of which directly expressed middle class values and the Protestant work ethic, he was to become one of the major influences on 'turning boys into men' well into the twentieth century. He was an enthusiastic supporter of eugenics and advocated outdoor activities and physical training to ensure the well-being and superiority of the British 'race' which, he held, was an elite among nations and had to be preserved at all costs. He deplored the sexual, regarded the feminine as a danger, and called for 'clean manliness in a dirty age' through male camaraderie and the creation of the archetypal scout ('clean in thought, word and deed') to serve unto death God, Queen and Empire.

The growing demand for spectacle

Enfranchised working class men began to exercise both political and leisure choices in the late nineteenth century, resulting in the emergence of an embryonic consumer society with an increasing desire for amusement, appearance and performance. This was fuelled by the expansion of 'mass' media from the 1880s in the form of popular newspapers, magazines and photography (including postcards and cigarette cards). Boxing and wrestling grew in popularity and 'strongman acts', long a feature of the circus, transferred to the music hall. Both Sandow and, later, the wrestler George Hackenschmidt toured Britain with their own shows, featuring strength displays, challenges and competitions. This coincided with a renewed nostalgia for the Olympian movement and presentations (using the new media of photography, slide shows and, later, silent film) of the ideal male body modelled on the warrior of antiquity displaying Herculean power. These purposely non-erotic poses (the erotic was reserved for photographs of scantily clad 'actresses') were often presented as 'living proof' of the physical superiority of the white, Anglo-Saxon 'race'. Accordingly:

> Sports, exercise, health policies, popular entertainment and military and moral concerns for the nation's physical well-being began to converge

within a jumble of attempts to salvage the physical body of the 'degen-
erate' British worker.

(Budd 1997: 119)

Increasingly, physical fitness was directly related to national and Imperial
well-being, military readiness and commercial success. Bourke (1996),
although referring to a later period, captures the thinking that has always
resided behind physical training for the masses:

> Physical training was patriotic and chauvinistic: it prepared men's
> bodies for war . . . The male body required physical discipline not
> solely for the sake of a state threatened with military and economic col-
> lapse: it also required discipline in the pursuit of social harmony.
>
> (Bourke 1996: 176, 179)

In the latter half of the nineteenth century rapid physical improvement in the
name of nation and Empire became a patriotic necessity. There was an
urgent call for improved recreational facilities for young, city men, as well
as the working class. Indeed,

> rather than percolating downward from the elite schools to broader
> society, the ethos for bodily reform developed within different classes at
> the same time.
>
> (Budd 1997: 17)

Moreover, the latter half of the nineteenth century witnessed a growing
interest in orthopaedics, specialist training and displays of physical skills,
seen in the foundation of the National Physical Recreation Society in the
early 1880s, the appointment of specialist army gymnastic trainers and the
start of the Royal Tournament as a celebration of strength, teamwork and
competition.

Imperial man's damaged masculinity

In our time there is a widely accepted view that Imperial masculinity was
damaging to its upholders, in particular the repression of feelings. Tosh
(1991), for example, refers to the 'brittle masculinity' of the generation of
middle and upper middle class men that grew up in the latter half of the nineteenth century. They experienced unaffectionate, duty-obsessed fathers and
associated tenderness with nannies, mothers and sisters. They came to
regard such feelings as unmanly and so suppressed them. Tosh's study of one
'true Arnoldian', Edward White Benson, reveals the contradictions behind

the public face. Through phenomenal hard work and self-denial, Benson rose to become a leading ecclesiastic. He epitomized the new man of his time, following Arnold's quest to establish a new middle and upper middle class, based on public service, piety, high-mindedness, sobriety and 'moral manliness'. Tosh demonstrates the damage done to Benson's long-suffering wife and sons, who later sought in relations with young men the intimacy denied to them by their career-driven father. Edmund Gosse's *Father and Son* (1907) captures many of these negative pressures, such as the gap between the over-stern father and the loving mother. This had a disastrous impact on many men, who thereafter hid behind a stiff upper lip and emotionally strangulated lives, a point vividly made in the *Reputations* television series broadcast on BBC2 in 1997 on Lord Kitchener and Robert Baden-Powell.

Imperial man, argues Rutherford (1997), was undermined by sexual uncertainty. Typically he was a women-avoiding and mother-obsessed person, surrounding himself with young male followers with whom he had strong **homosocial** friendships (Sedgwick 1985). Rutherford (1997) points to three particularly damaging facets of Imperial masculinity, namely, blind passion for the Imperial mission, boyhood and 'boyishness', and homoerotic tension.

Blind passion for the Imperial mission

The embracing of a masculinity-fit-for-Empire was an escape from the domestic and feminine into a world of male camaraderie, incited by the lure of adventure, heroism and even possible immortality in the cause of the great Imperial mission. If fate deemed that this meant dying like an Englishman for the good of the British race, then so be it. Rutherford comments:

> The Imperial mission, the 'white heights' of English manliness . . . became a divinity, an autoerotic pleasure offering itself as an object of love.
>
> (Rutherford 1997: 34)

Boyhood and 'boyishness'

Rutherford sees an infatuation with boyishness lying at the heart of Victorian manliness:

> The story of Empire is full of mother's boys – repressed, sentimental, loving boys in general because it was a way of loving the boyishness in themselves.
>
> (Rutherford 1997: 26)

Imperial men, he argues, were 'emotionally repressed, sexually confused, mother-fixated, women-fearing men and that this fostered in them a morbid nostalgia for 'the brave, bright days of his boyhood' (Rutherford 1997: 26). The figure of the boy in the adventure stories of the time came to represent for these men a longing 'for all that they had been forced to renounce – maternal love, their own bodies and sexual desire' (Rutherford 1997: 27). Of J.M. Barrie's *Peter Pan* (1904) he writes that it 'revealed what had been repressed and denied them in the Imperial fantasy of manly racial supremacy' (Rutherford 1997: 25).

Homoerotic tension

It is hard in a sexually liberated age to appreciate the degree of abhorrence held towards homosexuality in the latter half of the nineteenth century, which culminated in Oscar Wilde's trial in 1895. It is ironic, therefore, to note the sexual ambivalence and homoerotic overtones in the descriptions of the natives in much male adventure literature. Rutherford argues that 'the homophobic boyhoods of Englishmen exacerbated the autoerotic desire to spy on the bodies of "primitive" others' (Rutherford 1997: 32). Similarly, it is interesting that Skovmand (1987) concludes that far from being a straight-forward depiction of chivalrous masculinity, much Victorian literature dis-plays a 'beleaguered, defensive sense of masculinity . . . a pervasive sense of unease about gender identities' (Skovmand 1987: 56, 58). If there is one novel in which the anxieties about Victorian masculinity are laid bare, then it is, of course, R.L. Stevenson's *The Strange Case of Dr. Jekyll and Mr. Hyde*, published in 1886. Far from the Imperial imaginings of R.M. Ballan-tyne or Rider Haggard, it explores masculinity's underbelly, the savage and elemental in the context of the squalor and vice of the Victorian city.

The demise of Imperial man

Imperial man reached the acme of his popularity in the years leading up to the First World War. Rudyard Kipling's famous poem *If* was published in 1910 and is a celebration of Imperial masculinity and its doctrine of physi-cal and moral courage and self-reliance. It reads as a series of instructions: if you do this and if you do that then, eventually, you will become a good and proper man. Likewise, Sir Henry Newbolt's *Vitae Lampada* appeared in 1912 and presents a picture of courage, honour and selfless devotion to king and country even unto death. The masculinity depicted in both poems, viewed from the twenty-first century, appears obsessive, emotionally repressed and duty bound to the point of pathology. After the carnage of Passchendaele and the Somme, such blind heroism had an increasingly hollow ring: the idea that war was a glorious game played by gentlemen could never again be taken seriously. Indeed, the 'soldier and hero' quickly became the 'soldier and victim' (Fussell 1975; Bourke 1996), a sentiment wonderfully captured in Wilfred Owen's poem *Disabled* (1917).

Yet, in spite of all this, 'imaginings of Empire' continued in literature for juveniles in the interwar years, along with an extolling of the virtues of the chivalrous English (even British!) gentleman, a point noted by George Orwell ([1939] 1957) in his essay on the weekly 'penny dreadfuls' like *The Gem* and *The Magnet*. Boyd (1991), however, notes a shifting of emphasis in storybooks and comics from Empire to the home front. She examines a wider range of interwar storybooks and comics than Orwell. She sees them functioning to render boys from across the class spectrum 'British'. Working class boys, for example, are depicted forgoing the freedom of the streets and heeding the advice of teachers and, increasingly, employers to 'learn to be obedient, to compromise and to submit to the greater knowledge of their elders and community' (Boyd 1991: 145). Moreover, interwar adventures tend to be located not in exotic parts of the Empire, but in the more prosaic surroundings of school and playground. Participation in sport is greatly encouraged. In these dangerous years (which witnessed the General Strike of 1926 and the Depression of the 1930s), she argues that boys' comics played a key role in promoting the myth of 'one-nation Britain' by reinforcing traditional sources of guidance (especially fathers and the family, along with teachers and education), stressing the value of community and delineating the class based nature of what was expected of (British) manly boys.

Contemporary echoes of Imperial masculinity

Imperial man is still capable of shaking a jingoistic fist in times of national crisis (as in the Falklands War of 1982). He features widely in the heritage industry or in films like *Zulu* (1964). However, the rapid disintegration of the British Empire after the Second World War deprived him of his role. By the latter 1950s he was lampooned as an anachronism and little of him now remains: he is no longer part of the structures of feeling that shape contemporary masculinities. However, although Imperial man may be dead, something of his masculinity lives on in the stories of past colonial endeavour that still regularly surface in the media (see Chapter 6) and a continuing fascination with at least some of the great heroes of Empire. Dawson (1994) throws an interesting light on this. He takes two Imperial heroes, one of the nineteenth century and almost entirely forgotten (Sir Henry Havelock of Lucknow) and the other of the early twentieth (T.E. Shaw, better known as 'Lawrence of Arabia'). Why, he asks, does the latter ('the blond Bedouin') have continuing appeal in our postmodern times while the former has been reduced to a largely ignored statue in a corner of Trafalgar Square? The answer, Dawson argues, lies in his ambiguous, enigmatic character and mystery-shrouded life and death, with the result that it is 'impossible to fix Lawrence in any one position . . . [he] has become a locus of the phantasies of others . . . a battlefield for contesting forms of imagined masculinity' (Dawson 1994: 210, 213, 218). But it is in sport that the strongest echo of Imperial man survives. His sense of racial superiority and destiny has no place in multicultural, multiethnic, postcolonial Britain. Modern professional sport, with its win-at-all-costs ethic, has clearly abandoned the Corinthian ideal of playing the game for the game's sake. Yet sport remains one of the main arenas for the acquisition and expression of socially approved and desirable masculinity (Holt 1989; Lowerson 1993; Coakley 1998; Rowe 1999; McKay *et al.* 2000). It links masculinity and nationality and, at its worst, it can engender the worst kind of nationalistic xenophobia, well captured by Parker (1996):

> At football abroad . . . ill-educated and courageous young Englishmen in flimsy shorts and T-shirts, drawn from anonymous towns and suburbs and incapable of any meaningful contact with local cultures, are still aggressively on the prowl. Fortified by drink and the knowledge that they are English – and together – they guilelessly attack the best armed and most violent police forces on the Continent. Most of them also fully expect to 'win' those confrontations.
>
> (A. Parker 1996: 231)

In unpublished studies Magor (1999) and Gerrish (1999) trace echoes of Imperial masculinity in the play-the-game discourses surrounding gentlemanly rugby football and bodybuilding respectively. It is in the latter that Imperial man's voice is most clearly heard and it is to this that I now turn.

Men have long held muscles, especially of the biceps, neck and shoulders, to be signifiers of 'proper masculinity' (Wacquant 1995; Schacht 1996). This celebration of masculine power and invincibility based on muscle lives on (Johansson 1998) and stretches back through 'strongmen' (both actual and filmic) like Arnold Schwarzenegger, Sylvester Stallone, Dave Prowse, Steve Reeves, Charles Atlas, George Hachenschmidt to Eugene Sandow and then back even further into antiquity to Hercules. Schwarzenegger (see M. Harris 1997) and Sandow, although a century apart, share similar body shape and similar roles, both representing an enduring myth, namely the masculinist fantasy of unstoppable physical power and authority. While Imperial man has been confined to the giant dustbin of history, his desire for a hard, 'warrior body' survives. Men now find themselves in situations in which great physical strength is no longer required, but for lower economic men physical combativeness has always been and remains a major signifier of masculinity. Many invest an enormous amount of time and energy in working out with weights in order to attain the desired muscularity (Hargreaves 1987; Wacquant 1995; Johansson 1998). Moore (1996: 77) comments that 'what drives competitive bodybuilders is the desire for absolute physical wholeness, the complete development of almost every voluntary muscle and neck-to-toe physical perfection'. Bouncers, for example, are highly visible contemporary icons of raw machismo (James 2001), while steroid abuse among those hell bent on being 'big' (and thereby acquire the connotations of health, strength and sexiness) has reached dangerously high levels in both Britain and the United States. Both print and the visual media repeat Sandow's (1894, 1904) self-help message that to take one's body in hand is to do something positive about one's life and empower oneself both physically and mentally.

Further reading

Budd, M.A. (1997) *The Sculpture Machine: Physical Culture and Body Politics in the Age of Empire*. London: Macmillan.

Chandos, J. (1984) *Boys Together*. London: Yale University Press.

Dawson, G. (1994) *Soldier Heroes: British Adventure, Empire and the Imagining of Masculinities*. London: Routledge.

Mangan, J.A. and Walvin, J. (eds) (1987) *Manliness and Morality: Middle Class Masculinities in Britain and America, 1800–1940*. Manchester: Manchester University Press.

Mason, P. (1982) *The English Gentleman: The Rise and Fall of an Ideal*. New York: Morrow.

Phillips, R. (1997) *Mapping Men and Empire: Geographies of Adventure*. London: Routledge.

Roper, M. and Tosh, J. (eds) (1991) *Manful Assertions: Masculinities in Britain since 1800*. London: Routledge.

Rutherford, J. (1997) *Forever England: Reflections on Masculinity and Empire*. London: Lawrence and Wishart.

3 | UNDERSTANDING MASCULINITIES

Quit ye like men, be strong.

(Corinthians 16: 13)

the fillers look and work as though they are made of iron. They really do look like iron. They really do look like iron – hammered iron statues – under the smooth coat of coal dust which clings to them from head to foot. It is only when you see miners down the mine and naked that you realise what splendid men they are. Most of them are small (big men are at a disadvantage in that job) but nearly all of them have the most noble bodies; wide shoulders tapering to slender, supple waists and small pronounced buttocks and sinewy thighs, with not an ounce of waste flesh anywhere.

(George Orwell, The Road to Wigan Pier, 1937)

Introduction: critical work on masculinity

I start by briefly locating this chapter in critical work on masculinity before drawing upon work in sociology, anthropology, social psychology, cultural and media studies, film and literary studies to pursue four themes:

- socialization into masculinity and the ways commonly associated with being a man in the west
- masculinity in other times, a historical approach
- masculinity in other places, an anthropological approach
- the mediation of masculinity, specifically its representation in film and how cinematic masculinity might be analysed.

I conclude with a case study of how masculinity was lived and experienced at a particular time and in a particular place, 1950s Britain, and how it was represented in the literature and film of the time. This chapter is complemented by Chapter 7, in which I examine practical ways of researching masculinity.

Bourke (1996) provides a succinct summary of the ways in which masculinity has been approached:

- *Biological*: what men are is tied to biology and masculinity is a natural outcome of biology.
- *Socialization*: masculinity is a product of socialization and those who are not 'proper men' have not been properly reared.
- *Psychoanalytical*: male subjectivities are formed in sociohistorical and cultural contexts.
- *Discourse*: masculinity in all its variety is the product of discourse and discursive regimes.
- *Feminist*: **patriarchy** oppresses and damages women and also men themselves.

The early work on masculinity in the United States (for example, Pleck and Sawyer 1974; Brod 1987; Kimmel 1987, and which is reviewed in Clatterbaugh 1990) proved highly influential for scholars in Britain. It opened up new areas of study in sociology (long dominated by class) and was enthusiastically embraced by the emerging areas of cultural and media studies. Indeed, critical work on masculinity in Britain accelerated in the late 1990s, but dates back over two decades to Snodgrass (1977) and Tolson's (1977) pioneering studies. The latter advanced an economic and class-centred analysis of postwar British masculinities and appeared not long after Paul Willis's influential book *Learning to Labour* (1977), which remains one of the most compelling studies of the formation of young British working class masculinity in Britain. He argues that rebellious, irreverent and subversive masculinity is the principal means by which the young men in the study were trapped into a life of labour. To provide an indication of how masculinity has been studied to date is not an easy task for a number of reasons.

Masculinity's history of being studied indirectly

Masculinity has long been studied within the social sciences, but indirectly. For example, there is a history of sociological work on youth subcultures which, although it does not focus on masculinity *per se*, has much to say about it. Indeed, sociology has long acknowledged the importance of masculinity but, until recently, has failed to interrogate it and has tended to assume it to be both homogeneous and stable. The fact that sociology started to take masculinity seriously was largely a result of the feminist critique. Many early studies of male youth culture, for example, implied a high degree of homogeneity whereas, in fact, there has always been considerable diversity within young masculinity.

Masculinity approached via a variety of theories

The study of masculinity goes on within disparate subjects like cultural and media studies, sociology, psychology and social psychology, criminology, anthropology, literary studies, film studies, women's studies and, of course, men's studies. A number of theoretical stances towards masculinity are taken, from feminist, gay scholarship and, more latterly, **queer theory** through to psychoanalytical, Marxist, structuralist, semiotic and symbolic interactionist. Models used to study masculinity are usefully surveyed by Brod and Kaufman (1994) and Edley and Wetherell (1995). The importance of such work is that it moves beyond the descriptive to the analytical as in, for example, Mac an Ghaill (1994, 1996).

'Masculinity' as a very large umbrella

Such work, of course, contradicts the commonsensical assumption that masculinity is 'fixed', 'natural' and 'universal'. It has been extended into diverse areas, for example, on power (Brittan 1989), violence (Miedzian 1992), crime (Messerschmidt 1993), law (Collier 1995) and child abuse (Hearn 1990). Meanwhile, Westwood (1990) studies the interplay between racism, ethnicity, class and masculinity, while Edwards (1994) writes about gay men, sexuality and the advent of AIDS in this context. A number of studies in the 1990s focus on the **commodification of masculinity** (for example, Mort 1996; Nixon 1996; Edwards 1997). A still-growing development within the social sciences is queer theory, which provides a valuable critique of the heterosexual assumptions of much theorizing about gender. Those who adopt this approach analyse the social practices whereby heterosexuality dominates in a wide range of institutions, as well as charting gay, lesbian and trans-gender lives and experiences. This focuses upon how masculinities are constructed, experienced and enacted at particular times in particular ways in a range of socio-historical contexts. As a consequence there are numerous references to history, literature, film, popular culture and ethnography. Masculinity is presented as a highly diverse and fragmented text, not as a fixed essence chained to biology, but rather the outcome of socio-historical and cultural struggle and change. As Edley and Wetherell (1996: 106) aptly comment, 'manliness is a contested territory: it is an ideological battlefield'.

I now turn to the four themes mentioned at the start of the chapter, namely socialization into masculinity, masculinity in other times, masculinity in other places and the mediation of masculinity.

Socialization into masculinity

Sociology, in particular, has contributed to our understanding of how factors like class, culture and ethnicity impact on masculinity, which is seen to be shaped by the institutions in which men and women are embedded. Male aggression, competitiveness and emotional inarticulateness are held to reflect their position in the economic system. Capitalism places men in a network of social relations that encourages sets of behaviour recognized as masculine. Masculinity is thus viewed as a set of practices into which individual men are inserted with reference to upbringing, family, area, work and subcultural influences. Socio-economic positioning profoundly impacts upon the masculine sense of self so much so that men's identities are constructed through social structures which exist over and above any actions of the individual (Edley and Wetherell 1995). Sociology, too, has incorporated the feminist emphasis upon the historical production and reproduction of men's power over women and other men.

The still widely accepted view among the general public is that men and women fundamentally differ and that a distinct set of fixed traits characterize archetypal masculinity and femininity. This is reflected in popular sayings such as 'Just like a man!' or 'Just like a woman!' and in the kinds of features found in popular magazines along the lines of 'How manly is your man?', with a list of attributes to be rated or boxes to be ticked. Masculinity and femininity are often treated in the media as polar opposites, with men typically assumed to be rational, practical and naturally aggressive and women, in contrast, are held to be expressive, nurturing and emotional. Minor differences are often accorded great significance and misrepresented. Traits are treated as something that can be accurately measured and scientifically proven to be the defining features of gender. Differences between men and women have been expressed in terms of traits as diverse as cognition, esteem, sociability, achievement, motivation, dominance, aggression, compliance, nurturing, verbal ability and spatial and perceptual awareness. McMahon (1993) makes the point that because of the difficulty of defining masculinity, writers often quickly resort to such a list of assumed traits, which themselves have a cultural history. Being hard, physically powerful and mentally strong, competitive, aggressive, dominant, rational, unemotional and objective are often advanced as typical indexical markers of the masculine (Ochs 1992). These traits, traditionally attributed to masculinity, present it as a superior state to femininity, whose attributes of softness, emotionality and nurturing are seen as wanting in comparison and, as a result, often employed in censure. For example, shell-shocked men in the First World War were accused of being 'womanly' and having unmanly hysterics

(Bourke 1996). Many of the stereotypical male traits are artfully combined in mediated constructions of masculinity, as in the 'image-ing' of the ever-in-control, cool Hollywood hardman (like Clint Eastwood, Charles Bronson, Sylvester Stallone and, latterly, the 'gangster chic' of Vinny Jones). But in real life things are different and, as MacInnes (1998: 15) points out, 'any empirical individual's identity is always complex and contradictory rather than something that can be defined by any list of qualities, no matter how comprehensive or carefully defined'.

Work on the engendering into being a man naturally focuses on the role of home, school, community, peers and media during childhood and investigates why, typically, the masculine has come to be associated with assertion and aggression and, conversely, the feminine with gentleness and emotionality. Unsurprisingly, socialization theorists have often been attacked for promoting a very static, unitary concept of gender differences and for not taking sufficient account of the variety of masculinities (and femininities) resulting from social class, ethnicity and historical location. Writers point to how aggression and competitiveness often elicit approval and are reinforced in the male child. Archer (1994), for example, explores the sociobiological basis of gender and male aggression, drawing on social identity theory to examine how boys are socialized into men. From this research masculinity emerges as fragile, constantly forcing men into displaying and proving it. The outcome is that many men suppress the feminine in themselves and some even turn against women as a way of denying feelings of dependence (Frosh 1987). Early childhood influences and relationships with parents is a recurring area of interest. Whereas girls are much more likely to identify with the mother's role, boys are much more likely to break with the mother and identify, instead, with the often distant father (Chodorow 1978). A particularly interesting study is that by Browne and Ross (1995), who observed children in infant and nursery school classes and found that as early as the age of 3, children appeared to have mapped out which toys and activities were 'for girls', which were 'for boys' and which could be described as gender neutral. Girls were observed to be happiest playing with dolls, dolls' houses and felt-tip pens, whereas boys concentrated on Lego and wood-work. Books, puzzles and sand-play were viewed as neutral. Boys engaged in active and constructional play. Girls, in contrast, engaged in more creative play. This bifurcation appeared to cross cultural, linguistic and ethnic divisions. Even when using the same materials boys' and girls' play differed: for example, when working with Lego, boys gave doors, windows and base-boards to girls to build houses, whereas girls handed wheels and rotatable connectors to boys to build vehicles. Also, whereas boys approached constructional play as an individualized activity, girls were more collaborative and social in their play. If boys were more intent on making things, girls were more concerned with the process of social interaction itself.

The role model depicts men and women not as free agents but like actors following pre-scripted roles: so to 'be a man' is to play a certain masculine role. To take the theatrical metaphor further, masculinity is a performance, a set of stage directions, a 'script' that men learn to perform. Socializing agents like the family, school and the media inculcate and validate gender-appropriate behaviour and the boy learns the male role through observation, initiation (even indoctrination) and feedback (Bandura 1977). In this process stereotypical expectations (like girls playing with dolls, boys with toy cars) are reinforced.

While Brannon (1976), Pleck and Thompson (1987) and Moore and Gillette (1990) identify some typical male roles (for example, being a 'big wheel', 'sturdy oak', 'no sissy stuff'), it is Ian Harris (1995) who provides the most comprehensive study to date of the socialization into roles perspective based on extensive interview data with large numbers of men in the United States gathered over a number of years. In many ways Harris' study is problematic but is, nevertheless, a very comprehensive 'map' of contemporary American masculinity in the words of men themselves. The socializing 'messages' emanate from parents, teachers, peers, the media, organizations like church and the Scouts, and constitute a series of 'scripts', or guidelines, by which men live their lives. They can be grouped as follows, telling men they must strive to become

- *standard bearers*, who do their best and achieve as much as they can
- *workers*, who become good breadwinners and develop a strong work ethic
- *lovers*, whether as faithful husbands and partners, or as playboys
- *bosses*, by overcoming all possible hurdles and taking control
- *rugged individuals*, who are prepared to engage in dangerous and adventurous acts, having faith in their abilities.

These guidelines can give off contradictory messages (for example, the need for real men to be both conformist achievers and faithful partners as opposed to hedonistic playboys and rebels). If the study is good at detailing the nature of the voices, it is less so on how these are received, interpreted and enacted as **life scripts** differently by men in different circumstances.

Masculinity in other times

Historians have largely taken masculinity for granted and, therefore, it has passed largely unquestioned. As we saw in Chapter 2, it is only comparatively recently that some of them have embraced the fact that it, too, has a history, one which reveals a complex interweaving of both imagined and lived masculinities. As a result there is an increased interest in explicating the socio-cultural history of masculinity, in particular how competing forms characterize different historical periods and locations. As Roper and Tosh (1991: 12) put it: 'while the artisan of the 1880s gained manly pride from his breadwinning wage, the post- [Second World War] manager . . . expressed masculinity directly in product fetishism'. They argue that masculinity cannot be treated ahistorically, but must be placed in a historical context and examined in the light of social, economic, political and cultural circumstances. This view is echoed by, for example, Seidler (1989), who emphasizes the valorization of reason and rationality in the eighteenth century Enlightenment movement as crucial to relating the history of western masculinity. Reason and feeling were separated and masculinity came to be associated with the objective, the practical, the scientific and the technological. Similarly, increasing male control over women following the Industrial Revolution is attributed to the growth of cities and the consequent separation of home and place of work in the burgeoning nineteenth century factories and textile mills. Roper and Tosh (1991), however, argue that while nineteenth century patriarchal masculinity stifled women, neither did it serve the real needs of men. Indeed, in satisfying the demands of Empire, the military, industry and commerce, men's potential for personal growth and fulfilment was also decimated. The result was that the later decades of the twentieth century witnessed a determined drive by feminists and pro-feminist men to overthrow these deforming aspects of patriarchy, perceived as harmful both to women and men alike, that had originated in the eighteenth and nineteenth centuries. The outstanding collection of papers assembled by Roper and Tosh (1991) strives to render men visible as historically gendered subjects, providing as examples case studies of a range of time-situated masculinities associated with the nineteenth century professional man; the nineteenth century man of letters; Imperial man; the 'respectable' working class; post-Second World War public school men; and the 1950s 'company man' (referred to above) who expressed his masculinity in terms of work-related products.

Doyle (1989), building upon the work on the history of American masculinity, identifies six generalized 'ideal types' of historical masculinity, namely the heroic, the spiritual, the chivalrous, Renaissance man, the hedonist and the he-man. Doyle presents them as crystallizing their times although their relationship to the real lives lived by men is problematical and it is as well to remember that it is unlikely that any man conformed rigidly to any one of these templates. They serve, nevertheless, to highlight the cultural and socio-economic foundations of masculinity. Of course

many more such retrospective ideal types could be postulated but, importantly, they delineate themes which continue to echo in men's lives now,
though obviously not in these stark, clearly delineated forms. I look at each
of Doyle's ideal types as follows.

Heroic man

Heroic man is epitomized by the masculinity celebrated in the epic sagas of
ancient Greece. He is the courageous man-of-action, the warrior par excel-
lence, displaying physical strength, skill and courage in battle and, of course,
loyalty to leader and cause. His is a masculinity based on superiority over,
and rejection of, 'the feminine' in all its forms. It is the case that women
appear in the sagas only as peripheral figures, there merely to serve men's
needs (see also Gardner 1986; Cantarella 1987).

Spiritual man

Spiritual man is the non-violent masculinity associated with the figure of
Jesus Christ and based on celibacy, self-renunciation and service to others.
He willingly sets aside earthly pursuits in favour of spiritual ones. Women,
in this world, are presented as a seductive and dangerous threat.

Chivalrous man

Chivalrous man was the product of European feudalism and the rise of a
new military class based on trade and the growth of towns. His masculinity
is captured beautifully in the figure of the medieval knight undertaking
crusades against the devilish unbeliever, the Infidel, and displaying great
valour in the process. His quests are undertaken for a lady (a secularized and
asexual version of the Virgin Mary) to whom he is devoted, although his
devotion is largely cerebral and unconsummated. This courtly ideal is captured in Chaucer's portrait of the knight in *The Prologue to the Canterbury
Tales* who follows 'chivalry, truth, honour, generosity and courtesy' and is
of 'noble graces' and 'sovereign value':

> And though so much distinguished, he was wise
> And in his bearing modest as a maid.
> He never yet a boorish thing had said
> In all his life to any, come what might.
> He was a true, a perfect gentle Knight.

(Coghill 1960: 19)

Renaissance man

Renaissance man is the free thinker of the seventeenth century, searching for knowledge as the Roman Catholic Church's authority over people diminished and European expansion and trade propelled the emergence of a moneyed middle class. As we have already noted, the Enlightenment stressed the value of scientific inquiry which became incorporated within the modern conception of 'the masculine'. The physical prowess of the heroic, courtly knight gave way to the artistic and scientific achievements of Leonardo and Michelangelo.

The hedonist

The hedonist is best associated with the rise of the privileged middle class in the eighteenth century and its celebration through a pleasure-seeking masculinity based on ostentatious wealth and display. This was entrepreneurial masculinity in a hurry to succeed, prepared to risk all in business ventures and take pleasure in the fruits of his endeavours.

The he-man

He-man masculinity is illustrated by Doyle (1989) by reference to what he terms the 'strenuous life' in the United States in the period between the end of the Civil War up to the 1920s. Men turned to all-male activities in order to bolster their flagging sense of masculinity. The frontier had finally been closed; men were leaving the land in droves and migrating to the industrial and commercial life of the cities; patriarchy was being attacked by the early feminists; and increasing domestication was resulting in a softening of the masculine. Here is Ernst Thompson, one of the founders of the Boy Scouts of America, on this matter:

> Realising that manhood, not scholarship, is the first aim of education, we have sought out those pursuits which develop the finest character, the finest physique and which may be followed out of doors and which, in a word, make for manhood.
>
> (quoted in Doyle 1989: 41)

All-male company and activities (like the development of baseball, American football, boxing and athletics) was a means of reasserting the masculine, a riposte to fears of a process of emasculinization debilitating the nation. The hardening of the male body and mind and the formation of a masculine character through manly pursuits, particularly in the great outdoors in the company of men (and the exclusion of women) was epitomized in the figure of President Teddy Roosevelt and his outriders, his band of hard-riding followers. This 'rediscovering the masculine' is a theme which has been resurrected in our time by, in particular, the American writer Robert Bly (1991).

Masculinity in other places

There is a problem in looking at masculinity in other places because most of the literature about masculinity is about British and American men by British and American men and women. Studies of masculinity in other cultures are few, but are extremely valuable for the light they throw on masculinity as a cultural phenomenon. For example, Vale de Almeida (1996) records the daily enactment of masculinity in Pardais, a Portuguese town, detailing male interaction and behaviour in the cafés, nightclubs and even at the bullfight. Anthropology starts with the assumptions that there is nothing natural or inevitable about gender identity and that men in different cultures conceive and experience masculinity differently. It is all too easily assumed that contemporary western masculinity is the universal norm. Indeed, in the past any deviations from it were often held as indicative of inferiority: for example, it is well documented that the British in nineteenth century India held natives to be 'lesser men'.

Gilmore (1990) is one of the leading studies of masculinity on a global scale to date, examining ideologies of masculinity from a sample that traverses socio-economic categories. His previous experience as an anthropologist led him to believe that, since men everywhere appeared to be preoccupied by anxieties, the similarities seemed worthy of further exploration. His data are drawn from the Mediterranean to the South Pacific, Central New Guinea, East and South Asia, Tahiti and Semai, the Amazon in Brazil to East Africa. He readily acknowledges the limitations of the study: it is written, for example, from a male perspective in that most (but not all) of the data were collected by men. Furthermore, there is an absence of extended examples from aboriginal North America, the Arctic, Australia and Northern Europe. Nevertheless, the study covers masculinity in its many guises, from hunting-gathering bands, horticultural, pastoral tribes and peasants through to the enactment of masculinity in postindustrial societies. He starts with a definition of culture as an adaptatory device, maintaining that 'the genius of culture [is] to reconcile individual with group goals' (Gilmore 1990: 225). Gender ideologies are analysed in terms of what Durkheim (1964) termed **social facts**, collective representations that put pressure on people to act in certain ways. He argues that male aggression and toughness serve the same function as a female tenderness and gentleness as 'problem-solving behaviours'. As a consequence, masculine ideals both ensure continuity of the social system and integrate individual men into the community. In this paradigm 'manhood scripts' are specific responses to structural conditions (as are the divisions of labour): they are not just personal and psychological, but 'codes of belonging . . . modes of integrating men into their societies' (Gilmore 1990: 224).

So, in the final analysis, what does it mean to be a man in different cultures around the world? Gilmore comes to no conclusive answer, apart from noting that in most societies manhood demands that men do three things: impregnate women, protect dependants and provide materially for both. As a result, boys must be hardened and inducted into a masculinity based on self-reliance, discipline and self-direction so that 'underlying the surface variation in emphasis or form are certain convergences in concepts, symbolizations and exhortations of masculinities in many societies, but – and this is important – by no means in all' (Gilmore 1990: 5). He finds, for example, Tahitian and Samai men timid and concludes that male aggression is not innate, but culturally constructed. Given that life in most places in the past has been (and for many still is) hard and demanding, men took on the tougher tasks because of their anatomy. As a result, the stress on aggression, stoicism and sexuality is almost universally shared by men who, otherwise, have very little in common. Perhaps more significant than his 'findings' are his opinions. He expected to confirm the old stereotypes that conventional masculinity is hard and uncaring, femininity nurturing and passive. Instead, he advocates that men are every bit as much 'nurturers' as women, depending upon how the term is defined:

> men nurture their society by shedding their blood, their sweat and themselves, by bringing home food for both child and mother, by producing children and by dying if necessary in faraway places to provide a safe haven for their people. This, too, is nurturing.
>
> (Gilmore 1990: 230)

He continues:

> Manhood ideologies always include a criterion of selfless generosity, even to the point of sacrifice. Again and again we find that 'real' men are those who give more than they take: they serve others. Real men are generous, even to a fault.
>
> (Gilmore 1990: 230)

His conclusion is that a system of real manhood is necessary to ensure the voluntary acceptance of appropriate behaviour in men. Indeed, the 'manhood ideal . . . is not simply a reflection of individual psychology, but part of public culture, a collective representation' (Gilmore 1990: 415).

This far-ranging study has attracted both favourable and critical responses in roughly equal measure. For example, Cornwall and Lindisfarne (1994) accuse Gilmore (1990) of heavy handed positivism and for assuming that 'maleness' is unitary, grounded in innate psychological and biological factors. They challenge any universal category of masculinity and, on the contrary, switch the focus to the social contexts in which masculinities are shaped and enacted. In presenting Gilmore as oversimplistic they comment that 'by looking in detail at every day usage and the contexts in which people talk of masculinity its complexity soon becomes apparent' (Cornwall and Lindisfarne 1994: 2).

The mediation of masculinity: 'cinematic man'

Masculinity is constructed and represented in various guises throughout the mass media, whether on television, in film, advertising, literature, magazines, the tabloid and broadsheet press, pop music, even on the internet. By 'mediated masculinity', therefore, I mean the way in which popular media representations (in film, television and pop music in particular) provide highly crafted, alluring and accessible role models for boys and young men. I focus on the cinema here because elsewhere I look at how masculinity is mediated in literature (later in this chapter and in Chapter 7); in 'style mags' (Chapter 5); in the broadsheet press (Chapter 6); and on television and in comics (Chapter 7). Turning now specifically to the cinema, it is obvious that cinematic masculinity comes in visually crafted, carefully packaged and frequently idealized forms. These representations often have a more powerful impact than the flesh-and-blood men around the young and with whom they are in daily contact. Screen images are likely to be far more exciting and seductive than fathers, teachers, neighbours and older brothers. Indeed, masculinity as it is enacted is a mixture of the situation and previous experience and always has an imagined element because 'how men would like to be has obvious implications for the ways in which they act in everyday life' (Roper and Tosh 1991: 14). Two analytical frameworks provide valuable ways of making sense of the cinematic construction of masculinity. Although both Craig (1992) and the Cohan and Hark (1993) collections contain many insightful papers on cinematic man, most useful for my purpose here are the models provided by Kirkham and Thumin (1993) and Donald (1992).

Kirkham and Thumin (1993) look at the filmic construction and representation of masculinity in four arenas, namely the body, action, the external world and the internal world.

The body

In epics, adventure and sports films, the male body is connotative of power and strength, celebrated as manly spectacle in opposition to womanly gentleness and beauty. At its extreme it can be sexualized and eroticized, either openly (for example, the muscled, oiled and loin-clothed torso of Johnny Weissmuller as Tarzan, or quietly, as in the style-setting lounge suits of a Cary Grant or a Gregory Peck). The male body is eroticized for the admiring eyes of women and the approval of men and is rarely, even now, displayed in homoerotic terms.

Action

Appearance is relatively unimportant in the all-action movie where there is a sexualization of violence, as in numerous Clint Eastwood and Sylvester Stallone films. Skill, toughness and endurance are valorized and physique is important, allowing a star like Rock Hudson to be both 'soft-yet-manly'. Male violence is seen both as 'natural' (for example, Clark Gable's famous rape scene with Vivien Leigh in *Gone with the Wind* (1939), a scene applauded at the time but now unacceptable) and barbaric (for example, scenes of wanton rape and pillage in Vietnam War movies).

External world

'Proper' men exercise authority and behave courageously in adversity and sport. War often acts as a performance ladder to fame, fortune, popularity and success. Masculinity is, also, often depicted through the treatment of women, either through chivalrous, gentlemanly behaviour or a masculinity based on fighting, drink, sex and drugs. The epic leader, whether high or low born, leads by example and is defined by his actions, not by his birthright, often displaying superhuman strength, determination and resourcefulness to survive. The cowboy genre often celebrates the hero-as-loner determined to defeat evil, as in *Shane* (1952) and *High Noon* (1952).

Internal world

Masculinity is something men must aspire to and be prepared to defend but, more often than not, it is impossible to live up to and the result is a terrible sense of failure by men. Dyer (1993) observes that there is likely to be a disjuncture between the masculinity signified and the signifier, the actual man himself. Primarily shaped for women, masculinity is seen as largely an impossible fiction. What is often depicted as the flawless surface of conventional masculinity is more often than not a 'false skin' hiding deep insecurities. Dyer points to screen icons like James Dean and Rock Hudson, whose actual lives were in sharp contrast to their filmic representations. The figure of the 1940s private detective at first appears as a courageous figure of stability and integrity in a world that has gone badly wrong (Letort 2000). He is brave, incorruptible, overcomes a series of tests and fights greed, evil and self-interest. Honourable 'private eyes' like Philip Marlowe and Mike Hammer regard a woman's sexual appeal as a threat to their integrity. Thereafter, masculinity on screen became far less sure of itself and in the 1970s and 1980s Robert Redford and Jack Nicholson portrayed a succession of troubled losers (for example, the latter in *Chinatown*, 1974), but the best examples of men in psychological turmoil are found in the films of Martin Scorsese, in particular the characters of Travis Bickle in *Taxi Driver* (1976) and Jake La Motte in *Raging Bull* (1980) and in whom a very thin line is drawn between being in control, losing control and being out of control. Travis bodybuilds, arms and admires in the mirror the image of himself he has created, that of an impregnable urban warrior. Inside he is lonely, confused and totally unable to understand or communicate his inner turmoil and hatred, both of the squalid world of the New York underbelly through which he drives and of himself (Taubin 2000).

Donald (1992) provides a different approach to analysing filmic masculinity. He examines how 'the warrior' is depicted, with particular reference to the Vietnam War movies from the late 1970s into the 1980s and identifies a number of phases: induction, absent women, homophobia, being tough and emotionless.

Induction

Young men have to be introduced to the brutalities of army life by means of a **rite of passage** (Van Gennep 1960). They are separated from their families and the feminine, stripped and shaved and, thus, rendered vulnerable. They are then put through a series of rituals and tests, such as flogging, burning, immersion and combat tests (as in *Full Metal Jacket*, 1987). The aberrant are rooted out and vilified (for example, the recruit thought to be homosexual in *Biloxi Blues*, 1987). When they are instructed in appropriate warrior behaviour, they must follow orders unquestioningly, even if these are degrading. Only when they have successfully passed all the induction tests will they be finally admitted as full GIs and kitted out in the appropriate uniform. They have been dehumanized and turned into efficient 'killing machines'.

Absent women

Masculinity in war films is defined through the absence of women and the suppression of the feminine in men and there is usually a strong misogynist ethos. Women are regarded as a danger, both physically (messing up men's bodies with venereal infections) and emotionally (messing up their heads by inciting feelings of lust and love). They are best kept away from the combat zone, but when they do appear they fall into two distinct roles. First, as wives, daughters and lovers left behind and expected to look after home and hearth, remain chaste and faithful, act as emotional anchors and be a momentary escape from the war experience in their letters to the soldier hero. Second, as less-than-human chattel to be abused, raped or killed, given that rape is part of the victor's rewards as spoils of war (*Platoon*, 1986). In the late 1990s film *G.I. Jane* (1997) a woman is admitted to the Marines, but to do so has to behave in the same way as a male counterpart and adopt a masculine stance.

Homophobia

Masculinity in war films is strictly heterosexual: homophobia rules and sets the sexual boundaries. In *Platoon* (1986), for example, anyone who protests against the raping of Vietnamese girls is labelled a homosexual. If men show affection – what Easthope (1986) terms 'male femininity' – they do so through banter, or they cradle fallen colleagues and the dying. However, a manly code of conduct must be adhered to and to deviate is to invite the insults of being a woman, poof, faggot, queer or queen. In *Full Metal Jacket* (1987) recruits are called 'girls', 'ladies' and accused of being homosexual.

Being tough

War is presented as an exclusively male experience and masculinity defined in terms of being tough and selfless, having courage, guts and endurance, a lack of squeamishness, a high resistance to pain and discomfort and tight control in emotional matters. 'Hard men' must have physical toughness and the ability to employ violence, but they must also have skill, endurance, perseverance and control. Masculinity has to be earned by obeying orders and doing brave things. If a man does something considered cowardly, he must follow a masculine formula for redemption by engaging in an act of heroism in which he is either killed or regains his reputation. This is a world in which real men never back down, a sentiment strongly expressed by John Wayne in *The Shootist* (1976): 'I won't be wronged, I won't be insulted, I won't be laid a hand on . . . I don't do these things to others and I require the same of them' (quoted in Donald 1992: 136).

Emotionless

The warrior is hugely stoical, quiet, dignified and self-controlled, an uncommunicative man who does not play around with words. He is the upholder of what Mellen (1978) terms an invulnerable 'unfeeling masculinity' in a brutal environment in which the slightest weakness is picked upon and exploited. Emotions (fear, in particular) are signs of weakness that cloud a man's judgements on the battlefield and so must be hidden. The archetypal warrior must instead be an 'iceman', remaining cool under extreme pressure. The only emotions such a man is expected (indeed, allowed) to show are those associated with patriotism and lusting after women. Men bond in adversity and war films are far from devoid of affection, which is expressed in terms of duty such as willingness to trust buddies, being prepared to lay down one's life for them and doing one's job as a member of a unit or a platoon. Personal grief at the death of a buddy is weakness and the solution to this is the militarized grief of the ceremonial burial, with a dedication of the next kill to the fallen one. Revenge is held to be more effective than conventional grieving, which is considered unmanly and bad for morale. Being a soldier means a willingness to lay down your own life as well as accept the death of friends and men channel their emotions into a love of the regiment, squad, unit or platoon. At its most extreme this is encapsulated in the notion that the dead are immortal, that they live forever in glory (as in *Full Metal Jacket*, 1987) and will never be forgotten, a sentiment memorably expressed by Laurence Binyon (1919) in his famous lines following the First World War in his *Poems For the Fallen*:

> They shall grow not old, as we that are left grow old:
> Age shall not weary them, nor the years condemn.
> At the going down of the sun
> And in the morning
> We will remember them.

'The pathological silencing of women': 1950s masculinity

For many the 1950s is the transitional decade of the twentieth century as Britain came to terms with the fact that its Imperial role was coming to an end. Instead Britain faced an uncertain future in a world dominated by the United States and Russia. At home many of the old, patriarchal **male certainties** were still securely in place, yet to be attacked by feminism. Indeed, for Segal (1988), the period was characterized by what she terms the 'pathological silencing' of women. In spite of calls for a new partnership in the home (for example, Newson and Newson 1963), men and women were trapped together as unequals, occupying segregated domestic roles and living largely separate lives, albeit under the same roof. If women desired solid, dependable breadwinners, men wanted homemakers and housekeepers. Childcare was solely the province of women and, certainly for working class women, the only diversion from the domestic regime was daily shopping for necessities and occasional trips to the cinema. If they were lonely and oppressed within the home, their husbands were oppressed outside it (Hoggart 1957). Working class jobs were dirty, dangerous and difficult. At the weekends men turned to the male comradeship of the saloon bar and to sport, especially football, which was still maintaining its postwar boom. The fact was that behind the closed doors of Harold Macmillan's 'You've never had it so good' Britain, for most families across the United Kingdom there was tension, isolation, boredom and a desperate longing for something better, more exciting, more meaningful, an escape from the mutual entrapment of men-as-breadwinners and women-as-mothers (Bott 1957). It is not surprising that the journalist Kenneth Allsop's (1964) description of the 1950s as a sad, dishonest and neurotic decade is often quoted.

Segal (1988) identifies a number of masculinities current at the time. One of them was the tragic figure of the wartime survivor who had had his young manhood snatched from him. Traumatized by what he had been through (this was a time long before counselling), he now found himself unable to readjust to postwar society, often resorting to heavy drinking as a means of escape. Time quickly passed him by and he no longer recognized the world in which he lived. In working class communities the stereotypical working class patriarch ruled the hearth. He was often mean, lacking in affection, callous in sex and equally harsh and uncompromising to wife and children alike (Young and Willmott 1957). At work all day, men in the home were emotionally distanced from their families. In the mean time young men conscripted for National Service found themselves exposed to a violent, dog-eat-dog world of bullying and homophobia (Johnson 1973). Slowly but surely a new, family-centred man was emerging with his recently acquired television set (bought for the 1953 coronation of Queen Elizabeth II), a growing interest in do-it-yourself (DIY) and, if he could afford it, motoring. Then there were the upwardly mobile, clever, working class grammar school pupils recorded by Jackson and Marsden (1962). The first of their families ever to get near a university, they entered the professions only to find that, in order to get on, they had to hide their lowly origins. They 'married up', but found themselves rootless and unhappy as a result, comfortable neither in the middle class world of their wives or back in their working class child-hood communities.

In an original and insightful study, Roper (1991) looks at well-educated middle class men who left the armed services after the Second World War and became industrial managers in the late 1940s and 1950s. This was the generation who were to be replaced, at the end of their careers in the 1980s, by business school graduates. Whereas they had acquired hands-on know-ledge about products and production procedures, their successors spurned experiential knowledge in favour of financial expertise. Roper's central thesis is that an intense bond developed between the 1950s managers and the products they had designed, championed and produced. Class-based interpretations of masculinity lay at the heart of the manual–managerial divide. While Willis (1977) charts shopfloor culture, here we have middle class managerial job satisfaction and a masculine identity invested in actual products, nothing less than a masculine delight in mechanical things. If such 'product fetishism' exists today, then it is to be found not in heavy industry (long since decimated), but in technological innovation and e-commerce initiatives. But these men of the 1950s reminisced fondly about products like timing belts, welding equipment, landing gears and process equipment, goods they had produced and which were at the centre of their work, their emotional life and even their gender. Such products were landmarks in their career and they had nostalgic memories of a world of heavy production engi-neering management infused with a strong masculine ethos. At a time (late 1940s through to the mid-1960s) when accountants, advertising and public relations people were viewed almost as 'lesser men', the creativity and energy invested in what was interpreted as the aesthetic beauty of these products was held as proof of masculinity itself. As Roper makes clear, there was a dovetailing of product, company, loyalty, identity and, crucially, masculinity and class, for these postwar managers 'despised gentlemen, pre-ferring a masculine stereotype bound up with the drama of production, tech-nical competence and product fetishism' (Roper 1991: 207). By the 1980s corporate culture had finally destroyed family capitalism and the share-holder profitability of corporate culture took centre stage: in the process it also destroyed this kind of distinctively 1950s masculinity.

Before turning to how masculinity was represented in some of the litera-ture and cinema of the period, it is important to make the point that the 1950s was a decade which witnessed considerable cultural change, led by the growth of the media (especially the spread of television from 1953 on)

and the emergence of a pop music based teenage culture. Levy (1999) provides an interesting slant on this by looking at the Rat Pack (the leading
members of which were Sammy Davis Junior, Frank Sinatra and Dean
Martin) and which was the very epitome of 1950s, Las Vegas based 'cool'.
This was the showy, irreverent 'high life' the returning GIs had dreamed of
and striven for throughout the late 1940s and early 1950s as they worked
long hours to achieve affluence and stability in their lives. Indeed, the Rat
Pack

> spoke to men who had survived privation and war and congratulated
> them on the size of their bank accounts, the security of their jobs, the
> modernity of their homes, the voluptuousness of their women, the
> dazzling technology they invented.
>
> (Levy 1999: 352)

However, as Levy points out, Elvis Presley was waiting in the wings ready to
elbow the Rat Pack off the centre of the stage. His gyrating body was to be
seen and admired not only by women, but also by other men. In Britain, Bill
Haley led the invasion by a succession of American 'rock 'n' rollers' and set
the scene for the emergence of British teen idols like Tommy Steele, Billy
Fury, Joe Brown, Adam Faith, Cliff Richard and Marty Wilde. As the 1950s
gave way to the 1960s a still-unified youth culture based on pop music and
fashion (soon to be joined by football) had got under way.

What does the literature of the period have to say about 1950s masculinity? Davies (2000) points to the symbolic importance of Britain's involvement in Suez in 1956 in that, thereafter, British men had to take on board
the country's diminished global status and the loss of Empire. In many
novels written subsequently an incapacitated male ruminates on his decrepit
position in life (as in Ian McEwan's *Enduring Love*, 1998). Many look at the
British male novelists of the 1950s (for example, Alan Sillitoe, David Storey,
Angus Wilson, Kingsley Amis, Colin MacInnes and Bill Hopkins) and note
a tendency to blame women for the uncertainty emanating from the break
up of the traditional male kinship structures. Ferrebe (2000), for example,
identifies two main literary reactions, 'quietism' and 'radical individualism'.
By the former is meant that it was no longer a viable ambition in the 1950s
to aspire to be a 'great man' as this smacked of fanaticism, even fascism. The
latter, however, were engaged in a renegotiation of the tenets of received
'English' masculinity. The outcome of this was that 'reaction to or against
these two styles of masculinity fathered every fictional Englishman in male
novels to come' (Ferrebe 2000: 11). Indeed, contemporary male literary
anxieties can be traced to the male-authored fiction of the 1950s. Another
literary phenomenon of the 1950s, especially in **kitchen sink literature**, was

the figure of the 'angry young man', forever epitomized by the figure of Jimmy Porter in John Osborne's play, *Look Back in Anger* (1956). Brook (2000: 5) sees **angry masculinity** as a response to the experience of social mobility and the fear of becoming middle class and, therefore, the fear of becoming emasculated. It was aggressively heterosexual and was 'a way of asserting an oppositional identity which did not rely on claiming a particular class identity or political affiliation'. Brook sees no evidence of a shared, anti-establishment or political stance. Indeed, 'angry masculinity was a common representation of masculinity which substituted for political commitment but was read as a political position' (Brook 2000: 5).

Turning to film, the 'silver screen' was a magnet to a 1950s British public who had been starved of entertainment during the war years. British cinema of the time must be viewed in the light of the huge popularity of the American male stars, from the established (for example, James Stewart, Gregory Peck, Gary Cooper and Clark Gable) to the newcomers (James Dean, Marlon Brando, Montgomery Clift and Rock Hudson). Jackson (2000) tells the astonishing story of the most popular of all 1950s stars, Bristol-born Archibald Leach who, after making his way to Hollywood, reinvented himself as Cary Grant. He quotes Grant:

> I pretended to be someone that I wanted to be and I finally became that person. Or he became me . . . Everyone wants to be Cary Grant. Even I want to be Cary Grant.
>
> (D. Jackson 2000: 19)

In the 1950s Grant's debonair, urbane, sophisticated masculine persona was the epitome of desirable, romantic masculinity, the man all men wanted to be and all women desired. This 'masculine masquerade' was based on a self-constructed and Hollywood-promoted persona. He always had to be seen to be the kind of masculinity he represented on screen, while the 'real' Grant (or Leach) was never allowed to surface.

I am going to comment on a few selected strands of 1950s screen masculinity. Following Donald's (1992) framework examined in the previous section, I want first to comment on British war films of the era. War films satisfy our desire for danger, violence and horror and the warriors therein are powerful role models as they fight for good causes and to make the world a better place. The 1950s in Britain was when the Second World War was refought on screen in distinctively British films like *The Wooden Horse* (1950), *The Cruel Sea* (1952), *The Colditz Story* (1954), *The Sea Shall Not Have Them* (1954), *Cockleshell Heroes* (1955), *The Dam Busters* (1955), *Above Us the Waves* (1955) and *Reach for the Sky* (1956) to name but a few. It was as if the nation's filmmakers were not only celebrating the defeat of the Third Reich but also, at the same time, expanding the public's awareness of the enormous heroism and sacrifice that had taken place. The trend continued into the 1960s with *The Longest Day* (1962), *The Great Escape* (1962) and *The Battle of Britain* (1969), films now employing an international cast, providing bit-parts for a number of established British and Hollywood stars. One view of the stereotypical, essentially British war hero is of an emotionally repressed and buttoned-up masculinity based on incredibly brave and selfless actions for king and country by sea, air and on land. Yet today these films can be viewed **against the grain** and be seen, rather, to be about young men as victims of circumstances, stripped of normal lives and, instead, living on the edge, ordinary young men coping with extraordinary circumstances and being physically and emotionally destroyed in the process. Steven Spielberg's *Saving Sergeant Ryan* (1998) was praised for its realism and for showing the real horror of the Normandy beaches in 1944 as if for the first time. This is somewhat to underestimate the previous achievement of, for example, David Lean in such films as *The Bridge on the River Kwai* (1957) and *Ice Cold in Alex* (1958) which, while not being so action-packed or graphic, nevertheless memorably captured the terrible, emasculating psychological damage inflicted on men by war.

Another strand of 1950s British cinematic masculinity is the emergence of the urban tough, depending on his quick wit and fists who has long been the central masculine figure in American popular culture. Spicer (1999) throws an interesting light on 1950s Britain (and its obsession with class) in his essay on the packaging of the Welsh actor Stanley Baker as a 'tough guy' in the American mould to replace the Bulldog Drummond-like figure of the traditional British gentlemanly hero. This was evident in his first film, *The Cruel Sea* (1952), based on the bestselling novel by Nicholas Monsarrat, in which he played a tough, working class first lieutenant clearly ill-at-ease in the company of his more middle class fellow officers. Four years later Baker played his most memorable 'brute' role in *Hell Drivers* (1957) as an ex-convict haunted by his past in the aggressively masculine culture of dumper truck driving. In pioneering a new breed of British male anti-hero Baker demolished what Green (1960) terms the 'paralysed and paralysing hegemony of gentlemanliness' (quoted in Spicer 1999: 91). This was also evident in the 1950s British 'new wave' movies featuring dissenting iconoclasts. Albert Finney came to epitomize a new generation of non-gentlemanly rebels, often (as in *Saturday Night and Sunday Morning*, 1960) placed in the industrial North of England, itself depicted as 'authentic' and grittily masculine in contrast to the affluent, effete and softly feminine South. In these bleak northern settings, new working class heroes 'contested the dominant middle class paradigms of British culture in the 1950s' (Spicer 1999: 91).

All was to change in the 1960s, however, when accepted 1950s notions of masculinity began to be attacked. In a highly revealing study Shail (2000) examines the two decades by tracking the long and successful career of the British actor Dirk Bogarde. Bogarde moved from the representation of traditional masculine qualities in the late 1940s and throughout the 1950s as in, for example, *Doctor in the House* (1954) and *A Tale of Two Cities* (1958) to far more ambiguous roles in such films as *Victim* (1961), *The Servant* (1963), *Modesty Blaise* (1966) and *Accident* (1967), concluding with his masterpiece, *Death in Venice* in 1971. By abandoning in his parts the reassuring and apparently stable masculinity of the 1950s, Bogarde questioned not only the sexual and class identity of his characters but also, in the process, of himself.

The next chapter critically investigates the oft-repeated assertion that both men and masculinity are currently in 'crisis' and what the nature of that crisis might be.

Further reading

Berger, M., Wallis, B. and Watson, S. (eds) (1995) *Constructing Masculinity*. New York: Routledge.

Brod, H. (ed.) (1987) *The Making of Masculinities: The New Men's Studies*. Boston, MA: Allen & Unwin.

Craig, S. (ed.) (1992) *Men, Masculinity and the Media*. Newbury Park, CA: Sage.

Edley, N. and Wetherell, M.S. (1995) *Men in Perspective: Practice, Power and Identity*. Hemel Hempstead: Harvester Wheatsheaf.

Gilmore, D. (1990) *Manhood in the Making: Cultural Concepts of Masculinity*. New Haven, CT: Yale University Press.

Harris, I.M. (1995) *Messages Men Hear: Constructing Masculinities*. London: Taylor & Francis.

Kimmel, M.S. (ed.) (1987) *Changing Men: New Directions in Research on Men and Masculinity*. Newbury Park, CA: Sage.

Kirkham, P. and Thumin, J. (1993) *You Tarzan: Masculinity, Movies and Men*. London: Lawrence and Wishart.

MASCULINITIES AND THE NOTION OF 'CRISIS'

On a searingly hot day in July, 2000, I escaped into the air-conditioned haven of the Barnes and Noble bookshop in Kansas City. Near the display stand promoting Harry Potter's spectacular arrival in the USA was another, equally strident stand proclaiming 'the crisis of our boys and young men'. Arranged on the stand were about a dozen or so newly published volumes. Each proclaimed, in one way or another, that America's boys and young men were in deep trouble, thanks to poor parenting, fathering, bad schools, sink neighbourhoods, escalating crime, drugs and more drugs, the corrupting media, the triviality of popular culture, sexual abuse, teen suicide, racial prejudice, bullying and violence, etc., etc. Half an hour spent dipping into the books at the stand convinced me that the richest and most powerful country in the history of the world was in an advanced state of trauma when it came to its young males.

(John Beynon, *Missouri Journal*)

Introduction: 'Crisis! What crisis?'

This has been a difficult chapter to write. Although claims that men and masculinity are currently in crisis are constantly and vociferously made, the precise nature of the **crisis in masculinity** (that is, how it manifests itself and is actually experienced) is ill defined and elusive. In order to shed some light on the matter I proceed as follows. First, I start by raising questions about the 'crisis'. Indeed, given the absence of much field based evidence, it is inevitable that this chapter will raise more questions than it can possibly answer. Second, I examine what is commonly quoted as evidence of the crisis, during the course of which I delve into a possible reason why, worldwide, most crimes of violence are by men upon men. Third, I look at the most frequently advanced reasons for the crisis, namely the loss of masculine rights and changes in the pattern of employment. Finally, I examine whether the crisis is new or part of a broader historical pattern and ask, also, to what extent is it actual and to what extent discursive?

The idea that masculinity, in one guise or another, is in a state of deep crisis has become widely accepted as a 'fact'. But is it the case that something, repeated time and again, is assumed to exist on the 'no smoke without fire' principle? Moreover, if there is a crisis, then there are three possible explanations, namely that it is new and unique to our times, that it has existed in the past, either in the same or different forms, or that it is constitutive of masculinity itself. These three possibilities and the questions I now raise ought to be borne in mind throughout the chapter.

- Is the so-called crisis inflicted upon men rather than emanating from them? Who says there is a crisis-in-masculinity? Do men recognize it and go around proclaiming it? If there is a crisis-in-masculinity, then do all men experience it and do they do so in the same way? Is the crisis a matter of interpretation? Is there a genuine crisis, or is something created, at least in part, by the media as a **moral panic** (Goode and Ben-Yehuda 1994), a convenient catch-all in which to lock the most recent negative stories about men into an ongoing 'male crisis' narrative?
- Are we talking about men-in-crisis or masculinity-in-crisis or both? This is not always made clear and the two are often confused and conflated. Men, either individually or in groups, may be plunged into crisis, but their sense of masculinity can, nevertheless, remain relatively secure. The young men in 'Cityton' Prison (Chapter 7) may be in dire circumstances, but they retain a strong, binding sense of masculinity based on crime. Also, what may appear to be a crisis to an outsider may not necessarily appear so for the subjects themselves. What have they to say on the matter?
- What is meant by 'crisis' (or are we talking about crises)? What form does it take? What are the causes, as opposed to the symptoms, of the alleged crisis? How does it manifest itself and how is it experienced? Do all men experience the crisis uniformly or is it experienced differently across socio-economic and cultural groups? Historically, how do crises-in-masculinity reflect their times? Finally, how can the alleged crisis-in-masculinity best be studied? What sources can be employed? For example, of what use are film, literature, statistics, the press and television?

The 'evidence' for 'men-in-crisis'

In the 1990s men have been seen to be in the forefront of social concerns about jobs, changing family patterns, failure in school and violent crime. Coward (1999: 52) aptly comments that they have simultaneously appeared as 'both cause and symptom of a society in crisis'. But what evidence is there to substantiate the so-called crisis in masculinity? The following are certainly often listed as contributory factors:

- Men face constant job role changes, the threat of unemployment and job-related stress daily. The advent of **postmodernity** has resulted in redundancy and downsizing: less than 50 per cent of men aged 55 and over in Britain are in work and many such men die prematurely.
- Many remain bad at acknowledging and expressing feelings and are trapped between old-style, machismo and nurturing 'new man-ism' (see Chapter 5).
- The rise of the gay movement, along with the commercialization of male appearance and the widespread acceptance of more androgynous identities, has left men acculturated into traditional masculinity confused, especially the non-metropolitan, the older and the poorer.
- Men are generally far more reluctant than women to face up to and respond to physical and psychological problems. They suffer deep depression at the loss of the breadwinner role and the status that went with it.
- Men are four to five times more likely to commit suicide than women (Men's Health Forum, 1999) and there is an epidemic of young male suicides, which is of particular concern. Approximately 80 per cent of all suicides are by men and young male suicide in Scotland has trebled since 1970 (Professor Stephen Platt of Edinburgh University, reported in Harding 2000). Among the 25 to 35 age group, suicide now accounts for nearly 30 per cent of all male deaths and appears to be triggered by relationship problems, unemployment, drug and alcohol abuse, low self-esteem and mental illness. This grim picture must be contextualized in the overall rise in male suicide of 76 per cent since 1971 and, also, a steady rise in female suicide over the same period.
- Men die sooner and are three and a half times more likely to suffer from heart disease. For example, to herald Men's Health Week in June 1999, the *Western Mail* (Wales' premier daily paper) undertook an extensive survey which claimed that 66 per cent of men in Wales were depressed by their physical appearance and 86 per cent were worried about the state of their health. Men reported that stress at work was affecting their health and relationships and that work dominated their lives. About 80 per cent were reported as trying to improve their health and take up regular exercise. Altogether half reported they had suffered from depression, the vast majority had never sought advice or consulted a doctor. Men across Wales indicated their concerns over general fitness, weight, heart attacks, cancer and high blood pressure, hair loss, infertility and loss of libido.

- Men are falling out of family life in ever greater numbers and many end up in a lonely, angst-ridden limbo. More and more men are ending up isolated socially and psychologically, finding it difficult to ask for help. At least 50 per cent of marriages in the United Kingdom now end in divorce and men are mostly responsible for marital breakdown. Women initiate approximately 75 per cent of divorces and have demonstrated that they can bring up children without men.
- Nine out of ten fathers involved in divorce leave the family home and become non-resident. As Clare (2000) puts it, fathers are being 'airbrushed' out of the family picture:

  > The visiting father is a shadowy, displaced figure trying to avoid becoming an ex-father, who stops but does not stay, who is no longer a man of the house, but a visitor who comes and goes.
  >
  > (Clare 2000: 150–1)

- Weldon (1998, quoted in Coward 1999: 60) refers to the **redundant male** heading for economic, social and biological redundancy, a point underwritten by Cohen (1996). Clare (2000) writes:

  > The rise in the number of single mothers suggests not merely that men are inadequate as partners and fathers, but that they are simply redundant. Women are asserting that they can conceive and rear children on their own. They don't need men to father their children . . . woman can do without them in the workplace. Even more significantly, they can do without them in their beds.
  >
  > (Clare 2000: 100)

- Young men in the United Kingdom are responsible for most crime, whether burglaries, car thefts or violence. An increasing number are becoming 'absent dads'. Indeed, it appears some absent themselves from households simply because they feel they are no longer needed.
- Women are seen to be living more meaningful, successful and fulfilling lives, so much so that Hill (1997) talks of the future being female. 'Being a man' can no longer be defined in counterpoise to 'being a woman', both of which have changed out of all recognition since the late 1960s. Young men especially can no longer say with any certainty what masculinity actually is.
- Many men have been left behind by the **feminist movement**. Moreover, the loss of an automatic, patriarchal dominance and the advent of greater equality in heterosexual relationships have left some men high and dry. Moreover, 'confessional journalism' has been monopolized by feminist journalists who, it is claimed, constantly cast men in a negative light and have played a leading role in rendering masculinity problematical.

- Young men are underachieving in school. This was evident in the British broadsheet press in August 2000, when boys' GCSE and Advanced Level results were significantly depressed compared to girls. This was attributed to the attraction of 'lad culture', endlessly promoted by the media, for young men. A black British academic, Tony Sewell, ignited a storm by arguing that black youth's particularly disappointing examination showing was due to the adverse influence of black 'rap culture' (see Lightfoot 2000; Martin 2000). Janet Daley in the *Daily Telegraph* took up the gauntlet on Sewell's side and argued that:

  > by rendering invisible and quiet the achievements of black women and decent black men, the media cult of the black delinquent prevents young Afro-Caribbean men from seeing themselves as succeeding in any arena other than the criminal street.
  >
  > (Daley 2000: 16)

- Men commit most crimes of violence, both in the street and in the home and rates continue to rise. In the United Kingdom the upward spiral of acts of gross violence by men, including loss of life (whether manslaughter or murder) is of especial concern. This is an issue taken up and pursued later.

The summer of 2000 could justifiably be described as the 'masculinity-in-crisis-summer'. While bookshops across the United States were full of 'boy-crisis books', the press in the United Kingdom carried endless articles on the subject following the publication of Anthony Clare's book. Clare (2000) writes:

> At the beginning of the twenty-first century it is difficult to avoid the conclusion that men are in serious trouble . . . It is true that patriarchy has not been overthrown, but its justification is in disarray . . . In a world of equal opportunity for the sexes, can men renegotiate the relationship with themselves and with women?
>
> (Clare 2000: 3, 4, 8)

He sees the crisis manifesting itself across the whole landscape of social life – in crime, family breakdown, domestic violence, ill-health, suicide, education and work, including redundancy and early retirement. These can be clustered under three headings, as follows.

Masculinity is out of fashion

Masculinity, certainly as it has been traditionally understood, has become unfashionable and the 'crisis' has been created by a reversal in value of 'male' and 'female' traits. Being logical, disciplined, rational and competitive are

> now seen as the stigmata of deviance . . . [whereas] the very traits which once marked out women as weak and inferior – emotional, spontaneous, intuitive, expressive, compassionate, empathetic – are increasingly seen as the markers of maturity and health.
>
> (Clare 2000: 68)

Men are victims of a voracious economic system

For Clare (2000: 212), 'at the heart of the crisis in masculinity is a problem with the reconciliation of the private and the public, the intimate and the impersonal, the emotional and the rational.' This is, of course, a predicament shared with women, namely protecting the personal and private against the intrusions and excessive demands of a voracious economic system:

> It is a struggle between the world of personal love, intimacy, empathy, magnanimity and self-sacrifice and the terrible pressures of conspicuous consumption to achieve, possess and display.
>
> (Clare 2000: 215)

The 'male gender script' is still too narrow

Some see the crisis created because young men are allowed 'only one groove along which to travel' (A. Katz, 2000: 4); indeed, while it has been widened for girls, it has remained too constricted for boys. Young men are being labelled as problematic and end up living up to this in a self-fulfilling manner. The only way forward is to demolish the narrow strictures delineating what it is to be a man. Men are in crisis because they are fearful of exploiting the opportunities that the weakening of patriarchy has created.

At the end of this litany of shortcomings, how should men respond to the crisis in masculinity? Clare (2000) has surprisingly little to say on this matter except that they should attempt to live more fulfilling lives by relinquishing their pursuit of power, achievement and their fixation with possessions and, instead, rediscover the value of intimacy. They must, for example, learn to express tenderness and engage more seriously in fatherhood.

Defending 'male honour'

Violence is predominantly a masculine phenomenon as the contributors to the volume edited by Bowker (1998) amply testify. The spiralling rates of male violence are often cited as being part of the male 'crisis'. But why do (some) men maim and even kill? It is estimated that men engage in eight times as much violence as women and in Britain one in four women have reported domestic violence. Much violence is undoubtedly the result of machismo, a culture of male honour particularly associated with the Mediterranean basin and the Hispanic New World. 'Macho man' is compelled to be dominant and controlling and refuses to tolerate any disrespect or challenge to his honour and feels obligated to respond with threatened or actual violence. Clare (2000) puts it this way:

> Such men rate highly their competitiveness, their pride, their strength, their independence, their refusal to be pushed around . . . Their very honour as men is at stake in every challenge, in every act of disrespect. Such men are truly men only if they are prepared to fight like men.
>
> (Clare 2000: 36)

Criminologists have been slow to look at crime through the lens of masculinity. This is surprising since most murders are committed by men and in cities all over the world violence is dominated by young men, both as perpetrators and victims (Silverman and Kennedy 1987; Falk 1990; Johnson and Robinson 1992). Stanko (1994) makes a useful distinction between two broad categories of violence, namely expressive and instrumental.

- *Expressive violence*: unpremeditated, blind rage. Examples would be blind rage occasioned by jealousy, losing face, a sexual insult, or when an intimate relationship ends.
- *Instrumental violence*: violence is used in a planned and calculated manner for a specific purpose (for example, in a robbery or in revenge).

Men dominate both categories, especially young men at the borders of society, employing violence to resolve a conflict or in the course of another crime. Indeed, for many men the experience of violence in one form or another plays a central part in their lives, something they constantly have to display and be prepared to display (Connell 1987; Seidler 1991; Morgan 1992). While men commit most violent crimes, they also constitute the majority of its victims (Shepherd 1990). It is easy, therefore, to understand why violence is widely held to be a part of 'normal' masculinity. Regrettably, for some there is much male pride to be earned in displays of terror-as-power (J. Katz 1988) and dominance over people and places. Indeed, some feminists see all men as having a biological capacity for violence and rape (Brownmiller 1975; Scully 1990). Certainly young men appear to have difficulty controlling their aggression, especially after they have been drinking: most weekend violence is in public streets in the vicinity of pubs and clubs, as well as in the private venue of the home.

Fighting has long been a culturally sanctioned and distinctively male way of conflict resolution and, in this respect, violent men can be viewed as over-conformists (Brod 1987). For men at the foot of the socio-economic ladder, their lack of resources render their sense of masculinity problematical; a recourse to violence is one of the ways they have of confronting powerless-ness and exerting authority over other men and women. Unsurprisingly, hierarchies of power, based on violence, are most common among poor, working class men, so much so that Daly and Wilson (1988: 287) argue that young men with few prospects 'have good reason to escalate their tactics of social competition and become violent'. In short, for economically margin-alized men or those in manual settings the threat of violence is the major vehicle for both establishing, retaining and asserting masculinity by placing other men on the defensive. Here is Messerschmidt (1986) on the matter:

> The marginalized male expresses himself through a collective tough-ness, a masculine performance observed and cheered by his buddies. Members of the macho street culture have to maintain a strong sense of honour.
>
> (Messerschmidt 1986: 186)

Commentators have noted that many killings and cases of severe grievous bodily harm by men inflicted on other men or women often flow from an apparently trivial altercation. One explanation for these instances (obvi-ously not all) is that they arise from a defence of male honour, a deeply felt cultural imperative to defend male status (Daly and Wilson 1988; Polk and Ranson 1991). Given that violence is largely a masculine matter, how do confrontations start? Katz (1988) sees 'confrontational homicide' as the outcome of a number of spontaneous elements, of which humiliation is one, male aggression another. Daly and Wilson (1988) argue that men get involved in homicide around the issue of masculine standing and that, in cer-tain situations, masculinity depends not only on the threat of violence, but also on its performance. In short, male-on-male violence is often reducible to contests of masculine honour. Affluent, better educated middle class or older men are more likely to attack their opponents with a court injunction or seek retribution in a more sophisticated fashion than a street altercation. Polk (1994) reports on data (mostly prosecutors' briefs and coroners' reports) gathered in Victoria, Australia, tracking 380 homicides between

1985 and 1989, of which 22 per cent were confrontational homicides. She poses two questions: 'What happens between men to make them killers?' and 'What transforms the scene so that the taking of a life occurs?' The data revealed that an often trivial event triggers a spontaneous outburst in leisure and public settings. Alcohol was a common factor, along with the interpretation of the event as an insult to masculine honour by the killer. The three components of the fatal cocktail thus appear to be lower socio-economic position, a humiliated sense of the masculine, and a public setting. Polk (1994: 188) observes that 'extreme violence in defence of honour is definitely masculine'.

The triggering event is a 'homicide drama' in which the challenge to man's manhood, his nerve, strength, intelligence, or the insulting of a wife or girlfriend becomes a major matter that has to be 'settled' there and then. Sometimes the violence expands to include onlookers and the ultimate victim can even be peripheral to the initial insult. Obviously the chance of violence is heightened when large numbers of young men congregate in one place, but it can then spill out into surrounding public spaces like parks and stations and on to trains and buses. It can involve ethnicity, the safeguarding of territory, appearance and lifestyle, but it is the slur to male honour that is the trigger that activates and sets in motion the unfolding combat. Polk's conclusion is that confrontational violence is 'distinctively masculine' (or, if performed by a woman, then she behaves like a man). Sometimes the victim or perpetrator initially leaves the scene only to return with a weapon and the resulting homicide frequently occurs late at night after heavy drinking when inhibitions have been lowered. In such settings an inconsequential remark can be the catalyst which 'transforms the scene to the point where taking of the life of a person otherwise remote to the offenders becomes a possibility' (Polk 1994: 167).

So what are the origins of the crisis? Broadly speaking, the origins of the crisis are attributed to two principal sources: first, the loss of what had long been accepted as masculine 'rights' (this being largely the result of the feminist critique of masculinity) and, second, changes in male employment. I shall comment on each in turn.

The loss of masculine 'rights'

In the recent past the authority and dominance of men were simply accepted. It would appear that contemporary men have certainly lost rights (especially in the worlds of law, finance, politics and business) that they had previously enjoyed solely by virtue of their sex. Indeed, men's rights have, many argue, been subsumed by women's rights. The breadwinner ideology is no longer credible; work dependent upon muscle power has declined; and there has been a sharp growth in western economies of part-time and female labour. Moreover, generally speaking, men must now treat women as equals and participate more fully in domestic matters, including childcare, although the extent to which they actually do so is debatable. The material progress of modern capitalism has undermined patriarchy, so much so that MacInnes (1998: 55) feels justified in claiming that, even compared to the recent past, it is now 'a bad time to be a man', although he goes on to comment that 'this is a thoroughly good thing.' Furthermore, the way in which masculinity is publicly perceived has dramatically changed.

> What were once claimed to be manly virtues (heroism, independence, courage, strength, rationality, will, backbone, virility) have become masculine vices (abuse, destructive aggression, coldness, emotional inarticulacy, detachment, isolation, an inability to be flexible, to com-municate, to empathise, to be soft, supportive or life-affirming.
>
> (MacInnes 1998: 47)

Stereotypical female qualities (for example, empathy and gentleness) are now widely accepted as superior to stereotypical male ones (emotional reticence and aggression). He accounts for contemporary masculine insecurity by identifying a disjuncture between what he terms 'the core principle of modernity' (that all human beings are essentially equal) and 'the core tenet of patriarchy' (that men are naturally superior to women). He defines masculinity as an ideological response to the threat posed to the survival of the patriarchal division of labour by the rise of modernity. Men had previously been able to justify their monopoly of power and resources by reference to their sex, further justifying this by reference to 'their socially constructed gender identity which expressed some undefined natural difference' (MacInnes 1998: 45).

Germaine Greer's (1999) broadside on masculinity aggressively asserts that to be male at the present time is to be full of queer obsessions about fetishistic activities and fantasy goals. It is often claimed that, as a result of such feminist critiques of patriarchy and the kind of controlling masculinity on which it was based, men have been plunged into 'crisis' and that, as a consequence, there is now widespread confusion as to what, precisely, being a man actually entails (Buchbinder 1994). The causes, nature and impact of the alleged crisis occasions endless speculation in the press, particularly in the broadsheets (see Chapter 6). Feminists have challenged the traditional model of masculinity and forced (some) men to re-examine masculinity (both their own and others') critically so that from the 1970s on, but gathering momentum during the 1980s and 1990s, masculinity has become a major object of study, particularly in cultural and media studies and sociology. But the impetus for this was undoubtedly early, pioneering feminist work on the subordination of women by men. Much feminist work focused on the clearly distasteful outcomes of traditional masculinity (rape, pornography, child abuse and domestic violence) and presented it as a neurosis, damaging not only to women, but also to men themselves. They pointed to the harm that men did both to themselves and others as they strove to be 'real men' and how patriarchal masculinity mutated and reproduced itself. However, patriarchy, defined as men's control of women's bodies and minds, could not be reduced to crude acts of aggression. Rather, it was deeply entrenched in rituals, routines and social practices. Moreover, since men, it was argued, continue to occupy positions of power it was difficult for them to be reflexive about the negative aspects of masculinity. They held on to an ideology which obscured distorting inequalities of gender and were blind to the damage done to both women and men in a patriarchal society, including the stifling of the authentic expression of feeling (Morgan 1992). Sexuality was seen to be at the heart of men's authority and domination, along with sexual harassment, which was less about sex than about the brutal exhibition of male power (Hearn 1990; Hearn and Parkin 1993). Women, it was asserted, were exploited in the private and undervalued zone of the home. Dominant masculinity in the workplace was complemented by an unequal division of labour in the home where most men still avoided most domestic responsibilities. Domestic tasks were gendered: men typically engaged in DIY, car maintenance and reading children bedtime stories, whereas women undertook most of the endless tasks of cleaning, washing, ironing, cooking, clearing up and childcare.

The earliest responses by men in the United Kingdom were by pro-feminist men (of whom Seidler (1989) is among the most notable.) In the United States men's studies emerged, but was widely castigated as middle class, self-pitying and removed from the lives and concerns of ordinary Americans. But there were notable early texts, such as Pleck and Sawyer (1974), which called for men to raise their consciousness about what was largely taken-for-granted, namely their masculinity. Others reacted negatively to feminist thought, seeing the privileges of masculinity under threat. Yet others argued that men were in need of rediscovering their lost masculine essence (or 'deep centre') in a world that was changing too fast for them to comprehend (Bly 1991). Meanwhile, some viewed patriarchy as too reductionist and categorical a concept and pointed to the need to research the sites (whether private, domestic or public) in which it operated (Walby

1986, 1990). Some present-day feminists still point to men's continued domination of power relations and some are of the opinion that the changes to the old patriarchal order are superficial rather than actual: men have not yet given up enough and women must be ever on their guard against what Faludi (1991) describes as the **male backlash**. In short, in spite of all feminism's achievements, patriarchy is still firmly in place. But others (for example, Coward 1999; and, later, Faludi 1999 herself) question this, having some sympathy with the view that men have, in fact, become victims of the many successes of feminism. It is no longer a simple matter of male advantage and female disadvantage: indeed, it is not always women who are now being disadvantaged. Coward (1999), for example, takes a more sympathetic stance towards contemporary men and is dismayed by a tendency to blame them for all society's problems. This echoes Weldon's (1998) controversial description of men as the 'victims', a view strongly attacked by Toynbee (1998). Coward (1999) goes on to claim that there is now more evidence of exclusion of men from traditionally female jobs than of the exclusion of women from traditionally male jobs. Neither are women any longer confined to poorly paid work, but have made significant advances in the professions and business. She surmises that men's complaints are, indeed, more than 'squeals of masculine protest' (Coward 1999: 63). It is **womanism** (defined as 'feminism's vulgate' and lacking the complexities of mainstream feminism) which still sees women as victims and engages in an easy blaming of masculinity for everything. She concludes that 'if men are oppressors, then they are vulnerable ones . . . the power and emotional certainties that went with the old patriarchy are on the move' (Coward 1999: 86).

A major source of any 'crisis' in masculinity is the transformation of the world of work and it is to this that I now turn.

Men, masculinity and the changing labour market

The 1970s, 1980s and 1990s witnessed major economic, industrial, business and cultural reconstruction (Osgerby 1998). One of the main reasons for the alleged crisis in masculinity is undoubtedly the transformation that has taken place in the labour market throughout the western economies. The following factors are often identified as being at the forefront of the changing nature of employment:

• The almost total disappearance of **family capitalism** as smaller firms were swallowed up, heralding the emergence of large corporations and their anonymous senior management.

- De-industrialization and a loss of jobs due to the introduction of new technology and the demise of old, heavy 'smokestack' industries.
- The transition from an industrial to a postindustrial economy, from a Fordist to a post-Fordist context.
- The massive de-layering and downsizing of the 1980s and early 1990s which had an impact upon all sectors of the workforce, including middle and senior management.
- The adoption of market-led economic policies since the early 1980s and the effects of an increasingly global economy.
- Greater employment opportunities for women and the implementation of equal opportunity policies, along with the extension of part-time working.

These changes have had a huge impact, given that work is central to masculinity, providing money, power, a job or career, as well as the opportunity to develop and exercise skills, expertise and authority. It is surprising, therefore, that earlier studies of men in the workplace did not focus upon masculinity *per se* (for example, Walker and Guest 1952; Whyte 1956; Dalton 1959). The paradox is that while many working men were alienated from their work (Willis 1977), nothing has proved more damaging to them and their sense of the masculine than unemployment, which took away independence and control over family finances. Unsurprisingly, unemployed men suffer intense feelings of disempowerment, emasculation and loss of self-esteem. The men in the McKee and Bell (1986) study, for example, regarded themselves as victims of the state, reduced to nothing less than 'scroungers'. A similarly painful picture is documented by both Marsden and Duff (1975) and Gaillie *et al.* (1994). For the workless, doing housework while being supported by a working wife was the ultimate humiliation (Bernard 1981; Kelvin and Jarrett 1985). The psychological impact of unemployment can be profoundly adverse (Henwood and Miles 1987) and men in the Willott and Griffin (1996) study of the long-term unemployed in the West Midlands of England experienced feelings of personal inadequacy and emasculation because they could not afford to go out or provide their family with treats, gifts and holidays. They felt their exclusion from the consumer society acutely and feared their wives or partners might leave them as a result. Meanwhile, Cockburn (1983) records the trauma occasioned by the demise of the physically demanding 'hot metal' skills of printers and linotype compositors (demanding a long apprenticeship and historically the exclusive property of men) in the early 1980s and their replacement by, in comparison, 'feminine' computer based printing technologies (which could be operated by women). Technology became a weapon of powerful capitalists to exert power over disempowered men and the women who took their place.

Two of the most popular British films of the 1990s were about the crisis faced by workless men during the mine closures of the Thatcher era, namely *Brassed Off* (1996) and *The Full Monty* (1997). Both addressed the crisis inflicted upon working men by the demise of coal mining in the North of England, but whereas the former falls into nostalgia and elegy, the latter is about survival and creative initiative as the group of redundant men fight back. The masculinity associated with mining retains its association of heroic endurance, so that at the end of *Brassed Off*, although a victory of sorts has been won, it is a sad, hollow, futureless one (Lloyd and Thacker 2000). *The Full Monty*, in contrast, witnesses a group of working men, full of doubts and fears, regaining some self-esteem in a world where the nature of work and gender roles have been forever transformed. Indeed, if *Brassed Off* is informed by class politics, *The Full Monty* is informed by sexual politics (Lloyd and Thacker 2000), so much so that Talmon (2000) claims that:

> Spectacular masculinity of the 1990s is no longer articulated on the battlefield or in car races but, rather, in drag or strip shows, where unemployed and 'incompetent males' perform to satisfy female appetite.
>
> (Talman 2000: 12)

Many working men, deprived of a job in heavy industry, also felt demeaned by the nature of the new jobs that were developed in regions of high unemployment. The **feminization of employment** is a term used by a number of commentators (notably by Jensen *et al.* 1988, repeated by Yeandle 1995) to indicate the movement into the labour market in the second half of the twentieth century of increasing numbers of women. But it can also be seen to refer to changes in the nature of work itself with women, for example, able to occupy roles (through, for example, the replacement of 'muscle' by technology and machines) previously dominated by male labour. Interestingly, one man interviewed during the 'Hilltop' Hospital study (briefly alluded to in Chapter 7) described many of the jobs that had, in his experience, replaced heavy industry as 'women's jobs':

> I worked at the coal face for thirty-five years, man and boy. I was a foreman engineer and had a lot of responsibility. When the pits were closed and I couldn't get another job underground. I got very depressed, went very low. I was fifty-three and felt I had been thrown on the scrap heap before my time. For every job there were ten, fifteen, even twenty younger men standing in front of me in the queue. The only thing I could get, in spite of all my skills and experience, was a job packing chicken portions in a tray, covering them with cellophane and then scanning on the bar code. A trained monkey could have done it, honest,

and that's insulting the monkey's intelligence! But it kept body and soul together, so I did it for five years until I was sixty. But I never regarded it as a proper job. To me it was a woman's job, that's the way I saw it anyway. There was none of the technical challenges, dangers and male camaraderie I'd been used to underground. Nothing but pop music blaring out and bits of bloody chicken staring at you all day!

(Beynon 1987: see Chapter 7)

So far all the attention has been upon working class unemployment, but middle and senior managers, too, have increasingly experienced their own form of alienation as they have been excluded from decision-making in a world of corporate take-overs. Throughout the strata the hands-on, **old patriarchs** have been replaced by the accountancy and business studies trained **young pretenders** (McDowell and Court 1994; McDowell 1997). Peter Jachimiak's current research draws a parallel between the crisis of masculinity and what he perceives as a crisis in middle management. Taking his cue from Roper (1991) on the growing alienation of middle managers, Jachimiak argues that the technologization of the workplace and the loss of any guarantee of a job for life has undermined manual workers and middle managers alike, so that both now share a deep sense of uncertainty and instability. He documents the emergence of a new kind of middle manager in whom masculine forms of management exist alongside softer, more feminine styles. His speculative conclusion, based on ongoing fieldwork, is that 'perhaps a hybrid, "overtly masculine/overtly feminine" younger generation of managers is in ascendancy, where a feminized exterior shields a particularly ruthless male interior' (Peter Jachimiak, personal communication 2001). A similarly original approach to white collar management is that taken by Striff (2000) and to whom I refer again in Chapter 7. She points out that the popular image of the business world is intimately linked with cultural assumptions about hyper-masculine, goal-directed behaviour. Indeed, failure in business defines the 'non-man' (often dismissed as 'a woman'). The true 'company man' takes on the cloak of masculinity with a vengeance by engaging in blood-on-the-carpet power games. 'Hard' business success is everything, with intimacy reduced to an institutionalized homosociality, while genuine ('soft') relationships are placed firmly on the back-burner.

Is the 'crisis' new?

Is the notion of a crisis of masculinity new, or is it just that each generation experiences it in different ways? The evidence would suggest the latter.

Indeed, one view is that the crisis is constitutive of masculinity itself. This is certainly Mangan's (1997) view:

> Crisis is . . . a condition of masculinity itself. Masculine gender identity is never stable; its terms are continually being re-defined and re-negotiated, the gender performance continually being re-staged. Certain themes and tropes inevitably re-appear with regularity, but each era experiences itself in different ways.
>
> (Mangan 1997: 4)

But what evidence is there for this? Have there been periods of masculine crisis in the past and how do these compare to the current alleged crisis?

Fletcher (1995) charts an acute male crisis in Tudor and early Stuart England based on the fear of women and of the threat they were perceived to pose to men and, consequently, how best they might be controlled. Similarly, Kimmel (1987) talks of two centuries of male anxiety centred around a fear of the feminine and points to two earlier periods when there were major shifts in relations between the sexes and in domestic relations, namely in Restoration England (1688–1714) and in the United States (1880–1914), which witnessed the splitting up of men into pro-feminist, anti-feminist and pro-male. The influx of more women into the labour market in the early decades of the twentieth century in the United States resulted in mounting concern. Moreover, men have long suffered from the number and variety of demands made upon them. Roper and Tosh (1991) demonstrate how Victorian masculinities were distorted by the demands made upon men in all classes by burgeoning industry, business and of service to Empire. Many (for example, Horrocks 1994) hold that the gender roles that industrial society forced men and women to adopt were equally damaging to both. There have, too, been regular bouts of societal angst over the behaviour of young men. For example:

- In the Edwardian era concern over the morals and physical condition of young men led to the foundation of the Boy Scouts and the Boys' Brigade.
- In the 1930s, over the presence of teenage gangs in London, Glasgow, Manchester and Liverpool.
- In the 1950s over the arrival of Teddy Boys, followed in the 1960s by Mods and Rockers and by Punks in the 1970s.

An interesting approach to masculinity and crisis is the ways in which nations consciously engage in 're-masculinization' after traumatic, 'un-masculinizing' events. Examples would include, first, the rise of Fascism and of **Fascist masculinity** in Germany in the 1920s as a response to national humiliation in the Treaty of Versailles following the First World War. Mosse

(1996) presents Fascism as a reassertion of a fanatical, militaristic masculinity at a time of political and economic turbulence. The 'superiority' and 'purity' of Aryan man was established in contrast to 'lesser people' like Jews, blacks, homosexuals, lesbians and Gypsies. In addition to conquest of territory he was celebrated in technology, sport, art and, for example, the 'masculinist' architecture planned by Hitler's architect, Albert Speer, for a new Berlin as a capital worthy of the Third Reich.

A second example of re-masculinization is the United States in the 1980s and the election of Ronald Reagan as president. This occasioned an assault on the soft, debilitating 'pinko ideals' that were seen both as a product of the 'hippy 1960s' and the (allegedly) weak and indecisive presidency of Jimmy Carter. Meanwhile on screen the humiliation of the Vietnam War was reversed as the cyborgian figure of Rambo 'zapped' the Vietcong and, in the process, dealt a decisive blow against the emerging figure of the pro-feminist, sensitive 'new man' (Jeffords 1989).

Ferrebe (2000) discerns a crisis-in-masculinity in Britain in 1945–6 as men returned from the Second World War to civilian life and found that the United Kingdom they had striven to protect had changed beyond recognition in their absence (see Turner and Rennell 1995). It was a country that, by necessity, had been designed to function without them. Moreover, Britain was already turning to a new agenda of priorities (enshrined in the **Beveridge Report**) and establishing the welfare state, as well as experiencing the start of what we now recognize as consumerism. The result was that

> the older generation felt itself to be disinherited from the public sphere, just as the country they had remembered seemed increasingly diminished in importance and, by no stretch of the imagination, a world power.
>
> (Ferrebe 2000: 11)

Ferrebe sees this crisis reflected in postwar novels which are

> littered with older role-models clinging to out-moded traditions of honour, of failed fathers and, increasingly, with covert examples of the ultimate challenge to masculine homogeneity, homosexual man.
>
> (Ferrebe 2000: 11)

Likewise, a revealing mirror of crises in masculinity is film: for example, many 1940s and 1950s British and American films explored the problem of a whole generation of men returning from the Second World War. Prior to counselling, these often highly traumatized men had to do their best to acclimatize to civilian life (Cohan 1997). For example, Chibnall and Murphy (1999) in their study of British crime films of the period identify two themes:

first, a sensitivity to the loss of military agency and readjustment encountered by these ex-servicemen expressed in the contrast between them and the unpatriotic and cowardly 'spiv' who had avoided war service, stayed at home and grown rich through black marketeering. One way in which the unrewarded demobbed man could regain wartime heroism was by standing up to them. The second theme was the loss of masculine status due to the rising profile of women in postwar society and a nostalgia for a prewar society in which male privilege was assured. There was, also, the ever-present danger of being lured by a femme fatale into a life of crime. This, then, was a filmic depiction of masculinity-in-crisis,

> crime melodramas of masculine crisis . . . [where] men had to tread softly . . . to dance with crime . . . [and become] fugitives, intruders in a post-war society that would not accommodate them.
> (Chibnall and Murphy 1999: 65)

Meanwhile, Hunt (1998) asks (somewhat naively, given the wealth of evidence of the historical nature of the male crisis): 'When did postwar British masculinity have its first crisis?' His answer is during the 1970s as a result of the accelerating break up of the old Fordist heavy industries, deteriorating labour relations (culminating in the 'winter of discontent'), the impact of first wave feminism and the rise of the gay movement. He talks of the decade's 'uncertain maleness', he points to the emergence of skinheads and gays, 'sissy' Bowie boys and glam rock's ambivalence, in particular Gary Glitter's uncertain and camp hyper-masculinity. He notes a split emerging between the older 'safari suit man' and the younger men, because this was a decade in which (some) middle class men clearly felt the need to engage in consciousness-raising as a response to feminism and the embryonic 'men's movement' in the United States. This initial fragmentation of a relatively consensual 'manly vision' by popular culture gathered momentum throughout the 1980s and 1990s, plunging masculinity into its deeper, contemporary crisis. Hunt (1998: 73) concludes: 'whenever masculinity's "crisis" actually started, it certainly seems to have been in place by the 1970s and the signs of it were everywhere.'

Similarly, Gregory (2000) scrutinizes the 'glam rock' phenomena of the early 1970s, with its emphasis upon artifice and high drama which subverted established images of masculinity. He captures the spirit of glam rock when he writes:

> Male performers, some adopting glamorous pseudonyms and alter-egos, espoused a distinctive, visual style where glittering, soft and shiny fabrics were worn with platform soled boots, heavy make-up and

quasi-'feminine' hairstyling. Using transvestism and camp, Glam artists assumed sexually ambiguous identities which were fuelled by media speculation.

(Gregory 2000: 15)

This subversion of the traditional images of masculinity was extended in the 1980s in terms of menswear and magazines. Indeed:

anxieties surrounding the legalisation of homosexuality and the growing women's liberation movement found expression in effeminate representations of masculinity in popular music culture.

(Gregory 2000: 15)

Does the 'crisis' actually exist?

The assertion of the crisis afflicting men and masculinity is loudly voiced everywhere, if not the hard evidence. Indeed, in the 1990s men have repeatedly been redesignated as the fragile sex and numerous books have appeared calling for sensitivity and emotional literacy to be at the heart of the new masculinity. But how far is the crisis an actual or primarily a discursive one, created and sustained through unremitting press amplification (see Chapter 6) and 1990s popular literature (for example, Hornby 1992, 1995; Parsons 1999)? Do these outpourings create the crisis rather than reflect it? This would appear to be the view of the television personality and writer David Baddiel (1999: 1), who attacks the whole notion of masculinity-in-crisis as a bogus media product, the stringing together of a few statistics, news items and photographs. The stereotypical emotional illiterate male does not exist, but is a 'straw man' created only to give columnists something to write about! Men, argues Baddiel (1999), may feel concerned about their health, economic position and personal circumstances, but rarely about their gender. Others doubt the authenticity of the crisis: Segal (2000a), for example, sees the link between heterosexuality, men and power firmly still in place and argues that it needs to be made clear that not all men are failing, unemployed or unhappy. By any measure men remain the dominant and threatening sex; talk of a crisis is a way of sidelining more important issues like poverty, racism and structural inequalities. Outside academe and the media in the so-called real world neither masculinity nor crisis is a burning issue in people's everyday lives. The advent of gay iconography and men's changing power relationship with women have undoubtedly been a contributor to the notion of crisis. For Edwards (1997: 134), however, 'masculinity is indeed in crisis, yet not from the scrutiny of sexual politics, more from the market'. Another angle is provided by Plain (2000), who points to the 'discursive unsexing' of men in literature. She takes as her example the collapse of the cynical, hard-boiled male detective in a world that no longer values his brand of masculinity: for example, the contemporary novelist Ian Rankin's detective is an unattractive, divorced, near alcoholic and lonely figure. An interesting recent perspective upon the alleged crisis is that by Talmon (2000), whose work covers cinema and television in both Israel and the United States. She makes the point that media representations of new masculinity do not merely reflect changes in society, but legitimize them. The result is that former clear distinctions between the masculine and the feminine are being renegotiated daily on screen. The old master narratives and ideologies have collapsed, along with the masculine paradigms that underpinned them. Popular films and television shows, videos, advertisements and magazines are full of images and narratives of weak men unable to cope with the demands made upon them. These are, indeed, 'men-in-crisis', freed of an 'all-male, mission-oriented, nation-bound collective identity' and, instead, urged to retreat into 'sentiment, relationships and romance' (Talmon 2000: 4). These representations of men are very different from the former male paradigms of husband and breadwinner.

Faludi (1999) argues that the crisis has been precipitated by the fact that men have been enmeshed in an **ornamental culture** of display so that they have been forced to become more like women. American men are in crisis primarily because they have been rendered 'feminized' consumers rather than 'manly' producers. Robinson (2000), responding to the Faludian thesis of 'ornamental entrapment', suggests that the 'ornamentalization' of men need not be such a bad thing and asks whether the crisis in masculinity is a good or a bad thing and for whom? If it results in us rethinking the nature of masculinity (and femininity), then it could be an entirely positive outcome. The whole idea of men-as-victims is unsurprisingly regarded with considerable scepticism by feminists. Robertson (2000) suggests that men are busy establishing a litany of 'wrongs' in order to then claim 'rights'. The notion of crisis, therefore, is nothing less than a strategy by men to reoccupy the central stage and regain patriarchal status and power. As MacInnes (1998), in a seminal section of his excellent book, points out, the current state of masculinity is variously located on a continuum between 'the pessimistic' and 'the optimistic'.

The pessimistic

Masculinity is in rapid transition and, for many, change is painful, especially for older, less well off and less well educated men. The unquestioned authority of men (along with other former 'male certainties') has evaporated, leaving a deep sense of being lost, so much so that 'it is hard to avoid the contemporary inference that masculinity no longer implies an automatic superiority, but almost its opposite – difficulties, problems, inferiority' (Coward 1999: 88).

The optimistic

Economically privileged, self-confident, well-educated men are coping well; they have the resources to explore a more varied set of masculine scripts and are far better positioned to exercise choice than their older and poorer counterparts. For them it is a very good time indeed to be a man as the old patriarchal barriers are disintegrating and such men are experiencing new-found possibilities. The cramping masculinity born of nineteenth century industrialization and militarism has given way to a situation replete with novel possibilities. In a transformed world there is a need for new kinds of masculinity and femininity, for new kinds of men and women. In this process there will be losers. Young (especially economically privileged) men increasingly live lives that 'channel hop' across versions of masculinity, while (as previously pointed out) even less privileged young men adopt a more various bricolage style of masculinity than did their fathers (Beynon 1996).

Conclusion: a 'crisis' in need of research

A number of points with which to conclude. First, there is a misleading tendency to assume that the alleged crisis is new and unique to our times. This, as I have demonstrated, is untrue, although what may be unique today is the nature and the scale of the alleged crisis. Second, there is imprecision in identifying the nature of this crisis, which has consequentially become a contemporary cliché, a catch-all container into which anything negative about men is simply poured. In fact, 'masculinity' and 'crisis' have become so closely associated in some sectors of the media that they are in danger of becoming synonymous. The implication is that no self-respecting man can be without a crisis: it has almost become a male obligation! Undoubtedly many men (certainly not all) are encountering emotional, personal and professional problems, but there is an unseemly haste to attribute these to masculinity *per se*. Third, the causes of the crisis remain vague and have been variously attributed to feminism, changes to the labour market, economic restructuring, globalization and the global economy, technological innovation, the gay movement and consumerism. Fourth, there is a tacit assumption that the crisis has engulfed all men. Undoubtedly many men are currently experiencing major difficulties but, as has already been made clear, for very many men there has probably never been a better time to explore a widened range of 'masculine scripts'. Fifth, are we talking about a crisis of men or a crisis of masculinity, given that one is not necessarily indicative of the other? Moreover, does the notion of crisis really advance our under-standing of men or of masculinity? Indeed, is the term too easily brought into play to describe the changed relations between men and women (and, indeed, men and men) and, in the process, push aside more established concepts like educational achievement, status, regional positioning, cultural difference and, most notable of all, class? As Segal (2000b: 4) comments, 'Once you bring class back into it you see that many of these problems have been around for a long time, but were understood differently'. Indeed, are we dealing with one generalized crisis, or a series of very different crises which impact upon men in different ways in different places? Perhaps the only thing that can be concluded at this stage is that rather than referring to a monolithic masculinity-in-crisis, the notion of different crises (both actual and discursive) differentially affecting a range of masculinities is likely to be a more apt description. What is certainly the case is the pressing need to research what is really happening to men in a variety of walks of life and whether (and, if so, how?) they perceive their masculinity, or themselves as men, to be in crisis. Connell (2000) makes a start on this in his important book *The Men and the Boys*.

In conclusion, I started with the Crisis-of-American-Boys stand in the Barnes and Noble bookshop in July 2000, and it is appropriate that I should end by returning to that theme. In the *New Yorker* that same month Nicholas Lemann (2000) points out that young American males have long been deemed to be in crisis, at least on screen, from *Blackboard Jungle* (1955) to *American Beauty* (1999). He then takes a closer look at the cur-rent 'boy crisis books', dividing the debate into two sides, which he terms the 'red team' and the 'blue team':

- the red team presents boys being oppressed by the traditional expec-tations of masculinity
- the blue team believes that the real danger comes from the damage done by a generation of feminist attack.

Lemann cites an example of each, namely *Real Boys' Voices* (Pollack with Shuster 2000) and *The War Against Boys* (Sommers 2000). Pollack with Shuster (2000) believe that boys are prisoners of a rigid **boy code** that places enormous pressures upon them to succeed and prevents them from ex-pressing their anxieties. The unremitting demand to be tough and in control is deeply damaging. Sommers (2000), on the other hand, sees American 'teenager-hood' as being profoundly unfair to boys because of 'anti-boy feminists'. She argues that 'natural' masculine traits have been pathologized and attacks pro-feminist education which she sees as having resulted in reverse sexism in schools. Boys are constantly confronted with the notion that men are by nature brutal and emotionally damaged. Furthermore, the championing of female styles of communication and the rise of the thera- peutic 'talk-show culture' have colluded to render traditional male com- municational reserve dysfunctional. Lemann (2000: 83) comments that Sommers 'dreams of a world in which boys, rather than being subjected to training in self-esteem and emotional openness, would receive manly, Kiplingesque "character-education" '. Only then will they be able to with- stand what she presents as the onslaught of feminism.

The biggest influence on masculinities since the 1980s has been the com- mercial and it is to this that I turn in the next chapter.

Further reading

Bowker, L.H. (1998) *Masculinities and Violence*. London: Sage.

Clare, A. (2000) *On Men: Masculinity in Crisis*. London: Chatto and Windus.

Connell, R.W. (2000) *The Men and the Boys*. Cambridge: Polity.

Faludi, S. (1999) *Stiffed: The Betrayal of the Modern Man*. London: Chatto and Windus.

Jeffords, S. (1989) *The Remasculinization of America: Gender and the Vietnam War*. Bloomington, IN: Indiana University Press.

Mosse, G.I. (1996) *The Image of Man: The Creation of Modern Masculinity*. Oxford: Oxford University Press.

Newburn, T. and Stanko, E.A. (eds) (1994) *Just Boys Doing Business? Men, Mas- culinities and Crime*. London: Routledge.

Sommers, C.H. (2000) *The War Against Boys*. New York: Simon & Schuster.

THE COMMERCIALIZATION OF MASCULINITIES: FROM THE 'NEW MAN' TO THE 'NEW LAD'

5

Young men are being sold images which rupture traditional icons of masculinity. They are stimulated to look at themselves and other men as objects of consumer desire. They are getting pleasures previously branded taboo or feminine. A new bricollage of masculinity is the noise coming from the fashion house, the marketplace and the street.

(Frank Mort, *Boy's Own*, 1988)

Loaded's senior staff have moved on . . . but what of the generation they have left behind? Pretty soon the lads with the mummy's boy dream of abundance and no interference . . . will have to wake up. And they will have to face the fact that their own utopia is not very different from John Major's creaky old village-green idyll, only their particular folly features sports cars, bimbos and recurring nosebleeds.

(Ian Penman, *Over-Loaded*, 2000)

Introduction: masculinity from the 1980s

If the 1990s was the decade in which masculinity was extensively deconstructed by academics world-wide, then the 1980s was most certainly the decade in which it was extensively reconstructed. What do I mean by this? Masculinity was more extensively transformed by economic and commercial forces in the 1980s than at any previous time. This postmodernist transformation of masculinity has been extensively documented by three writers in particular, Frank Mort (1996), Sean Nixon (1996) and Tim Edwards (1997). I refer to each repeatedly throughout this chapter and record my debt to them at the outset. Let me emphasize that this chapter is effectively theirs, not mine. I can only hope I do their work justice. I proceed as follows. First, I place the 'new man' in a brief historical context before examining the 'nurturer' and 'narcissist' strands. Second, I explore the narcissist strand of new masculinity by drawing upon Nixon's threefold model of analysis of the commercialization of masculinity in the 1980s by reference to menswear, visual representations (including advertising) and the men's **style press**. Third, I label the 1980s as the 'hello and goodbye' decade, specifically 'hello' to the **yuppie** and 'goodbye' to the 'old industrial man'. Fourth, I then move into the 1990s and on to the present time and examine the further commercialization of masculinity, this time in the form of the 'new lad' and **laddism,** a project particularly associated with the magazine *Loaded* and the advent of 'lad television'. Fifth, I then trace the new lad's ancestry and the considerable barrage of criticism that has been levelled at him. Finally, a question is posed, namely 'Who was (or is) the "new man"?' I draw upon the views of three influential commentators, Chapman (1988), Mort (1996) and Edwards (1997). I conclude by arguing that a generalized 'new man-ism' has now emerged in which elements from both the nurturer and the narcissus strands have been scrambled together.

'How "new" is the "new man"?' is a pertinent question to ask. He has been around in various guises for some considerable time. For example, George Bernard Shaw was musing about what form he could assume in the twentieth century as early as 1903! Also, the term has often been used by historians to indicate past shifts in masculinity. Two examples are the new man of the Renaissance (epitomized by Leonardo and Michelangelo) or, more recently, someone like the ecclesiastic Edward White Benson, the subject of John Tosh's (1991) fine biographical cameo. In spite of comparatively humble origins, Benson had, through iron discipline and hard work, risen to become one of the most respected public figures of his time. He epitomized the new man of the latter half of the nineteenth century in that a self-made meritocracy was slowly beginning to emerge in which social position was earned through effort rather than being dependent on family background and inheritance. However, the term the 'new man' belongs firmly to the 1980s and can be both a term of opprobrium (signifying a new and improved version of masculinity cleared of some, if not all, of the less endearing attributes of traditional, patriarchal masculinity) and one of jocular dismissal and humour (in which some of the alleged features of the new man, such as connecting with his inner self, are mercilessly lampooned). Some argue that there is little 'new' about the new man and that under the veneer he is the very same 'old man'. Some would even argue that he has never existed. Such a view is trenchantly expressed by Moir and Moir (1998), who maintain that the new man is nothing more than the creation of intellectuals and that he does not exist outside the academic mind and Gucci perfume ads! I now turn to the origins of the new man which is approached in terms of two strands, the nurturer and the narcissist.

Strand 1: the 'new man-as-nurturer'

The first strand in new man's heredity is allied to men's reactions to social change and the changing role of men in the 1970s and 1980s, particularly men's reactions to first wave feminisim. In the United Kingdom and United States pro-feminist men, sensing justice in the feminist movement and eager themselves for social change, attempted to raise both their own and their fellow men's consciousness and foster a more caring, sharing, nurturing man. They willingly supported the women's movement and taking a full role in the domestic arena (particularly in respect of child-rearing). These men were usually middle class, well educated, intellectuals: an example in the United Kingdom would be Seidler's (1989) early work and contributors to the magazine *Spare Rib*. Feminism attacked patriarchy and pathologized patriarchal masculinity as arrested development and, as Chapman (1988) makes clear, equated it with rape, war, incest, pollution and much else. Changing patterns in family life, with men marrying later or not at all, along with a willingness to take on a supportive role in a woman's career, resulted in the emergence of the new man as an ideal. He was the riposte to vilified 'old man', his father, and a refugee from the hardline masculinity epitomized by the paranoid, macho men with stifled emotions. They were enacted on the screen by Wayne, Bogart, Bronson and Stallone, with Stallone's Rambo character memorably depicted as 'bare-chested and alone, wading through the Vietcong swamp with not even a tube of insect repellent for comfort' (Chapman 1988: 227). Others reacted differently to the social changes taking place. One of the most lampooned images is of the new man as a tree-hugging, back-to-nature figure desperately searching for his real 'masculine self'. He will always be associated with Robert Bly, the American poet whose *Iron John* (1981) is still the subject of considerable debate and controversy. In it he calls on men to journey into nature, the great outdoors and engage in rituals in male-only groups to release long-suppressed emotions. Thereby, he feels, men can reclaim their souls and reclaim true manhood. He laments the decline of the father's influence in inducting the son into the ways of the world and argues that young men need older male mentors to help them connect with the wild, innate masculinity inside them. This is something modern man has lost contact with but which is preserved in ancient myths. Many read the book as part of an anti-feminist backlash, accused Bly of blaming women for alleged male emotional distress and discontent, feared it would distract anti-sexist men as they struggled against gender oppression and argued that Bly had failed to distinguish between gender and sexuality.

Although Christian's (1994) is a small-scale study, its outcomes, given the paucity of empirical evidence of any kind, are noteworthy. He interviewed some 30 men (non-macho and mostly non-gay, in the age range 21–54) who were attempting to live non-sexist lifestyles because they believed in the justice of increased equality between the sexes. Moreover, many of these men were aware of sensitive and vulnerable feelings which they believed helped them have better relationships with women and children as well as with other men. Among the key early influences in these men's lives were

- non-identification with traditional fathers and strong identification with nurturing fathers and parents who did not conform to conventional domestic roles
- a rejection of macho behaviour in school and a preference for the company of girls
- the generalized influence of feminism but, often, a relationship with one feminist in particular.

Christian (1994) reveals some apparent contradictions concerning the male breadwinner role. Since the 1960s women have become less prepared to accept dependence and there has been a widespread erosion of the male breadwinner role. However, many of the men in the study believed that a commitment to it was still compatible with a non-sexist lifestyle and aimed for a mixed breadwinner–homemaker role with their partners. Christian depicts pro-feminist men as a minority who may not be active in anti-sexist groups. Their importance lies in their attempts to relate to women in non-oppressive ways and try to be their allies in the struggle against gender oppression. Similarly, Kimmel and Messner (1992) depict anti-sexist men as active supporters of women's demands for equal opportunity, education, political participation, sexual autonomy and family reforms. Such men are clearly the product of recent economic, cultural and demographic changes which have rendered traditional masculinity less and less sustainable. As Christian (1994: 3) puts it, 'many men's experience and expectations of life and traditional ideas of masculinity have been seriously called into question in the late twentieth century'.

Widely criticized as being middle class, elitist, western-centric and remote from the lived experience of most men, the stereotypical image of the anti-sexist, caring, sharing man nevertheless gained credibility and strength throughout the 1980s. But how deep or widespread was the change? Was it no more than a media-driven illusion of change or, in fact, a genuine change in the consciousness and behaviour of men? What evidence there is would indicate that, in spite of his survival into the new century of the 'new man-as-nurturer', men's involvement in domestic labour has not significantly changed. Christian argues that the situation has been compounded by the increasing work demands of employers which have made it even more difficult for men to change long established masculine routines and expectations.

Strand 2: the 'new man-as-narcissist'

Before exploring this topic further, let me acknowledge again my indebtedness to Mort (1996), Nixon (1996) and Edwards (1997). This second strand of the new man is associated with **commercial masculinity** and the spectacular expansion of consumerism since the end of the Second World War (Shields 1992). The 'new man-as-narcissist' is clearly the son of his father's 1950s and 1960s rock and hippy generation, with its interest in clothes and pop music and far removed from the 'demob-suited', carbolic soap and Old Spice-scented generation. Although the commercialization of masculinity accelerated in the 1980s, the trend had its origins in late 1950s pop culture, especially in the United States, with the emergence of Elvis Presley and others who dressed to be looked at and admired. Mort (1996) pinpoints 1953–4 as the time when class based masculinities started to be replaced by style based ones as a series of take-overs and mergers set in motion a gradual erosion of the status quo of mass male (Burton's) fashion. Meanwhile, Ehrenreich (1983) identifies the 1950s *Playboy* as the ancestor of the 1980s yuppie. In the 1950s early marriage and the subsequent support of a wife and children were visible proof of 'normal masculinity', any deviation from this preordained route rendering the individual vulnerable to imputations of homosexuality. Hugh Hefner's *Playboy* magazine's heterosexual hedonism avoided this while still rebelling against the dominant norms of 1950s masculinity. Whereas mainstream 1950s masculinity was antithetical to the feminine aspects of consumerism, the 'playboy' revelled in the acquisition of fancy clothes, fast cars and beautiful women. It was this utopian vision that was to be picked up and exploited by 1980s consumerism.

If the 1960s set the scene for the fragmentation of a hitherto relatively uniform masculine text, the 1970s, which Hunt (1998) terms 'the decade that taste forgot', took it a stage further. The 1970s witnessed a disintegration of the relatively unified youth culture of the 1950s and 1960s and, as a result, male fashion, propelled by **creative advertising**, became what Mort (1996: 25) terms 'a hydra' and stimulated a 'desire to play about with masculinity, to re-arrange traditional icons of maleness' (Mort 1996: 203). York (1982) captured this when he observed the proliferating expressions of young masculinities on the streets of west London. Hunt (1998) notes that the young male icons of the time (like the footballer Charlie George and the singer Rod Stewart) displayed a 'hard–soft' masculinity which was easily copied. 'Rodness', for example, was readily available in that all a young man had to do to acquire it was to drink, sing, pull girls and like football. For Hunt the strike-strewn 1970s rather than the peacock 1960s marked the emergence in Britain of more varied, mobile masculinities. The rampant commercialization of masculinity that was to follow was founded on a number of 1970s stereotypes ranging from the traditional ('Old Spice Man', 'Tobacco Man', 'Bitter Beer Man') through to the new kids on the block (the permissive, swinging 'Safari Man', 'Hair Spray Man', 'Lad Fop' and 'The Gay'). As the 1980s got under way the commercial exploitation of men-as-sex-objects became very big business. The voyeuristic sexualization of the female body, its packaging as visual erotica, was now transferred to the male body with the same ultimate purpose in mind – to sell, sell, sell. Menswear shops proliferated, full of broad-shouldered, 'body armour' suits, with loud ties and flamboyant shirts; the male body became the peg on which to attach new fashion codes in an unprecedented way. Meanwhile, Ross (1999) describes how football and fashion began, at least at the mass end of the market, to be brought closer together, making more concrete a link already evident in the colourful career of the 'fifth Beatle', the footballer George Best, in the 1960s and 1970s. He describes how the football terraces became catwalks:

> The football fan of the early Eighties was no longer a rattle-waving, scarf-wearing wally or a toothless skinhead grunt, but a mass of label-wearing, style-coded casual wear freaks.
>
> (Ross 1999: 29)

The 1980s witnessed a change in the **politics of looking** as the 'male-on-male' gaze joined the 'male-on-female' (along with female-on-male and even female-on-female) as socially acceptable, especially among young, fashionable metropolitan men with high disposable incomes. Nixon (1996) employs a threefold model to analyse how this came about:

- *Clothing outlets for men*: male retail outlets proliferated in the 1980s, ranging from the exclusive, designer outlets to the merchandising of cut-price labels. The middle-ranging Next chain was one of the great marketing successes of the decade, their clothes 'speaking' aspirational lifestyle rather than class. In Next's hands the outmoded suit made a spectacular comeback, wreaking 'a vengeance against all forms of soft-focus effeminacy' (Edwards 1997: 21).
- *New visual representations of men*: in the 1980s new visual representations of masculinities appeared in advertising and on television. The male form began to be eroticized and objectified in ways that had previously

been applied to the female body. In the hands of photographers (for example, Ray Petri and Kevin Brody), advertising agencies (like Bartle Boyle Hegarty and in cards and posters (for example, those by Athena) a narcissistic new man emerged, self-confident, well groomed, muscular, but also sensitive).

- *Style magazines for men*: the emergence of the style press for men was arguably among the most notable features of 1980s popular culture. In their pages diverse and mobile masculinities were created: as Edwards (1997) puts it, in both layout and content these were new kinds of magazines for new kinds of men. They constituted a new commercial project and were 'lifestyle manuals . . . offering new ways of experiencing the city' (Nixon 1996: 155), in the process placing **men-in-the-mirror**, to borrow a term from Edwards' (1997) book. He documents the growth of style magazine publishing and the clever crafting of a range of visually sophisticated masculinities for the first generation to be brought up on colour television, one more visually literate than any before. Both Mort (1996) and Edwards (1997) are of the opinion that 1980s men were not changing because of sexual politics, but through commercial pressures. In fact, the style magazines had 'a lot more to do with new markets for the constant reconstruction of masculinity through consumption' (Edwards 1997: 82).

Gay men, predominant in the image and fashion industries, were at the forefront of these changes and were blamed for what some perceived to be the 'feminization' of men's fashion. These critics strongly objected to what they held to be the prioritization of the 'gay look' in fashion, including the sending up of macho masculinity in terms of hyper-masculinity. Conversely, some gay men resented what they regarded as the cheapening of their own distinctive visual style by the fashion industry. It is easy to overemphasize the significance of these skirmishes for the general British male populace, most of whom live outside London and for whom such metropolitan lifestyles are light years away from their own daily experiences. Indeed, Nixon (1996) concludes:

> Whilst it is true to say that the boundaries between gay and straight, or even between male and female, are becoming more blurred in terms of media representations, the marketing of up-market fashion and the consumption patterns of some affluent and professional groups, this barely marks a sea change in the entire population where the categories of male and female, straight and gay, black or white, remain remarkably stable.
>
> (Nixon 1996: 117)

The 1980s were characterized by two masculine archetypes:

- The ostentatious City and Wall Street yuppie, at his most triumphant a Donald Trump-like character, famously portrayed on screen by Michael Douglas in *Wall Street* (1985).
- Old industrial man, rendered redundant by the decimation of heavy industry, forever symbolized by the angry figures of miners confronting lines of police during the pit closures of the mid-1980s.

It is to these that I now turn in order to provide a picture of the 1980s as the 'hello and goodbye' decade.

'Hello' to the 'yuppie'

Although the term 'yuppie' was also applicable to women, its connotations were (and remain) essentially masculine. At his heart was conspicuous consumption and a ruthless, cut-throat determination to be seen to be successful, all 'driven by an excessive desire to spend money. Whether it was property, cars, clothes or personal artefacts, consumption was a dominant feature of the yuppie lifestyle' (Mort 1996: 172). Following financial deregulation, the City of London became an economic and style centre and his was an overtly commercial masculinity, which Edwards (1997) captures vividly:

> The yuppie was not only a product of the economic expansion of the financial sector, he was an advocate of the most striking conspicuous consumption since the Second World War, posing, parading and swaggering around the City in his pinstripe and power-look suits, ties and accessories, swinging his attaché case, talking animatedly on his mobile phone, endlessly flicking the pages of his Filofax, slicking his hair and using every excuse to get into and out of his suit, his tie, his striped shirt and, of course, his Porsche.
>
> (Edwards 1997: vii)

If he worked in the City, the yuppie lived (at least during the week) in the redeveloped fantasia of the London Docklands (P. Hall 1998) and patronized the chic new restaurants and café bars of the refurbished (some would say divested of character) Soho, newly invaded by a wave of young media and advertising executives. Mort (1996: 163) recreates *The Great Gatsby* ambience of this controversial 'regeneration' when referring to the transformation of the old Welsh Nonconformist chapel in Shaftesbury Avenue into an up-market nightclub where yuppies could show off their new-found wealth:

> Decorated with murals and with a strong emphasis on art and architecture, the Limelight enshrined its own caste-like hierarchy within the spatial environment. The VIP suite restricted access to celebrities or to those able to buy into celebrity status. From an elevated gallery the elite could either look out across London, or gaze down from a position of superiority on the dance floor below.
>
> (Mort 1996: 162)

London's Soho became the location for two distinct constituencies of 1980s 'imaged masculinity', namely yuppies and gays. In this 'heterotopic world' young men engaged in what Mort (1996) terms as 'experiments in masculinity':

> For the most part these were organised along an axis separating heterosexual from homosexual behaviours. However, at moments more hybrid forms of identity were generated, as ways of being and acting mutated from one group to another.
>
> (Mort 1996: 182)

Outside London 'yuppiedom' was comparatively thin on the ground. Yuppies, however, had their poor relations, what Edwards (1997) terms their 'underclass counterparts', who wore a uniform of trainers and down-market labels and counterfeits. Edwards (1997) recalls two dominant lifestyle images of 1980s yuppie masculinity, resonant with virility, sexual prowess and masculine sensuality:

- *The corporate power look*: the image of the aspirational yuppie in his wide-shouldered, double-breasted suit, striped shirt, braces, personal phone and BMW, shot against a background of a Docklands studio apartment.
- *The outdoor casual look*: the image of a muscular torso, stripping off his white T-shirt, or in an English gentleman's weekend clothes shot against his rural retreat far from the cares of city life.

Similarly, Nixon (1996) identifies two variants of the above, 'Edwardian Englishness' and 'Italianicity':

- *Edwardian Englishness*: this was an image of masculinity associated with the urbane, aristocratic Englishness of Empire, of class, colonial domination, prestige and power. This nostalgia for a colonial past and an Englishness tied to the Edwardian era was particularly strong in the 1980s, with a string of nostalgic films like *A Passage to India* (1985), *Room with a View* (1986) and *Maurice* (1987) and a number of television series, notably *Brideshead Revisited* (1981) and *Jewel in the Crown* (1982).

- *Italianicity*: this encapsulated the swaggering bravado of macho Italian masculinity, celebrated in numerous gangster movies and fashion photographs.

'Goodbye' to the 'old industrial man'

Millions of men in the advanced economies lost their jobs and economic authority in the succession of recessions throughout the 1980s and early 1990s. The message was clear: loyalty, faithfulness, dedication to employers no longer counted for anything when it came to the operation of raw capital. The turning point in Britain was the 1980s Thatcherite deregulation of the economy, her adoption of market-led policies and a refusal to provide state hand-outs to halt the all-too-evident decline of heavy industry. These policies reached their apotheosis in Chancellor of the Exchequer Nigel Lawson's 1988 budget in which he slashed the top rates of income tax and reduced the basic rate. This fuelled consumption and led to the mushrooming of out-of-town shopping malls, retail parks and the promotion of shopping as a primary 'leisure-pleasure' activity. The new man-as-narcissist rode on the back of this postindustrialism and burgeoning 'image industries' like advertising, media, promotion and public relations. As Mort (1996: 113) puts it, he was the logical outcome of the 'commercial narrative of gender', established through 'the sexual politics of advertising'. For the ordinary working man in areas of heavy industry (like the North East of England and South Wales) the pact between employer and employee based on mutual loyalty to a company was finally broken in the increasingly global marketplace. The traditional male career was attacked at all levels, but at least down-layered executives enjoyed high redundancy packages. The shift from manufacturing to servicing, and from industrialization to electronic technology, was immensely damaging for working class men. The old industrial labourers, along with skilled and semi-skilled workers, were rendered obsolete by the technological advances they had helped to implement. Jobs that depended upon physical strength vanished in their millions and in their place came, at best, short-term contracts and part-time work.

Why was the loss of often inhuman, exploitative jobs (like coal mining) so mourned? First, these were not just jobs, but benchmarks of working class masculinity. Economic and social changes destroyed these patterns of employment and, in the process, 'status, self esteem and the old moral authority which men used to have just by being men' (Coward 1999: 86). Second, this was not just a temporary 'laying-off' as in past industrial disputes: it was, rather, the end of the United Kingdom as a major venue for heavy manufacturing (like, for example, shipbuilding). Contracting out, downsizing and de-layering meant the end to stable patterns of working class employment (Coward 1999: 48). By the mid-1980s a rise in suicide figures and increasing male homelessness was evident. As Coward says of these men:

> Feminism had given the women the confidence to move into masculine areas, combining work and motherhood, seeing new opportunities in new work patterns. Men, by contrast, were experiencing their work changes, this so-called feminization of labour, more like a smack in the eye.
>
> (Coward 1999: 51)

What was going on in fashionable Soho was a million miles away from the lives and experiences of such economically and socially marginalized men. While shifting masculine scripts have impacted on all men, they did so unevenly. Increasingly style marked off young men from old, rich from poor, powerful from powerless, gay from straight. What emerged was a hierarchy of masculinities based on appearance and which abolished more traditional masculine divisions based upon work roles, ownership and sexual orientation. It became clear that men do not participate equally in the consumer society. Indeed, since the 1980s:

> wealthy, good-looking and well-located young men [have been] increasingly socially valorised over older, uglier or poorer men . . . those with the looks, the income and the time on their side have never had it so good in terms of the opportunities which the expansion of men's style and fashion have to offer them . . . But those without the luck, the looks or the time have never had it so bad and are consigned to looking and longing, or even exclusion and castigation for not playing the game. In this sense fashion is fascism: conform in the mirror of judgements, or else take the consequences.
>
> (Edwards 1997: 133–4)

Welcome to the 1990s: 'the lads are back in town'

We have seen how in the 1980s the male body was treated as an 'objectified commodity' (Healey 1994), much as the female body had long been. Appearance and possessions became vehicles to give off meanings. It was the growth point for a renewed consumerism and the niche-marketing of a sensuous imagery of young, affluent masculinity. The new, glossy men's style magazines were the principal vehicles for this commercial project based on male narcissism. As we shall now see, the 1990s marked something of a reversal, with an attack on the self-conscious gentility of the 1980s mags and the projection of a far harder and distinctly 'laddish' masculinity (Alexander 1997). What they had in common were that they were both overtly commercial ventures, carefully calculated to open up new markets and generate profits. Men's magazines in the 1990s toned down the masculine sensuality of the 1980s, although *Attitude* has tried to retain something of the sexual ambivalence opened up in the 1980s. Both *Arena* and *GQ* cast the 1980s aside by reintroducing a strong heterosexual script and stylish, soft-porn shots of women. But the great 1990s men's magazine success was undoubtedly *Loaded*, a publishing phenomenon, conjured up by James Brown and Tim Southwell in 1993 as an antidote to what they regarded as the effete style based men's mags.

In Southwell's (1998) lively and entertaining account of the *Loaded* story he talks of its genesis. In Barcelona with Brown for a European Cup match, Southwell writes:

> We'd just emerged from a fancy nightclub full of very attractive and very accommodating Spanish nurses. We were delirious with the joys of life. We were also very drunk. Rambling down the Ramblas, I began a high octane recounting of the night's amazing events . . . Suddenly James comes over all unusual, grabs me by the arm and fixes me in the eye with a strange, cold stare. 'Wait a minute,' he says, 'What you just said. There should be a magazine like this, moments like this . . . it should be all about the best moments you ever had'.
>
> (Southwell 1998: 2)

As the dust cover of Southwell's book puts it, *Loaded* celebrated the fact that 'the boys from the bike sheds were running riot all over the school'. It was, claims Southwell (1998: 255–6), about capturing 'the best time of our lives for readers.' He denies it had any political or social agenda, resented the way in which charges of 'laddism' were levelled against them and is still angry that what started out as 'blokes being honest' became confused with yobbish behaviour and football violence. He continues:

> There was no specific concept like 'let's abolish the "new man" and replace him with the "new lad" . . . ' [the magazine] existed to celebrate what it was like to be a bloke in Britain from 1993 onwards . . . I've never ever met a 'new lad' and the reason is quite simple: they don't exist.
>
> (Southwell 1998: 107)

However, it is left to Ross (1999) to attempt to explain *Loaded*'s popularity. He asserts that by the 1990s the high-living that had been at the heart of the lifestyle of the elite and celebrities from the 1960s onwards was now available, albeit in a less lavish form, to everyone, whatever their means, on the streets throughout Britain and the magazine captured this:

> men's lifestyles were [now] more concerned about good times than the stiff, fake 'new man' crap that the other titles had been peddling in the Eighties . . . Britain was learning how to party . . . *Loaded* was the men's mag that walked it like it talked it. It spoke the language of the bars and clubs of the UK.
>
> (Ross 1999: 41, 44–5)

As the 1980s moved into the 1990s, booming London continued to dress up, while depressed Liverpool and Manchester dressed down. He continues:

> everyone was on a blag, selling a lot of knock-off here, a bit of drugs there, robbing this and fiddling that. There was a huge black market economy going on . . . [this was] a million miles away from the cosy world inhabited by Thatcher and her Tory cronies.
>
> (Ross 1999: 31, 33)

Loaded left the needs of narcissistic new man to its competitors, turned its back on metropolitan chic and returned to basics:

> Lads into football, beer, rock and talking about birds were hardly marking a new demograph . . . It was just that it had been ignored by the mass market mags for years.
>
> (Ross 1999: 23)

Moreover, as Calcutt (2000: 271) observes, *Loaded* was 'the ideal format for boys who did not know how to grow up and so acted out a pantomime version of traditional masculinity'.

Ross (1999) places *Loaded* at the very forefront of young men's culture in the 1990s, claiming nothing less than that the *Loaded* effect has been one of the key cultural influences of the decade. Sales figures certainly appear to substantiate this assertion. In summer 1997, for example, the main 'lad mags' had between them a combined readership of some 1.5 million, as follows: *FHM* (504,959), *Loaded* (450,000), *Maxim* (185,000), *GQ* (148,574), *Esquire* (92,907) and *Arena* (77,107). *Loaded*'s popularity and sales figures climbed steadily at first from an average of 60,000 a month and then rocketed, making magazine publishing history in the process. In October 1996, it was selling 300,000 monthly; in summer 1997, it was 450,000; by January 1998, this was up to an astonishing 500,000; and the fiftieth anniversary number in May 1998, topped 600,000, with *FHM* as its nearest competitor some way behind. By the summer of 1994 *Loaded* was synonymous with irreverence and laddishness was in the air as a backlash against 1980s over-dressed, narcissistic new man. But this was not solely attributable to *Loaded*. Lads' programmes dominated television ratings, most notably *Men Behaving Badly*, with its two male lead roles played by Neil Morrissey and Martin Clunes, and *Fantasy Football League*. Then there was 'Brit Pop' (in particular, Oasis, Pulp and Blur), Chris Evans, Gazza, David Baddiel and Nick Hornby's (1992) eulogy to football obsession, *Fever Pitch*.

The 'new lad': his ancestors, friends and enemies

The new lad was a throwback to a time when men had been able to behave badly and not worry about censure. Laddism was a reaction both to the 1980s men's style press and a reaction to the growing assertiveness of women. His distant ancestor was the George Best and Stan Bowles working-class-hell-raisers-made-good of the 1960s and 1970s, while his more immediate relative was the 1980s 'lager lout', the yuppie's lower class alter-ego who, as Hunt (1998) notes, quickly moved from a folk devil into a consumer category. Another immediate ancestor from the 1980s was the 'toyboy', a sexualized young man happy to be the sexual plaything of older women. Of him Mort (1996) writes:

> By Christmas, 1986, it had all got too much for the tabloids. Lumping [these] disparate male markets together, they came up with the 'toyboy'. Pics and tales of young, stylish lads snapped in their boxer shorts, the supposed playthings of older women . . . After all, if forty eight year old 'rock granny' Tina Turner could 'boogie the night away' with her 'German hunk', so could any ordinary woman.
>
> (Mort 1996: 205)

The new lad had his origins in pop music and football and, as Edwards (1997: 83) comments, the link is hardly surprising 'as football has historically always been a bastion of blow-drying, smut-swaggering, sharp-looking English laddism.' The link between football and laddism was further strengthened in 'football fiction' by, for example, Nick Hornby and John King. While the former is football for family consumption, the latter's version is about machismo, violence and hooliganism. But although the new lad may be objectionable, selfish, loutish, inconsiderate, building his life around drinking, football and sex, he was just as concerned with consumerism and labels as his new man elder brother:

If the 'new man' sold muscles and scent, Armani and Calvin Klein, the 'new lad' sells t-shirts and trainers, Hugo by Hugo Boss and Prada . . . the style may have altered, yet the drive to consume remains the same . . . 'new lads' are just as much a phoney marketing phenomenon as 'new men'.

(Edwards 1997: 83, 249)

The success of *Loaded* was about selling magazines through the exploitation of working class machismo. In fact, the whole 'lad phenomenon' was a profit-driven, middle class version of the archetypal working class 'jack-the-lad'. Calcutt (2000) also points out that 'the lad' was not on his own. By his side was the 'ladette', girls behaving just like lads and, like Zoe Ball, 'willing to play ball with the New Lad culture if it will advance their celebrity' (Calcutt 2000: 263). There was also a 'yobocracy' of celebrity lads made up of such 1990s luminaries as Paul Gascoigne, Danny Baker and Chris Evans. Laddism was not just a reaction to constraints placed upon male behaviour by feminism but, certainly in the hands of *Loaded*, a counterblast to the stifling metropolitan chic of the 1980s men's style press. Many saw the attraction of laddism and *Loaded* (and the two have become synonymous) lying in the fact that young men were suddenly sanctioned to display the errant side of masculinity, a return to unreconstructed basics like flesh, fun and unselfconsciousness. As Southwell (1998) puts it:

Loaded had clocked on to the fact that there was another kind of Britain other than the Beefeater, f***ing around in Florence, that kind of high-brow Britain. *Loaded* clocked on to what we all knew anyway: there was another England, but no one had ever championed it.

(Southwell 1998: 61)

Loaded writers famously engaged in 'capers' by going out into the provinces or travelling world-wide in order to find out what was happening on the streets and in the clubs:

It was about having a laugh . . . about self-deprecation . . . what *Loaded* was really saying was that all those things that people like doing, things like getting drunk, they were all right. *Loaded* was all about being honest . . . we weren't trying to sell a lifestyle, we were having a laugh . . . If we did anything it was to make berkish behaviour acceptable. It was a big celebration . . . We were constantly receiving letters of thanks from people who'd followed the *Loaded* path after reading articles about travelling to the world's greatest festivals and cultural happenings.

(Southwell 1998: 73–4, 98, 175)

Laddism was a celebration of the irresponsible, of unreconstructed young-men-running-wild reduced to their crude basics and promoted in *Loaded* through jockstrap humour and 'bikini-style' photography. As Benwell (2000) shows, irony is at the heart of the 'new lad' discourse, an 'unrelenting omnipresence of a certain knowingness, self-referentiality and humour'.

Inevitably, the whole lad culture in general and *Loaded* in particular was charged with gross sexism, a charge hotly rebutted by Southwell (1998):

> We like football, but that doesn't mean we're hooligans. We like drinking, but it doesn't mean that as soon as the pub shuts we turn into wife-beating misogynists. We like looking at pictures of fancy ladies sometimes, but that doesn't mean we want to rape them . . . Men like looking at pictures of attractive women. Big Deal. Get over it . . . It's a class thing. *Loaded* portrayed women in a very mainstream way and had no shame about the fact that this basic element would appeal to our readers, most of whom would be men and most of them would, if they were anything like us, appreciate the inclusion of such pictures.
> (Southwell 1998: 101, 212)

Critics were numerous, as Southwell recalls:

> clubby-pubby, all lads together hedonism and a healthy disrespect for pretension and anything Soho . . . [a magazine] not for men-in-arms, but for men who are reverting to type and getting drunk on the profits.
> (Helen Birch, *The Independent*, quoted in Southwell 1998: 99)

> There's a feeling with lads that girls are fun; sex is great; and everyone is having a good time . . . sod the politically correct.
> (Rosie Boycott, *Daily Express*, quoted in Southwell 1998: 105)

> In 'ladworld', feminism and homosexuality barely exist.
> (Suzanne Moore, *Guardian*, quoted in Southwell 1998: 206)

> The choice facing men today is between simpering cissy and unreconstructed lout.
> (Tony Parsons, quoted in Southwell 1998: 209)

> [*Loaded* is] a regression to an infantile state of 'behaving badly' by fetishising the behaviour and culture of their adolescence.
> (Michael Bracewell, *Guardian*, quoted in Southwell 1998: 209)

As the 1990s drew to a close the criticisms levelled at 'laddism' increased in intensity. For example, David Baddiel (1999), himself a leading 'telly lad', attacked the culture he had in no small part helped create, dismissing *Loaded* as 'unreadably passé'. Others, for example Margolis (1995), objected to the way in which television has allowed itself to be engulfed by the vulgar and attacks the Tony and Gary figures in *Men Behaving Badly* as irresponsible, stupid, slovenly and disgusting. Indeed, all the 'celebrity lads' (Paul Merton, Frank Skinner, David Baddiel and Chris Evans, among others) have allowed themselves to be trapped inside laddist personas to such an extent that they have become depressing, even tragic figures. Yet others attacked the banality of the mags that both feed and feed off laddism. Early in 2001 the announcement that an all-party committee of Members of Parliament was to examine the rising rate of young male suicides in Britain led to the claim that the 'culture of laddism' was largely to blame because it fed young men a diet of excitement that they could not possibly replicate in their own mundane lives (BBC1, *Breakfast*, 7 March 2001). Surprisingly, one of the co-founders of *Loaded*, James Brown, appears to concur with many of his critics:

> *Loaded* was like being on tour with the Rolling Stones . . . We were young and . . . irresponsible and we were having the time of our lives. And when you're having that you don't think of the moral implications.
> (Jenkins 2000: 25)

However, if for most laddism is just another clever way of making money out of young male consumers by resurrecting the appeal of the working class jack-the-lad, hell bent on having a good time, others still regard it as a genuine rebellion, a reassertion of something 'fundamentally masculine'. But no one can deny its continuing influence, especially since it has been successfully exported to the United States. In August 2000, the American edition of *Maxim* broke the 2 million circulation level, making it the most successful ever magazine launch in the United States. Given their subject matter, it was appropriate that Goodwin and Rushe (1999) adopted a distinctly laddish tone to record the launch of the *For Him Magazine* in the United States:

> The troops are being assembled, the invasion plans are well advanced and the general is in place . . . to launch if not a full-frontal assault at least a semi-naked one, to liberate the sensibilities of the all-American male . . . For Uncle Sam, the count down to the acceptable face of totty-time has begun . . . a guy's a guy, wherever he lives . . . A testosterone-charged British sperm is swimming across the Atlantic . . . If the American 'new man' was ever house-trained by feminism to be considerate, sensitive and interested in women's minds rather than their bodies, he is about to be led wildly astray.
> (Goodwin and Rushe 1999: 32)

Who is (or was) the 'new man'?

The 'new man-as-nurturer' was a response to feminism, to male conscious-ness-raising and the activities of men's groups and the influence of both male and female intellectuals. Widely criticized as being middle class, elitist, 'western-centric' and remote from the lived experience of ordinary men, the stereotypical image of the anti-sexist, caring, sharing man nevertheless gained credibility and strength throughout the 1980s. But how deep or widespread was the change he initiated? Was it a media-driven illusion of change or genuine change in the consciousness and behaviour of men? Simi-larly, if some saw 'new man-as-narcissist' as an upholder of individualism and a bright new future for a more diverse masculinity, others dismissed him as little more than a gullible clothes horse. Indeed, there are sharply diver-gent views concerning the degree of actuality of the new man. Many, for example, would agree with York and Jennings' (1995) opinion that he was nothing less than the advertising industry's dramatization of its own self-image and driven primarily by commercial greed. Meanwhile, Polly Toynbee (quoted in Mort 1988: 17) is of the opinion that the new man is 'not here and does not seem likely that we shall see him in our lifetime'. Nixon (1996: 197) tends to concur, describing him as nothing less than a 'regime of rep-resentation'. There follows, in chronological order, three views of the new man, namely an early evaluation by Chapman (1988) and more recent ones by Mort (1996) and Edwards (1997).

Rowena Chapman on 'The Great Pretender'

Chapman (1988: 226) argues that the new man was a direct descendant of *Playboy* narcissism and hedonism and was 'a potent symbol for men and women searching for new images and visions of masculinity in the wake of feminism and the men's movement'. He was prepared to recognize the fem-inine within himself at a time when feminism had unhitched gender from biology and masculinity and femininity had become spaces available to both sexes and so it was in new man's interests to co-opt femininity in order to maintain male hegemony. Chapman writes:

> Looking and listening to the 'new man' we can see at once how partial the changes are. It is too easy to get utopian here. For in the images, as on the ground, many of the traditional codes of masculinity are still in place . . . The 'new man' is many things – a humanist ideal, a triumph of style over content, a legitimation of consumption, a ruse to persuade those that called for change that it has already occurred . . . while the

'new man' may well have provided some useful role models for those redefining their masculinity . . . [he] is an ideal that even the most liberated men would never lay claim to.

(Chapman 1988: 222, 226, 228, 247)

The new man epitomized the change in advertising from product to lifestyle and, if he continues to exist, then he does so only in stereotypical form. Narcissism quickly overtook him and he has now lost credibility and is regarded as little more than 'a gleam in an ad. man's eye' (Chapman 1988: 228). Always an uneasy mixture of both the nurturer and the narcissist, the 'sensitive man' (the product of feminism and 1970s humanist psychology) she sees as having been killed off by 'commercial man' so that by the mid-1980s 'the nurturant tadpole had become the narcissistic toad' (Chapman 1988: 232). She argues that patriarchy mutates, incorporating critiques of itself, and that embracing the feminine is little more than a strategy employed by men to retain control of women:

> the 'new man' represents not so much a rebellion, but an adaptation to masculinity. Men change, but only in order to hold onto power, not to relinquish it . . . the emergence of the 'new man' has been to reinforce the existing power structure by producing a hybrid masculinity which is better able and more suited to retain control . . . the 'new man' ideal is manipulated to become a reactionary figure, co-opted into the service of patriarchy . . . he is a patriarchal mutation, a redefinition of masculinity in men's favour, a reinforcement of the gender order, representing an expansion of the concept of legitimate masculinity and thus an extension of its power over women and deviant men. New masculinity, like the old, relies upon a fissure in gender and an unequal positioning of values.
>
> (Chapman 1988: 235, 247)

Even men dressing up as women (as in the case of a showbiz personality like Lily Savage) is held to be part of this masculinist strategy and nothing less than a 'new and insidious kind of masculinity . . . [that] allows men to hijack femininity, to have it when they want it and dispense with it when they don't' (Chapman 1988: 241).

Frank Mort on Cultures of Consumption

Mort (1996: 15) argues that the new man was a 'hybrid character, his aetiology could not be attributed to one single source. He was rather the condensation of multiple concerns which were temporarily run together'. Mort concludes that 1980s new man was composed of 'hybrid scripts', many antagonistic to each other (a 'contested pluralism') and reflecting differences in purchasing power, age, status, geographical location, ethnicity and sexuality. Mort asks whether the new man was anything more than a set of marketplace images, 'a symbolic form of representation crystallised in texts . . . associated with promotional culture?' (Mort 1996: 183). Mort's response is that in the 1980s sexual politics played a far less important role in the birth of the style-ridden new man than the 'dynamics of the marketplace . . . in shaping young men's wants and needs' (Mort 1996: 18).

However, it would be a mistake to write off new man as just a set of alluring images dreamed up by advertising executives in order to line their own pockets and those of their designer, tailor and publisher friends. He may not have changed the lives of the majority of men, but he was 'certainly not a chimera' (Mort 1996: 17) given that high street fashion reflects changes in our society and does not entirely instigate them.

> I am not arguing that the 1980s 'new man' is totally new. But nor am I saying that nothing has changed . . . For we are not just talking images here: images are underscored by the economics and cultures of consumption . . . [what] the 1980s [witnessed was] an intensification of that process and proliferation of individualities – of the number of 'you's' on offer.
>
> (Mort 1996: 207, 209)

Tim Edwards on Men in the Mirror

Edwards (1997), too, discusses whether the commodification of masculinity was a genuine development in the nature of masculinity and an advance in sexual politics, or just a crude marketing device? Masculinity has became something which is now marketed and is a 'design-driven affair', but how far is this proof of a genuine transformation in masculinity? Had the take-up of new man imagery resulted in changes in men's relations with other men and with women? Was it anything more than fun for a high-earning, young, metropolitan coterie of style-conscious yuppies? Was the new man primarily the stuff of visual imagery and imaginings, influential but lacking in substance? While there might have been some disruption to traditional masculinity, it is doubtful if there had been any lasting impact upon most men. Rather,

> the reconstruction of masculinity invoked in the concepts, representations and practices of consumerism in the 1980s demonstrate very few signs of post-feminist consciousness and many more indications of intensely sexualised and phallocentric muscularity.
>
> (Edwards 1997: 51)

He concludes that the new man was nothing less than a 'crystallisation of consequences – economic, marketing, political ideology, demography and, most widely, consumer society in the 1980s' (Edwards 1997: 39–40). Indeed, few would disagree that 'commercial signposts have come to occupy a prominent place in young men's narratives about themselves and their place in the world' (Mort 1996: 205). For Edwards (1997: 22), too, the suit has retained its importance 'not as much an end to the processes set up in the 1980s as much as a melting down . . . a masculinity secure in its own constant, narcissistic re-invention'. Moreover, 'iron-pumping narcissism [is] positively socially approved' (Edwards 1997: ix), while images of successful, sexy young men appear as frequently as their female counterparts in ads, mags and tabloids, not to mention film, video and television. Narcissism and the fetishization of male fashion and the male body is still big business and the recurrent male image in the 1990s is of well dressed, muscular masculinity. We are, according to Edwards (1997) increasingly asked

> not to see masculinity, rather to image-ine masculinity [for] . . . as executives consider their looks for corporate success and young men aim to gain muscles, masculinity is no longer simply an essence or an issue of what you do, it's how you look.
>
> (Edwards 1997: 54, 55)

In his more recent work Edwards (2000) distinguishes between what he identifies as three contemporary versions of masculinity in Britain, the 'old man', 'new man' and the 'new lad'. These ideal types can be characterized as follows:

- The 'old man' is relatively uninterested in fashion, is married and holding down a regular job, and remains somewhat sexist and homophobic in outlook.
- The 'new man' is narcissistic, progressive and ambivalent in his sexuality, yuppie-influenced and generally anti-sexist. When he first emerged he was viewed variously as the same old wolf, but in designer clothing, a revolutionary in his relations with women and his willingness to display the emotional side of his nature, and a marketing opportunity for new visual codes.
- The 'new lad' is defensive about fashion, ambivalent in his attitude towards women (he has pornographic notions of them rather than relationships with them) and he believes life should be one huge alcohol and drug-induced party.

All three are media-created, media-driven constructions and, certainly in the case of the latter two, the primary purpose is to make money. Indeed, laddism (with its direct appeal to old-style aggressive masculinity and the soft porn portrayal of women) was promoted in the media in a way that the 'new man' never was. Some see laddism as a regression in sexual politics in its display of sexist humour, loudness and violence, but his success lies in his opening up a new marketing space for the exploitation of young men. He remains a way of affirming masculinity without confronting or questioning it and it is mags like *Loaded* and *Later*, in which its purest expression is to be found, are for men but certainly not about them.

Conclusion: the emergence of 'new man-ism'

In Chapter 4 I distinguished between two strands upon which the notion of the new man is based. One (the nurturer) arose out of gender politics, particularly as a response to first wave feminism. The second (the narcissist) was a direct result of the commercial **image-ing** of masculinity in the 1980s. If the former was emblematic of the late 1960s and 1970s, the latter was a direct outcome of the market-led policies that have been pursued in the United States and western Europe since the 1980s era of Reagan-Thatcherite economics. Similarly, the creation of the new lad in the 1990s was a commercial project and a regression in terms of gender politics.

In March 1998, Jeremy Paxman, one of the presenters of BBC2's *Newsnight* programme, included an item in the 'new man' on the programme which revealed much about the media's fascination with categorizing and labelling of contemporary masculinity. Four men appeared, each fitting into a narrow stereotype:

- An angry 'old man', who vociferously argued that men had come off badly in the changes to the divorce laws and the activities of organizations like the Child Support Agency.
- A 'new man', Mark 1, circa the 1960s and 1970s, who talked of his efforts to tap into his inner masculinity and feelings.
- A 'new man', Mark 2, a child of the 1980s, responding to the changing roles and responsibilities of men in the consumer society.
- A 'new lad', who expressed the view that the new man did not exist in real life but was little more than a ruse by men to get women into bed.

New 'types' of men are constantly being invented by the media. In the lead-up to January 2000, 'Millennium man' was constantly mentioned, along with the 'dad lad' (that is, the 'lad' grown up and settled down). As I write this (in February 2001) I hear on the radio and read in the press of 'Colditz man', who wants to escape from 'dragon woman' and the onerous and stifling pressures of contemporary family life. As will be explored further in Chapter 6, these journalistic generalizations, while they guarantee their inventors a string of media appearances and might even put a finger on an element of truth, usually have very little evidence to substantiate them. It is also salutary to remind ourselves of the possible disjuncture between discourse and actuality. Easthope (1986) perceptively pointed out in the mid-1980s that the relationship between 'the discursive' and 'lives-as-lived' will always be ambiguous because 'men do not passively live out the masculine myths imposed by the stories and images of the dominant culture' (Easthope 1986: 167). However, he then went on to say:

> But neither can they live completely outside the myth since it pervades the culture. Its coercive power is active everywhere, not just on screens, hoardings and paper, but inside [their] heads.
>
> (Easthope 1986: 167)

While there is widespread acknowledgement that masculinity has changed considerably during the 1980s and 1990s, there is, I believe, no longer any clear consensus as to what the new man actually stands for. It is my contention that these two hereditary (in some ways antithetical) strands have been woven together in the public mind into a pot-pourri, nebulous new man-ism. The only defining feature we can point to with any degree of certainty is that he is certainly not 'old man', his father. The present-day young have all been touched by this new man-ism in one form or another. Conveyed by television, film, pop songs, radio, advertising and the press, as well as in everyday social interaction, new man-ism remains a highly pervasive and masculine 'message' (I. Harris 1995), one that bombards men in various forms from all angles.

I end this chapter by reporting a small-scale exercise (no more) that I undertook with a group of 50 students, 35 of whom were female. Without any elaboration or discussion I asked them to record what they took to be the defining features of what they understood as the 'new man'. While I am fully aware of the limited nature and shortcomings of such an exercise, it was interesting to note that the most frequently mentioned characteristics that follow straddle the 'nurturer–narcissist' strands previously explored. Even given its modest scale I believe there is some support here for my contention that a general, hybridized new man-ism is now widely shared.

Characteristics that fell under the nurturer strand were as follows:

• Is domestically competent and fully involved in domestic tasks, including child-rearing and childcare.

- Is emotionally literate, sensitive and in touch with his gentler, 'feminine side'.
- Understands, respects and relates well to women and is both caring and sharing.
- Is opposed to violence, is a good listener and relates to others in a thoughtful and democratic way.
- Is open about sexual matters and takes a liberal and supportive stance on gay and lesbian issues.
- Is into ecology, peace politics and is radical and forward-looking in his thinking.

Characteristics that fell under the narcissist strand were as follows:

- Is fit, highly body and health conscious and muscular.
- Is ultra-smart in his appearance and is into clothes, fashion and shopping.
- Is highly ambitious, careerist and driven by the need to achieve, to attain status and flaunt his material success.
- Loves expensive goods like watches, cars, and so on.
- Is interested in all gadgets and is immensely knowledgeable about all aspects of computing.
- Enjoys a good time and is a playboy and hell-raiser.
- Is adventurous, daring, brave and constantly up to all sorts of escapades.

In the next chapter I examine how masculinity was constructed and represented over the millennium period when newsprint galore was expended upon what was termed 'Millennium masculinity'.

Further reading

Calcutt, A. (2000) *Brit Cult: An A to Z of British Pop Culture*. London: Prion.

Chapman, R. and Rutherford, J. (eds) (1988) *Male Order: Unwrapping Masculinity*. London: Lawrence and Wishart.

Christian, H. (1994) *The Making of Anti-Sexist Men*. London: Routledge.

Edwards, T. (1997) *Men in the Mirror: Men's Fashions, Masculinity and Consumer Society*. London: Cassell.

Hunt, L. (1998) *British Low Culture: From Safari Suits to Sexploitation*. London: Routledge.

Mort, F. (1996) *Cultures of Consumption: Masculinities and Social Space in Late Twentieth Century Britain*. London: Routledge.

Nixon, S. (1996) *Hard Looks: Masculinity, Spectatorship and Contemporary Consumption*. London: UCL Press.

Ross, J. (1999) *The Nineties*. London: Ebury.

6

'MILLENNIUM MASCULINITY'

Clearly quite a lot of journalism is post-truth . . . More important, perhaps, is journalism's post-truth tendency . . . to make no propositions for which there is a possible 'true/false' response. This type of journalism . . . does not refer to an external world beyond the inter-textual sociosphere of contemporary symbolic culture, nor does it invoke a reality which takes precedence over its narrative renditions.

(John Hartley, *Popular Reality*, 1996)

While some journalists and critics are charging that the division between 'news' and 'entertainment' is becoming dangerously blurred, what form should a truly popular journalism take? At what point does 'serious' news reporting end and 'infotainment' begin?

(Stuart Allan, *News Culture*, 1999)

Introduction: the discursive construction of masculinity

The question underlying this chapter is, 'How was masculinity discursively constructed in contemporary British broadsheet press and popular books about masculinity over the millennium?' In addressing this I refer to data mostly gathered in 1999–2000, when there was a heightened press interest in reviewing masculinity at the onset of the new century. I identify and examine four 'discursive themes' (Foucault 1972, 1977) through which masculinity was both represented and scrutinized as we left the twentieth century and entered the twenty-first. The term 'broadsheet press' has long been associated with 'quality' journalism (for the 'thinking man/woman') as opposed to the tabloid press (in many senses a form of sensationalized adult comic). In the United Kingdom the main broadsheets are the *Daily Telegraph*, *The Times*, *The Independent* and *Guardian*, along with the *Sunday Times*, *Sunday Telegraph*, *Independent on Sunday* and the *Observer*. In addition, two further papers are referenced here, both of which straddle the tabloid–broadsheet divide, namely the *Daily Mail* and *Western Mail*. The broadsheet press is more discursive on the topic of masculinity than is the tabloid press but, of course, is read by far fewer people. However, its readership is likely to be the more influential 'opinion formers'. **Discourse analysis** looks at the linguistic features of a text, how language is selected and used to shape people as social subjects, its intertextuality and how it might be interpreted and 'read' (Heywood 1997). My emphasis here, however, is upon identifying broadsheet discourses on masculinity rather than analysing narrative and form in any detail. Suffice to say that a typical broadsheet article format is as follows:

- A news item or 'research' (very broadly defined) is discussed, focusing upon issues a journalist 'cherry picks' to highlight.
- The researchers themselves and/or 'experts' in the area are invited to comment.
- The article then ends with a 'punch line' that seeks to encapsulate the point/s being made but, in the process, frequently simplifies, even trivializes. In the process what is often little more than unsubstantiated conjecture attains, through such journalistic practices, the status of 'pseudo-certainty', even 'fact'.

Popular books on masculinity are aimed at an even wider readership, are highly 'readable', but usually claim a degree of academic respectability. I have in mind, for example, publications like *Men are from Mars, Women are from Venus* (Gray 1992) and *Why Men Don't Iron* (Moir and Moir 1998), which was accompanied by a television series on Channel 4. In 1999 two books appeared by Coward and Faludi: the former says much about men in the United Kingdom, the latter American men. They fall into the category of the well written and informed books about masculinity aimed at a wider readership than the academic. This is not to imply, however, that they should be dismissed as lightweight: far from it. Both authors have a considerable academic lineage and they were extensively reviewed in the broadsheet press. Clare's (2000) book falls into the same 'popular-serious' genre.

Four 'discursive themes' repeatedly recurred and dominated the delineation of British and American masculinity throughout the latter years of the decade and increased in 1999–2000 over the millennium period. These are as follows:

- Theme 1: the 'new man' and the 'old man'
  (a) the 'new man': health and appearance
  (b) the 'old man': nostalgia for a bygone age

- Theme 2: men running wild
  (a) men as (bad) fathers
  (b) antisocial and violent male behaviour
- Theme 3: emasculated men
  (a) disparaged and incompetent men
  (b) vulnerable men and hollow masculinity
- Theme 4: men as victims and aggressors
  (a) men-as-victims
  (b) angry men fight back

Theme 1: the 'new man' and the 'old man'

In this group of discourses the new man-as-narcissist, explored in Chapter 5, is set against nostalgia for unreconstructed 'old man' and the time-honoured masculinity he is held to have embodied.

The 'new man': health and appearance

The new man-as-narcissist was the most frequently repeated theme. Numerous examples point to new man's love affair with appearance, clothes, cars and possessions. 'Teenage boys queue up for cosmetic surgery' was the headline of a feature in the *Sunday Telegraph* on 7 January 2001 (Jarvie 2001). The Sunday broadsheet supplements are information banks of consumerism, with 'where to buy what' and 'what to wear when' the dominant themes. For example, the *Sunday Times* Supplement of 20 February 2000 was a celebration of male fashion with a detailed review of the Milan Menswear Show, along with an article on handbags for men. Male grooming as well as clothes is a recurring topic. Cook (1999), for example, comments on the booming market in men's cosmetics in the United Kingdom. By the end of 1998 the 'male market' was worth £560 million per year. Young men have become hugely 'brand aware' and men's skin care products and toiletries have contributed to the biggest growth in sales for the European cosmetics industry during the 1990s. Also, grooming for men has boomed: men spent £557 million on toiletries in one year, three times the expenditure in 1985, and sales of skin care products have greatly risen in that time. Aitkenhead (1999) regrets that men are being encouraged to be more like women and concludes that 'the finest beauty of men has been that they did not consider their greatest attribute to be their manicure'. In spite of the invocations for men to be more 'style literate', it would be a shame if appearance was to become for them as it has long been promoted for women, namely the measure of personal worth.

Cook (1999), in commenting on this, refers to Wolf's (1990) argument that in the west we live in a world in which beauty is increasingly a necessity in a way that bread and education are not. Youth and beauty are revered more than ever and both sexes feel ever more obliged to strive to conform to certain physical ideals. This is damaging, as is a society in which people believe they can purchase not only a new appearance, but a new identity. We seek 'to extend that period in which we feel young and attractive. Cosmetics are something we apply to re-create ourselves' (quote attributed to Martin Skinner, University of Warwick). More and more young men are now falling for the 'consumerist promise' that has long seduced young women and are increasingly preoccupied with looking young, fit, healthy and sporty, linking their self-esteem to their appearance. They are obsessed with the highly toned body as a symbol of sexual desirability and success. Dr Pat Hartley (of Manchester University), who notes the increase among young men of eating disorders, observes that 'we don't value the inner person to the extent of Eastern culture, which is why eating disorders are more common in the West'.

In April 2000, Mintel (the market research organization) reported that sales in men's toiletries were down by 2 per cent (from £502 million to £486 million). In commenting on this Ryle (2000) distances the newly emerging 'Millennium man' from the effete 'new man' of the 1980s:

> Sweet smelling 'new men' in touch with his feminine side are a figment of advertisers' imaginations. 'Millennium man' is happy with his nature, raw scent and rough skin.
>
> (Ryle 2000)

One of the publishing successes of recent years has been *Men's Health Magazine* (henceforth *MHM*), which was launched in 1995 and by 1998 enjoyed a circulation in the United Kingdom of a quarter of a million monthly (Gibson 1999). *MHM* speaks to overworked, overweight young to early middle aged men who wish to become more acceptable to themselves and desirable to the opposite sex ('Give yourself an MOT', the editor exhorts his readers, 'This year look like an Aston Martin not an Austin Allegro'). As Wollaston (1997) puts it, 'as readers of *MHM* move into their thirties and grow up a little, they still enjoy a bit of unbridled hedonism but don't want the beer gut that goes with it'. It thus connects with that version of the 'new man' in whom fitness and appearance are high on the list of responsibilities and, in the process, strongly echoes the nineteenth century physical culture tradition and the self-improvement ethic. With the right fitness routine and diet, *MHM* readers can attain not only a new body, but a new identity: 'cool, sophisticated and smart . . . (the "new man") cares about clothes, but he also wants a well-dressed mind' (Wollaston 1997).

For Landesmen (1997) *MHM's* discursive practices can be traced directly back not only to the health and fitness mags of the late nineteenth century and early twentieth century, but also to women's mags since the 1950s, where the headlines typically refer to success, strength, talent and health, but the subtext targets the readers' inferiority, an inferiority that can be remedied only by purchasing the magazine and the products it advertises (McCracken 1993). But *MHM* not only is about physical fitness, but also conveys useful, everyday advice for the professional man in a 'matey-pubby' style on what are perceived as 'men's matters' (for example, how to conduct an office romance, how to hold a drink, how to be successful with women and how to avoid being 'stabbed in the back' and so forth). *MHM* also provides a graphic insight into how the ideal physical image of manliness (what Hilton (1999) describes as a handsome confidence and upper arm development) is portrayed at the start of the twenty-first century, denoting health, strength, fitness and energy connotative of material success. Above all else, the *MHM* male body is celebrated as an object to be looked at with pleasure and admired. Healey (1994: 87) discusses this issue of male display and which constitutes 'a problem for straight male spectators, who are invited to approve and aspire to the masculinity he embodies'. In *MHM's* 'politics of looking' a careful course must be charted to steer clear of the homosexual and promote the desirability of heterosexuality.

Magor (1999) examines how the 'ideological scripting' of masculinity is achieved in a sample of *MHM* covers. A magazine's front cover is about the construction and presentation of genre identity and is obviously the chief selling point, indicative of how it wishes to present its take on the world and differentiate itself from its competitors. In summary, 'the cover serves to label not only the magazine, but the consumer who possesses it' (McCracken 1993: 19). Magor (1999) unwraps how 'the masculine' on *MHM's* front covers is assembled so that masculine-on-masculine looking is permitted and encouraged in a way which strictly conforms to the template of mainstream heterosexuality. This is achieved through not only body display (an almost exclusive focus upon the musculature of the upper body, especially the development of biceps and abs) but also its geographical location (typically in an outdoor setting, thus providing good reason for being semi-clothed, as well as being resonant of healthy, open air activity). Also, the linguistic texts accompanying the cover photograph are in marked contrast to the body depicted in the photographs (for example, 'be your own doctor . . . you can stay stress free . . . you can lose that half a stone and can beat your biggest rival', and so on), for this is a body not just to be admired but, importantly, attained with the minimum of exertion and discomfort.

The 'old man': nostalgia for a bygone age

A recurring broadsheet theme takes the form of a lament for the demise of the 'old man' of the recent past and in comparison to which the nebulous 'new man' is found wanting (Powell 1999). Coward (1999: 107) quotes a fairly typical onslaught on the latter from a columnist (in the *Daily Mail* in 1997): 'They're conditioning their pony tails. They're changing the nappies. They're whipping up coulis. They're going on courses in bonding and self-fulfilment.' Indeed, contemporary men are frequently presented as physically and mentally soft because they have been seduced into abandoning traditional masculine values. At its most extreme (certainly in the hands of those who wish to re-establish patriarchal hegemony) this takes the form of asserting that 'real masculinity' belongs to the past. Even in the view of some liberals there is an enduring nostalgia for hard and stoical, traditional masculinity, the antithesis of his narcissistic, fashion-driven contemporary. Here is Julie Burchill (1999) writing movingly about her late father:

> My dad took five years to die from asbestos poisoning, during which time he never uttered a word of complaint. At his death he requested that there be no flowers, no ashes, no headstone and no death notice in the local paper . . . He left no disease diaries on special discount for Christmas at Waterstones and no yellowing newspaper columns celebrating hypochondria. He left us no bad, or vaguely embarrassing memories. He left no sign that he was here at all. Nothing that is, except a giant shadow that will fall forever across all the men I have ever and will ever know, making puking, mewling moral pygmies of them all. That, then, was truly a man.
>
> (Burchill 1999)

A temporary reversion to a traditional masculinity was evident in the broadsheets in the spring of 2000 as they welcomed the emergence of a new magazine called *The Chap*. This nostalgically celebrated a kinder, gentler age when chaps puffed on briar pipes and wore leather patches on the elbows of their cardigans. Similarly, nostalgia for a lost gentlemanly 'sporting masculinity' was evident in the obituaries and articles written in February 2000, on the death of the footballer Sir Stanley Matthews. Michael Parkinson wrote of him:

> when judged not simply as a footballer but as a man who came to represent a vanished time, [then] Stanley Matthews stands alone . . . it took the death of a man who hadn't played for more than thirty years to remind us of a time when sportsmanship, courtesy, manners and good humour were not dead words . . . [his] career was a celebration of

the game when it was beautiful. His death a reminder of how ugly it has become.

(Parkinson 2000)

Others were similarly effusive about a sportsmanship that belonged to another era and contrasted him favourably with the footballing icons of more recent times like the former alcoholics George Best and Tony Adams, the laddish Gazza and the celebrity David Beckham. It was repeatedly pointed out that from the age of 17 to 50-plus Matthews was never once cautioned, even though defenders would resort to all manner of skulduggery against him on the pitch, leading Ponting (2000) to conclude that Matthews 'lit up his chosen game like no one could. His like will not be seen again'. Similar sentiments were expressed in the obituaries to the great Australian cricketer Sir Donald Bradman in February 2001.

Another strain in this nostalgia emerges from the fact that there is very little opportunity for male heroism in today's world of reduced physical labour. Even the sculptured, gym-produced body is now the product of the leisure/pleasure industry and is a parody of the labour-hewn, working class male body of the past. The heroic, over-muscled Herculean body has become just another element in the make-up of the male narcissist. Moreover, feminism has reinterpreted male heroism as an anachronistic neurosis, while militarism has been treated with the utmost suspicion since Vietnam. Yet in spite of this (or, perhaps, because of it) stories of male heroism, of bravery, endurance and old-fashioned 'guts' and determination still feature strongly in both the tabloid and broadsheet press, television and films. Indomitable, valorous masculinity (often interjected with a generous dose of British 'backbone' in the face of adversity) is still regularly celebrated. One example will serve to make the point. The *Daily Telegraph* (4 September 1999) published extensive extracts from Alice Thomson's biography of Charles Todd who, against enormous odds and crippling setbacks, constructed for Queen and country the world's longest telegraph through the centre of Australia in 1871, 'where an iron crow bar left for a few seconds in the sun became too hot to handle'. Similarly, the television programmes and popular publications by Ray Mears, the 'survival expert', rekindle the appeal of hard men combating the challenges of the great outdoors.

Theme 2: men running wild

This group of discourses expresses a fear of a rampant, untamed masculinity, of men running wild, and either behaving in an irresponsible way sexually and, thereafter, failing to take seriously their responsibilities as fathers, or literally being out of control.

Men as (bad) fathers

Too many bad dads around.
(topic of the *Kilroy* television programme, BBC1, 22 September 1999)

The relationship between fathers and sons is often highly problematical (for example, Morrison 1993). Furthermore, the oft-referred-to happy, patriarchal family of the nineteenth and twentieth centuries is now widely regarded as largely a myth, the purpose of which was to lock middle class men into paternal responsibility (Roper and Tosh 1991). At the start of the twenty-first century it appears outmoded as more liberal, democratic and companionate models of the family (with changed roles for both the father and the mother) emerge. Of course, as long as the nineteenth century patriarch provided for his family, he could regard himself a 'good father' and was, thereby, licensed to absent himself emotionally and, in the process, wreak huge damage on his family (Tosh 1991). Feminists have attacked his authority and the unearned dominance it afforded. Conversely, many men have blamed the influence of feminism for family breakdown and for women bringing up children alone. Some men's groups (for example, those featured in such publications as *Male View*) see more and more women off-loading husbands rendered 'legally defenceless' by changes to the divorce law. There has also been a loss of certainty about the father's role in the light of the feminist argument that he is effectively redundant, leading Lyndon (1993) to talk of the 'elimination' of the father. Similarly, Blenkenhorn (1995) coins the term **fatherless America** to refer to what he perceives as a nation of children growing up bereft of fathers around the home.

Murray (1990, 1994) sees increasing numbers of men with no role in their family or community and Phillips (1999) points to the negative psychological impact of absentee dads. This, of course, is the line adopted by Bly (1997) and the **new masculinists** in the United States, who lay the blame for gang culture and social disadvantage fairly and squarely on the absent father and the deterioration of paternal discipline and authority. Boys, they argue, are more susceptible to adolescent criminality without a paternal role model to emulate. In this conception of fatherhood masculinity is something to be passed on to sons through example and homosocial companionship. Because they have not experienced the attention of a father, Bly holds that many young American males are highly damaged, reduced to little other than 'perpetual adolescents'. The fecklessness of fathers who duck their

responsibilities and the Child Support Agency's attempts in the United Kingdom to locate and track them down is a recurring broadsheet item, tying in
with feminist pathologizing of the patriarch. Indeed, young fathers who
shoulder the responsibility of their actions are depicted as most unusual and
so worthy of attention (Freely 1999). The Mori Poll of June 1999 was
widely presented as an insight into how young male Britain was thinking.
On the basis of a representative sample of 400 young men, aged 16 to 25, it
was argued that 66 per cent of young British men would be reluctant to
marry if they got their girlfriend pregnant and 40 per cent (approximately
1.5 million men) would be unlikely to stay with a partner solely for the sake
of a child. While 26 per cent did not believe there was a need for two parents to bring up a child, some quarter of a million men believed that a father
had no responsibility to support a child financially. More than 1.8 million
children did not receive maintenance from their non-resident parent and the
resulting bill for the taxpayer (including child benefit) ran at £10.4 billion a
year.

The press labelled young men who did not feel obliged to stay with partners for the sake of their children as the 'not likely lads' (after *The Likely
Lads*, a popular BBC television comedy of the 1970s). Similarly, Moller and
Hemelrigk (1999) in the *Reader's Digest* castigated the 'deadbeat dads' who
avoided shouldering the responsibilities of fatherhood, arguing that:

- Children living in homes where the father is absent tend to do worse in
  terms of health, education and employment and there is an increased like-
  lihood of involvement in crime: the cycle of deprivation is thus perpetuated.
- Increase in crime attributable to the breakdown in traditional family life
  and absence of the father (see also Dennis and Erdos 1992).
- Young men under 18 are responsible for 28 per cent of all violent crime
  and 39 per cent of burglaries in the United Kingdom.
- Society has ceased to prepare young men to take responsibility for their
  own children and since 1983 the proportion of British families headed by
  a lone mother has doubled to 23 per cent.

A parallel discourse is the 'blame your father' one. The father–son relationship has long been recognized as a hugely complex and frequently problematical one. The traditional concept is of the father as a bridgehead into
manhood for the son. Faludi's (1999) argument in her monumental study of
men and masculinity (from Sylvester Stallone to ordinary men living ordinary lives) is that American men are aggrieved at being let down in the
sphere of work where their loyalty and endeavour have failed to be recognized. But behind this public hurt lies, she argues, a deeper hurt, namely that
their fathers had failed, even deserted, them. She writes that having a father

was supposed to mean 'having an older man show you how the world worked and how to find your place in it . . . He was a human bridge connecting the boy to an adult life of public engagement and responsibility' (Faludi 1999: 302). There was, she argues, something particularly disturbing about what she terms 'paternal desertion' in the years immediately after the Second World War, particularly the late 1950s and 1960s, an era of steady economic growth and material well-being:

> The sons grew up with fathers who so often seemed spectral, there and yet not there, 'heads' of households strangely disconnected from the familial body. The non-present presence of paternal ghosts haunted long after the sons had left home, made families of their own. An aching sadness remained and men spoke to me of waiting, year after year, for a sign, a late night confidence, a death-bed confession, even – desperately – a letter delivered posthumously, for any moment that would decode the mystery of their mute fathers.
>
> (Faludi 1999: 596)

She claims to have identified a disjuncture in expectations in that the world promised them by their fathers had failed to materialize. In spite of all their wartime heroics, the 1950s and 1960s fathers sacrificed their sons to an image-based, shallow, commercial world.

A complementary discourse focuses upon what is taken as the essential presence of a father and a close relationship with his children or stepchildren (as, for example, Phillips (1999) in her review of *Tomorrow's Men*, a study of young men). She argues the need for fathers ('highly involved men' or HIM) to spend 'quality time' with their sons who, thereby, will be far more likely to grow up into confident, successful adults:

> Nine out of 10 boys with 'HIM' in their life were in the top 25% of achievers in the survey, while boys at the bottom tend to have semi-detached fathers who tell them that 'boys don't cry'. The 'leading lads' were young men with plenty of what the researchers call 'can do', which allowed them to tackle life with enthusiasm with HIM as the key factor, building self-esteem and success. It is the quality of his relationship with men in his life which marks out the supremely confident.
>
> (Phillips 1999)

However, the HIM 'doesn't have to live with him, he doesn't even have to be dad, but he does have to take an interest.' Also important in building up young, 'can-do' achiever masculinity is an anti-bullying policy in all schools so that they are 'no longer places where *High Noon* (1952) provides the model of what a man's gotta do' (Phillips 1999).

A related discourse is of the celebrity dads, like David Beckham and Dennis Wise, who are eager to demonstrate their commitment to fatherhood.

Antisocial and violent male behaviour

This discourse centres on a terror of uncontrolled violence by men running wild. In its most savage manifestation it features rampaging men, totally beyond the control of civilized society, but nearly always (apart from the odd sadistic murder) located 'abroad', in the savage world 'out there', like Africa. The report of the systematic rape, torture and genocide of Tutsi women by Hutu military in Rwanda in 1994 (Hilton 1999) is one example, the excesses of the recent ethnic horrors in the former Yugoslavia another. This discourse presents inflexible traditional masculinity (where men cannot face failure or humiliation in any shape or form) as potentially pathological. To illustrate this I turn to an appalling family tragedy that occurred in South Wales in July 2000, when six members of the Mochrie family were found dead in their home. It appeared that Robert Mochrie calculatedly killed his wife and four children before killing himself. In the huge nationwide press coverage that followed the horror, the possible causes of the crime were explored. Here was a man, the psychologists approached for their views were quoted as asserting, who could not live with setbacks or blows to his authority in either his public or private life and it was this that drove him down the terrible, destructive road he eventually followed. There was, of course, no conclusive proof of this, but it neatly fitted into the **pathological masculinity** discourse, one that presented Mochrie as little more than a servant of the pathological masculinity of which he was the possessor.

The idea that men are innately violent surfaced in the British press in the autumn of 1999 in the form of a heated 'moral panic' (Goode and Ben-Yehuda 1994) over the release in the United Kingdom of the American film, *Fight Club* (1999). In spite of its 'happy ending' (the protagonist gets the girl and renounces violence) the film implies that the cure for the crisis-in-masculinity resides in re-masculinization through men fighting. Particular exception was taken to David Fincher, the director, who was quoted as saying that 'it deals with the riptide of being male in today's society . . . It's about fighting, it's about being alive, about not pretending to be somebody else'. Reactions were predominantly condemnatory. Young men fighting was grandiosely condemned as symbolic of nothing less than the 'malaise of a whole generation' (Gristwood 1999). Indeed, the fear that the film might encourage the spread of bare-knuckle fighting featured in both the tabloids and the quality press (for example, Ridley and Goodchild (1999) picked up on this with their portrait of Joe Savage, the appropriately named bare-fist boxing champion of Britain). A similar reaction was that male DNA is not to be satisfied by such tame pursuits as surfing the net or watching television. Ridley (1999), for example, argued that the film was a refreshing relief from the stultifying influence of 'pansy new men' in touch with their feminine sides and all-too-willing to express emotions. Let's be honest and admit, he trumpets, that men are biologically predisposed to aggression and that violence is fundamental to 'being a real man':

> If we tone down violence on the screen and tame the football terraces, we may find the aggressive instincts of young men displaced to the Internet or to something much more dangerous, to other people . . . I feel I have been lectured too often from the screen that men can be redeemed by touchy-feely therapy.
>
> (Ridley 1999)

In the United Kingdom, however, the fear of men running wild is regularly centred on the despised figure of 'the yob', dangerous, antisocial young men operating outside civilized society, with all the attendant fears of disorder and social disintegration. Coward (1999) contextualizes this historically in the fear of the 'residuum', the potentially 'out-of-control' who lived in the 'rookeries' (slums) of the Victorian city. She comments:

> The 1990's image of the council estate, with its gangs of alienated youths, abandoned mothers and violent homes, drug-dealing, drinking and chronic crime, is an update of an earlier version of the dark side of Britain's social landscape.
>
> (Coward 1999: 135)

Indeed, in this discourse the drugged up, anarchic yob is the ultimate upholder of macho values and the most potent contemporary symbol of moral (and national) decline (along with his female counterpart, the 'single mum', the specific target of the Tory Minister John Redwood's onslaught in the mid-1990s, when he was Secretary of State for Wales). There are two other discourses associated with this: first, that of the **underclass** (particularly associated with Murray 1990, 1994); and, second, the feminist rereading of alienated, criminal young men (as in Campbell 1993).

Charles Murray (1990, 1994) is a highly controversial figure in the United Kingdom who, nevertheless, had a major influence on the law and order policy of John Major's Conservative government (1992–7). Under Major (and his Home Secretary, Michael Howard) 'yob crime' came to be regarded as the direct result of moral breakdown, not economic failure. The **yob**, badly brought up and socialized by a cheap, morally bankrupt television and video culture into irresponsibility, was running out-of-control, spawning children and, in the process, rupturing the established family structure. He was a highly visible, easily identifiable danger to civilized society, the epitome of young, macho masculinity run wild. Murray's 'underclass' thesis remains hugely contentious and is rejected by many as grossly reductionist in that everything is boiled down to family breakdown, assumes single parents are, by definition, inadequate and demonizes all impoverished young men, without exception, as yobs. Campbell's (1993) feminist analysis, on the other hand, presents youth crime as a way of achieving the mantle of manhood, an escape route for young, unemployed men from the stifling confines of the domestic space and the marginal life of anonymous estates. Similar arguments have long been part of liberal criminology. The evil of unemployment, she argues, unleashes extreme forms of macho masculinity, a view shared by Coward (1999), when she writes:

> In less than a generation, many men have watched an entire edifice of everyday life, built on steady work and a regular wage, crumble . . . such helplessness breeds rage and aggression and the boys' rage erupts on the streets . . . It may be that the yob is carrying the weight of a masculinity which . . . middle-class society finds increasingly unacceptable and rhetorically dumps on to the men of the lower class. He is a classic scapegoat. Young men, perhaps the most vulnerable members of society, are targeted as its main problems.
>
> (Coward 1999: 145)

In contrast to this, others are of the opinion that it is entirely their own fault that these young men find themselves in these circumstances: 'What of the unemployed poor who are, nevertheless, decent, law-abiding citizens?', they ask.

Theme 3: emasculated men

The third group of discourses focuses upon the alleged utter incompetence of men, how hopeless and infantile they are, and how vulnerable and hollow is contemporary masculinity ('all show and no trousers' as one headline put it).

Disparaged and incompetent men

In the 1980s advertising images celebrating girls-on-top began to appear and men were increasingly presented as stupid and unattractive, even contemptible. The trend accelerated in the 1990s when 'male incompetence' (occasionally equated with jibes about 'male impotence' and falling sperm counts, even 'male incontinence') became a favourite topic for advertisers as they tabulated all the things men were charged with doing badly (like making a mess of household chores) or doing shoddily the practical, household things it was traditionally assumed men did well (like plumbing, electrics and decorating). The message rammed home is that men are generally lazy, slovenly and cannot be trusted. Fun was poked at 'manly' acts of physical endurance and men were shown to be not only emotionally inadequate and domestically cack-handed, but downright dim and useless at most things. Sexual humiliation at the hands of women became part of the humorous role-reversal beloved by advertisers (for example, women in an office gawk and make suggestive comments about a young man in tight jeans, or a stiletto heel is poised suggestively above a man's naked bottom). Coward (1999) concludes:

> Traditional masculinity has been rendered at best absurd and at worst something menacing – a quality which needs to be taught a lesson . . . the once desirable attribute of masculinity now seen as absurd, fair game for humour and sometimes disgust . . . Masculinity is no longer a position from which to judge others, but a puzzling condition in its own right.
>
> (Coward 1999: 91, 94)

It is asserted that men are incompetent at understanding women and, especially, female sexuality. Indeed, women have no real need for men any more as they move into arenas previously the sole province of men, best illustrated by the stories which swept through the broadsheets in the autumn of 2000 of MI6 being taken over by female intelligence officers, who were proving more competent and less of a security risk than their male counterparts. They can even play male roles on screen, as Hilary Swank does in *Boys Don't Cry* (1999).

In the 1990s, too, men themselves took to denigrating traditional masculinity: for example, Nick Hornby has dissected masculine obsessionalism in his novels *Fever Pitch* (1992) and *High Fidelity* (1995). Likewise, the male scriptwriters of the highly popular and laddish BBC television comedy *Men Behaving Badly*, although it presented the two principal male characters as comically likeable, ultimately depicted them as pathetic, ridiculous and inadequate. In doing so it linked itself to an ancestry of denigrating 'traditional' masculinity on British television stretching back to *Monty Python's Flying Circus* in the 1970s, through to comedians of more recent vintage (and well known to British audiences) like Ben Elton and Harry Enfield. A complementary discourse is that men are useless because they have failed to grow up and should be treated as such. For Burchill (1999) young men today are no more than 'adult babies'. She reserves special venom for 'bully boy rap stars' in whom

> infantilism takes a vicious turn. Whether raping the girls and making them cry, or blaming black women for the bad prospects of black men while worshipping capitalism, rap represents the ugliest aspects of all the male inability to grow up.
>
> (Burchill 1999)

Moreover, middle-aged women have now been landed with 'the tragic, thwarted, spreading body of the middle-aged man housing the spirit and soul of the surly, sulking, pre-teen brat'. Commercially driven laddism is 'a pleasure-crazed capitulation to the sensual pleasures of infantilism'. Lads are afraid of manhood and are threatened by the attention their babies get and sulk, 'hissing with sibling envy when the patter of tiny feet other than their own turns up'. She continues:

> Men have got it too soft these days . . . educated until they say 'when', with sex on tap, there simply seems no point in growing up. Add to this the appalling role models that came about with the advent of youth culture from James Dean to Liam Gallagher and what you have is a recipe for permanent Peter Panhood . . . They don't make them like they used to, that's for sure.
>
> (Burchill 1999)

Vulnerable men and hollow masculinity

Another discourse is one which equates masculinity with vulnerability and insecurity: the assertion is that men feel threatened by having to question what they previously could confidently have taken for granted. The old certainties are no longer in place and, on the face of it at least, the compensations appear minimal. Men in the west have been compelled to take a journey of personal transformation and this has, perhaps more so than in previous shifts in masculine values, not been easy (Townsend 1997). What Coward (1999) terms this 'heroism of the inner moral life' is far more than striving to become more emotionally literate and sensitive beings: it is about redefining masculine identity and the very idea of masculinity itself. For Faludi (1999) old style masculinity was rooted in the politics and community of a social system which has now been replaced by an 'ornamental culture' predicated upon electronic town squares, cyber communities and cafés and the image-obsessed, celebrity industries and their visual spectacles. Rather than facilitating greater social and political involvement, the celebrity culture has eroded it. There are now fewer meaningful jobs or jobs for life and it is harder to become a useful member of society. Formerly high employment workplaces (like mills, mines and docks) have been converted into low employment housing and heritage sites and, in the process, 'real jobs' have disappeared by the million. As Raven (1999) puts it:

> the men who worked at the shipyards and coal mines didn't learn their crafts to be masculine . . . their sense of their own manhood flowed out of their utility in a society, not the other way around. Conceiving of masculinity as something to be, turns manliness into a detachable entity, at which point it instantly becomes ornamental and about as innately 'masculine' as false eyelashes are inherently 'feminine'.
>
> (Raven 1999)

Faludi (1999) interviewed Sylvester Stallone and the little cameo that resulted illustrates her point both about the inauthenticity of the ornamental society and the inner emptiness that many men, it is argued, experience. Stallone was a skinny kid, pushed around by a sadistic father and who, when he was 13, became obsessed by weight-training after seeing Steve Reeves (a screen strongman of the 1960s and early 1970s) in the film *Hercules Unchained* (1959). But by 1996 his Rambo image had become a prison and, tired of his cinematic depiction as nothing more than a 'glob of muscle mass', he dropped out of training and turned down 'muscle moron' contracts in a desperate attempt to escape the 'blue screen' (against which his movies are filmed, the action scenes being computer generated and added later). A revealing insight occurred when she and Stallone were driving across the George Washington bridge into New York:

> 'See that?', Stallone said, pointing at the bridge's ornate ironwork, 'the incredibly detailed work that went into it. That's work. That's when men had a real craft, when they really built something. Imagine looking out and seeing this and thinking, I did that!'
>
> (quoted in Viner 1999: 15)

It is no wonder men are no longer sure who they are or should be because, Faludi continues:

> the internal qualities once said to embody manhood – surefootedness, inner strength, confidence of purpose – are merchandised back to men to enhance their manliness. The more productive aspects of manhood, such as building or cultivating or contributing to a society, could not establish a foothold on the shiny flat surface of a commercial culture, a

looking-glass before which men could only act out a crude semblance of masculinity.

(Faludi 1999: 543)

Men's self-image has been so battered that they inject themselves with synthetic testosterone (Sullivan 2000) and engage in extreme sports to compensate for a growing sense of inadequacy (Burke 2000).

Men have become increasingly vulnerable in sexual relationships with women. Out of the Michael Douglas and Glenn Close film *Fatal Attraction* (1987) came the term 'bunny boiler' to depict a woman who uses a sexual relationship as a weapon of power over a man and attempts to torment him when spurned. While welcome male attention and harassment (which is usually more about power than sex) can be differentiated, Coward (1999: 202) for one is highly suspicious of the feminist stance that women can never harass and argues that it a dubious double standard to assume that 'male sexual pushiness expresses male power while female sexual pushiness does not'. She continues:

We are being encouraged to think that it is acceptable for a girl to assert her sexuality by behaving provocatively and unacceptable for a man to respond as if that was an invitation.

(Coward 1999: 207)

Women adopt dress and poses which indicated they are ready for sex, but it does not follow they are. They dress for themselves, not for men and, as in pornography, they celebrate a power based on sexual attractiveness. There is 'a status to be had from demonstrating an available sexuality which is powerful enough to lure men but, at the same time, to resist them' (Coward 1999: 206). Men accused of rape have often interpreted (under the added complication of alcohol and drugs) female sexual display literally rather than virtually. While Coward distinguishes between women's sexual expression not as an act of invitation but of political defiance, she points out that both sexes are increasingly turning to the law to establish boundaries for them, boundaries they have failed to draw themselves concerning sexual display, response and behaviour in highly ambiguous and sexualized circumstances.

Theme 4: men as victims and aggressors

This group of discourses refers to a view that men can, with some justification, be regarded as 'victims', and men's anger and their attempts to fight back against what they see as unfair treatment (including a revival, albeit in mediated and symbolic form, of some aspects of 'old style' masculinity in laddism).

Men-as-victims

In some parts of the United States a man can be prosecuted for domestic violence even if the woman insists that she was not abused. It would appear that 'growing numbers of women who have otherwise welcomed the opportunities won by feminism are rebelling against such apparent injustices. Faludi (1999) adopts a similar stance towards **men-as-victims**. She argues that American men feel betrayed on a number of fronts (for example, as above, at having been let down both in terms of work loyalty and in their relationships with fathers). At the centre of her thesis is, however, the assertion that men have fallen victims to what she terms the 'ornamental culture' of global consumerism. In the 1980s and 1990s the 'real world' was swiftly replaced by one in which

> personal worth was judged in ornamental terms. Were they 'sexy'? Were they 'known'? Had they 'won'? Winning had been elevated to the very apex of manhood while at the same time it was disconnected from meaningful social purpose. Being first seemed to be all that mattered.
>
> (Faludi 1999: 186)

They found themselves locked into competition with women:

> Men felt trapped in Miss America's boudoir. She was now their rival, not to be won over by a show of masculine strength, care or protection, but only to be beaten in a competition where the odds did not seem to be on men's side.
>
> (Faludi 1999: 187)

Men and women, she concludes, have arrived at 'ornamental imprisonment' by different routes, women through being formerly powerless and men through a maniacal commitment to work and power-striving post-Second World War. This ornamental culture is founded on

> a competitive individualism that has been robbed of craft or utility and ruled by commercial values that revolve around who has the most, the best, the biggest, the fastest.
>
> (Faludi 1999: 187)

Glamour has long been commodified and peddled to women, although feminists have staunchly resisted the enslavement to femininity's 'merchandised façade'. Now ornamental culture has seduced and entrapped men as well. Men's magazines now outsell women's and, as many have noted, there is considerable truth in the dictum that 'being a bloke today is big business'. In the process masculinity has been commodified and incorporated into the ornamental culture.

Faludi (1999) argues that ornamental culture is equally damaging to both men and women and that they should stop fighting each other and, instead, unite to oppose a common enemy. In her view:

> the feminine power whose rise most genuinely threatens men is not the female shoulder hoisting girders at a construction site, not the female foot in the boardroom door of a corporation, not the female vote in the ballot box. The 'femininity' that has hurt men the most is an artificial femininity manufactured and marketed by commercial interests. What demeans men is a force ever more powerful in the world, one that has long demeaned women. The gaze that hounds men is the very gaze that women have been trying to escape.
>
> (Faludi 1999: 415)

Coward (1999) expresses a similar view. Young men in the United Kingdom are in thrall of a 'me-culture' based on pop music, computer and video games, consumerist desires, a high octane fashion consciousness and a week-end lifestyle based on clubbing, drugs, cars, football and more football. Furthermore:

> the moral status of masculinity, built on the foundation of hard work, a single career and the aim of providing for a family, has completely gone . . . Previously it was girls who, deprived of any pathway to achievement, dreamed of being plucked from the streets by a model agency or a rich husband. Now it is boys who dream of being spotted on the football fields or forming the ultimate boy band.
>
> (Coward 1999: 177)

Indeed, the ostentatious sporting of laddish qualities opens up the hope-against-hope possibility that one might be 'talent spotted' on the street, in the clubs, or on the football pitch, so much so that

> the most obvious and visible ways for young men to acquire power, status and money have nothing to do with model male citizens which the new moralists constantly harp back to. It is skill, strength, music, looks and style – embodied in the adulation of footballers and pop groups – that count.
>
> (Coward 1999: 177)

This idea that masculinity has become a commodity is the subject of Raven's

(1999) perceptive piece. She presents herself as a 'man-hater of the old school' and argues that:

> feminist man-hating wasn't a bar-room grudge, but a response to a political situation. It wasn't about individuals – most feminists got on fine with men even as we also denounced masculinity as an idea. These days the situation is reversed.
>
> (Raven 1999)

What does she mean? She talks of masculinity, at least as viewed through contemporary young women's eyes, as a 'gettable commodity':

> The modern man-hater hates specific men but worships the idea of masculinity . . . [and their views] . . . are founded on people not politics. Masculinity has been reduced to a 'gettable commodity' . . . [women] have got the car, the spike heels and the job, so why don't they have a right to expect the perfect men to match? . . . From the Diet Coke break girls to the thirty something fans of Mr. Darcy, women – grown women – are deserting the real in favour of a fantasy landscape in which men measure up. The fact that they don't in real life has less to do with men's real feelings than the way these are regarded by women who believe that perfection is gettable.
>
> (Raven 1999)

Angry men fight back

The tone for this is typified by the following:

> If I have one public hope for 1999, it is that this will be the year when men finally start to stand up for themselves. I would hope that individually and collectively men would begin to look at the society that they are alleged to dominate and ask themselves, Where is the evidence of such domination in a society which demonises and denigrates them at every turn?
>
> (John Waters, *Irish Times*, 12 January 1999)

One is reminded of the film *The Full Monty* (1997), in which a group of dispirited, defeated, unemployed working class men in Sheffield devise a stage act based on stripping as a way not only of earning a living, but also of regaining some self-respect as men in a world that has rendered them and their industrial skills redundant. Stripping becomes an act of defiance, a way of fighting back against injustice, of becoming (albeit for a moment) the exploiter rather than the exploited.

Whereas in the 1970s and 1980s the men's movement in North America was in sympathy with feminism, in the 1990s it has become far more masculinist, seeking to articulate men's concerns and reverse what they perceive as the continued emasculation of men. (The 700,000 'Promise Keepers' who descended on Washington DC in 1997 as part of a crusade to re-establish patriarchal 'godly masculinity' bore witness to the very strong feelings held in various quarters on this matter.) In all of this Robert Bly remains an influential figure and in his *Sibling Society* (1997) calls for the recovery of some of the old male certainties and bemoans the lack of a masculine presence in what he terms the United States' 'society of orphans'. In his view American men have been stripped of all moral authority, economically disadvantaged by the courts and are the victims of an uncaring matriarchy. In Britain, while feelings may not appear to run so high, men have still mobilized to fight what they regard as the loss of paternal power and rights, with particular reference to divorce, child custody and the much-publicized activities of the United Kingdom's Child Support Agency. They argue that repeated changes in the law have greatly favoured women and victimized men (Lyndon 1993; Thomas 1993). Faludi (1999) doubts whether men have the means to fight back because, whereas feminists framed their struggle as a battle against men, men have no clearly defined enemy who they can point to with certainty as oppressing them. Thus the male model of confrontation, appropriated so successfully by women is, ironically, now unsuitable for men.

A more recent advocate of 'men fighting back' is Newell (2000), who argues that men must now reclaim a more traditional form of masculinity, one which has (sadly in his view) fallen into disrepute. They must rediscover a new code of honour and balance action-based and contemplative virtues, given that they have been deprived of the traditional arenas in which the true 'art of manliness' were exercised. Technology has so transformed the battlefield that nobility in fighting and dying for a cause have been lost and, furthermore, statesmanship no longer demands the masculine virtues it formerly did. He sets out to provide a 'guidebook' for the reconstruction of the 'manly life', posing (and seeking an answer to) the questions, 'What is a good man and how should he live?' He documents three thousand years of the 'manly tradition' by drawing on extracts from essays, poetry and fiction from ancient Greek and Hindu texts to contemporary writers, via the likes of Shakespeare, Lord Chesterfield and Winston Churchill. For him the eighteenth century Romantic period exemplifies the classical manly virtues, namely chivalry and gentlemanliness, wisdom and statesmanship, a strong sense of familial duty and responsibility, and nobility and heroism.

Conclusion: a bleak outlook for masculinity

The four groups of discourses in this chapter provide an insight into how masculinity was being talked about in the public domain in the lead up to the millennium and into the twenty-first century. What jumps out is the overall negativity: a Martian arriving on Planet Earth and not knowing what masculinity was would quickly form the opinion that it was a highly damaged and damaging condition with very few, if any, redeeming features. In the hands of these writers it is something dangerous to be contained, attacked, denigrated or ridiculed, little else. There is none of the optimism shown by MacInnes (1998) and others that the proliferation of masculinities has opened up new opportunities for men. If masculinity has been successfully 'problematized' by academics during the 1980s and 1990s, here it is merely reduced to 'a problem' – for women, for men themselves and for society in general. If masculinity is not in crisis, then it is not for lack of trying by the broadsheet journalists! It ought also to be noted that while much broadsheet writing on masculinity is by women, it also appears to be largely for them. The fact remains that in spite of the huge amount written about masculinity, we still need to know how men perceive masculinity today; whether or how they experience masculinity-in-crisis, how they enact 'masculinities' and how they relate to other men and women. How it might be carried out is the subject of the next chapter.

Further reading

Blenkenhorn, D. (1995) *Fatherless America*. New York: Basic Books.
Bly, R. (1997) *Sibling Society*. Harmondsworth: Penguin.
Campbell, B. (1993) *Goliath: Britain's Dangerous Places*. Harmondsworth: Penguin.
Coward, R. (1999) *Sacred Cows*. London: HarperCollins.
Faludi, S. (1991) *Backlash: The Undeclared War Against Women*. New York: Crown.
Lyndon, N. (1993) *No More Sex War: The Failures of Feminism*. London: Mandarin.
Newell, W.R. (ed.) (2000) *What is a Man? Three Thousand Years of Wisdom on the Art of Manly Virtue*. London: HarperCollins.
Thomas, D. (1993) *Not Guilty: In Defence of Modern Man*. London: Weidenfeld and Nicolson.

7

RESEARCHING MASCULINITIES TODAY

> Go to the bookshelf and take down a book. Any book, don't hesitate for too
> long. Start reading. What does it tell you about men and masculinity?
>
> (Morgan, *Discovering Men*, 1992: 48)

Introduction: David Morgan's *Discovering Men*

The emphasis in this concluding chapter is very much upon researching masculinities and it proceeds as follows. First, I return to Morgan's (1992) *Discovering Men* which, as I made clear in Chapter 1, remains a seminal text
and still has much to say to potential researchers. Second, I identify six
'research modes' through which masculinity might be approached. Third, I
expand on these, presenting briefly examples of recent relevant research.
Fourth, I pay particular attention to ethnography (Mode 6) and summarize
some previous ethnographic studies of masculinity which I have undertaken.
Finally, I return again to Morgan's influential book.

  As I have said, Morgan's *Discovering Men* remains hugely thought pro-
voking on ways to study masculinity. Here I intend to focus on two areas in
particular, rereading existing texts and the enactment of masculinity in
everyday life. I'll comment briefly on each in turn.

Rereading existing texts

Recent critical studies address masculinity directly as a sociohistorical cul-
·tural concept, but older texts deal with it indirectly, even obliquely, and can
be profitably reread 'against the grain'. Morgan advocates rereading auto/
biographies, novels, sociology and literature in new, deconstructive ways: it
is not so much a question of an absence of texts about the male experience,
but a lack of familiarity by readers with reading texts in a particular way. He
advocates the rereading of such existing texts in new ways as a process of

'reading between the lines', seeking out 'themes which may not be explicitly stated, to read absences as well as presences, to decode the text or to discover hidden or suppressed meanings' (Morgan 1992: 50). He himself provides critical rereadings of two classic texts, namely Weber's *The Protestant Ethic and the Spirit of Capitalism* (1930) and Whyte's *Street Corner Society* (1955). The latter, an ethnography of an American-Italian slum community, is revealed as the study of a very macho society, containing a diversity of masculine types ('heroes', 'strivers', 'loners', 'street boys' and 'college boys', for example) and having much to say about male power and homosociability. Morgan also points to the possibilities of studying the construction and expression of masculinities through fiction, diaries, letters and historical studies, with autobiographies and biographies being especially fruitful sources.

The enactment of masculinity

Morgan advocates researching masculinities in a range of real-life settings, from schools and prisons, through to military establishments, in business, sport, unemployment and retirement, as well as in face-to-face interaction and conversational behaviour. 'Masculinity' thus becomes an analytical concept to gain purchase on a range of actual settings. He comments:

> do not consider masculinity as a characteristic that one brings uniformly to each and every encounter . . . [rather] gender and masculinity may be understood as part of a presentation of self, something which is negotiated, implicitly or explicitly over a whole range of situations . . . in short, we should think of 'doing masculinities' rather than of 'being masculine'.
>
> (Morgan 1992: 47)

Six research modes

How masculinity is constructed and enacted in a range of settings is already firmly on the research agenda (for example, Berger *et al.* 1995), but there is still a paucity of field-based work charting the 'experiencing' and 'living' of masculinity. The need now is to research and theorize men and masculinities in new and innovative ways and document how the subjective experience of masculinity is affected by age, class and cultural location, ethnicity, sexuality and geography, along with the reproduction of certain forms and practices of masculinity. Nixon (1996) makes a similar point when he calls for researchers to address a 'plurality of masculinities' and research men in different arenas of their lives (as fathers, lovers, workers and so on). How contemporary men are responding to rapid change and adapting to new circumstances needs to be recorded but, as Rutherford (2000: 35) aptly warns, 'contemporary methodologies of masculinity limit understanding of the changes taking place in **male subjectivities**'.

Bearing in mind these points (including Morgan's wise advice) and in an attempt to open up the research options available when studying masculinities I now detail the six 'research modes' (see Figure 7.1). In employing them a number of theoretical perspectives will clearly be brought to bear, from discourse and **narrative analysis** to semiotics, **symbolic interactionism, dramaturgy** and content analysis. Given the 'culturalist' bias of this book some readers may see this research map as limited (given that more quantitative approaches such as statistics, surveys, schedules, questionnaires, even tests and experiments) have not been explored.

- *Mode 1: the literary.* How is masculinity depicted in literature?
- *Mode 2: printed media.* How is masculinity represented in newspapers and magazines?
- *Mode 3: broadcast media.* How is masculinity represented in film and on television?

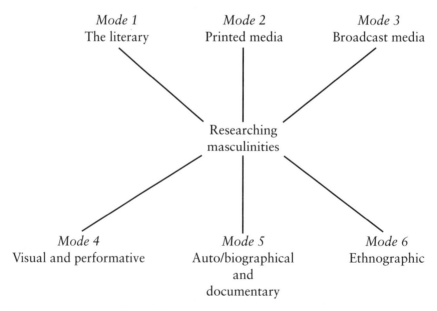

Figure 7.1 Research modes

- *Mode 4: visual and performative.* How is masculinity depicted in advertising, photography, painting and sculpture and performed in 'spectacles' like, for example, sport, dance and even military parades?
- *Mode 5: auto/biographical and documentary.* How do men experience masculinity in their lives? How has masculinity been experienced in the past?
- *Mode 6: ethnographic.* How is masculinity constructed and brought off in particular settings?

The data sources associated with each of these research modes are summarized in Figure 7.2.

I now detail the six research modes.

Mode 1: the literary

Throughout this book, but especially in Chapter 2, literature has been drawn upon as a valuable resource, providing insights into masculinity in different sociohistorical periods. Two recent books are excellent examples of this, namely Knights (1999), on masculinity as depicted in twentieth century British fiction, and Schoene-Harwood's (2000) study of **ecriture masculine** from Frankenstein to the new man (via, for example, the 'angry young man' of the 1950s). Another example would be Shakespeare's *Antony and Cleopatra* re-viewed through the glass of masculinity (Mangan 1997). For Caesar, true manliness is based upon martial skills and in expressing disgust at Antony's 'womanly' nature he articulates the Roman male's fear of female lasciviousness and inconstancy. In exposing himself to Cleopatra's 'effeminizing influence', Antony lays himself open to Camidius' jibe that 'our leader's led, And we are women's men' (Act 3 scene 7). Mangan also approaches *Macbeth* as being about what it is 'to be a man': Lady Macbeth offers one definition, one based on daring and having the nerve to kill. Meanwhile, contemporary novelists (like Kazuo Ishiguro, Graham Swift, Ian McEwan, Julian Barnes, Iain Banks, Irvin Welsh, Helen Fielding, Pat Barker, Alan Hollinghurst and Martin Amis) depict a wide range of 'literary masculinities' and, in so doing, often subvert previously taken for granted male qualities and the notion of a 'fixed' masculinity. For example, Graham Swift's *Last Orders* (1996) reveals the damage done to men through the internalization of dominant ideas about masculinity and its attendant codes of behaviour (such as heavy drinking, swearing, fighting, emotional repression and a reluctance to communicate). Ishiguro's *Remains of the Day* (1989) examines the intersection of notions of service, duty, nationalism and class and his portrayal of a repressed, stunted masculinity in the tragic figure of Stevens.

Mode	Data sources
Mode 1: the literary	Novels, poetry, plays, historical studies, travel and sports' writing
Mode 2: printed media	Tabloid and broadsheet press, magazines and comics
Mode 3: broadcast media	Film, television, videos, the internet and radio
Mode 4: visual and performative	Paintings, sculpture, adverts, photographs, cartoons, illustrations, sport, dance, pop music, ceremonies, rituals, spectacles, appearance, demeanour and speech
Mode 5: auto/biographical and documentary	Oral history, life history, biographies, autobiographies, diaries, journals, archival sources, audio and video tapes
Mode 6: ethnographic	Observation based field journal, interviews (formal, informal, individual, group), audio and video tapes

Figure 7.2   Research modes and data sources

Mode 2: printed media

Chapter 6 drew heavily upon the broadsheet press to examine how masculinity was presented and discussed over the millennium, given that little work has been done to date on press representations of masculinity (especially in the tabloid press). Similarly, Chapter 5 showed how the new generation of style magazines commercialized masculinity in the late 1980s. At a time when male power had been questioned, the male body was sexualized and visualized for profit as magazine publishers realised there was big money to be made from commodifying masculinity. Gregorio-Godeo (2000) casts an interesting light upon the depiction of masculinity by looking at magazines targeted at women (for example, *Marie Claire*, *Elle* and *Chic*). A number of conceptions of masculinity emerge, with the new man to the forefront, but more attention is also being paid to often disregarded forms of masculinity.

Comics are, for children and young people, an important means of exploring masculinity through narrative, character and visual effects. Mahawatte (2000), in a study of American comics since the 1960s, sees new images and models of masculinity being consciously subverted and aligned with new age philosophy. A new series of male characters have come into existence, marking a dramatic departure from normative models of masculinity. Hybridity has replaced the familiar stereotypes in comics.

Mode 3: broadcast media

The many paradoxes inherent in masculinity is a recurring theme in contemporary American and British films as their subject and in which the crisis in masculinity is a strong and recurring theme. Spielberg's *Saving Private Ryan* (1998), although set at the time of D-Day in June 1944, and depicting a duty-bound, nation-serving masculinity, raises a number of questions about contemporary masculinity. Other 1990s films like *Fight Club* (1999) and *American Beauty* (1999) offer a very different version of masculinity from the muscle-armoured, emotionless males seen on the screen in the 1980s. The former, along with a new genre of 'gangster chic' (for example, *Lock, Stock and Two Smoking Barrels* (1998) attempt to recreate a form of hard masculinity at a time when male status has been eroded. Striff (2000) also sees the desperate attempt to retain and exert male power in the depiction of male, white collar, middle management in such 1990s films as *Glengarry Glen Ross* (1992) and *In the Company of Men* (1997). Hyper-masculinized men reject the feminine and vent aggression in the workplace by means of fax machines and voice mail and reject any relationships not driven by competition.

Turning to television, a number of commentators have argued that the whole balance of intersexual relationships has changed towards female power. Pederzini (2000), for example, sees the character of Fox Mulder in the globally popular *X-Files* as psychologically (sometimes physically) dependent on his female partner. There is a preponderance of 'soft and tender' masculinity, whether in television programmes like *Blind Date*, or in dramas and comedies like *Friends*. Parham (2000) argues that new man-ism has even penetrated the traditionally male domain of sports coverage, in particular football and snooker. He shows how new man imagery features in trailers, post-match analyses and opening credits in order to 'speak' to a wider audience, especially women. Meanwhile, Patrick (2000) demonstrates how a variety of representations of black masculinity occur in current pop videos, from the polymorphous and perverse (as in the case of Michael Jackson and Prince) to the heterosexual and hegemonic (as, for example, in rap videos), to those employing Afro-centricism, postfeminism and queer politics to fracture master narratives of conventional masculinity.

Mode 4: visual and performative

The male body is a vehicle of meanings. By the 'visual' I obviously mean how the male body is depicted (in painting, photography and advertising, in sculpture and photography) and through clothing and the physique. Some of the studies of masculinity and the body which I have found most informative are Bordo (1993), Dyer (1997), on the construction of 'whiteness', and Pfeil (1995), on contradictions in the construction of white heterosexuality. An important book is that by Nixon (1996), who employs **semiotics** to decode and 'read' visual representations of the masculine in advertising and style magazines. Worth consulting is MacKinnon (1998) on the presentation of the male body in photography, film and on television, Johansson (1998) on bodybuilding and Blake (1996) on sport and the male body. The journal *Body and Society* is an excellent indicator of current work.

By 'the performative' I mean, obviously, the enactment of 'the masculine' through speech and body language in a wide variety of settings, examples of which are everyday encounters, pop concerts, military spectacles (like the annual Trooping of the Colour), rituals and pageants, dramatic performances and major sporting events. An interesting and original light thrown on the performance of masculinity is the emerging body of work on dance (Burt 1995, 1998, 2000; Hargreaves 2000; Roebuck 2000). In addition, a most important contribution is being made by sociolinguists in analysing men's language usage in social interaction (for example, Holmes 1995; Mills 1995; Bergvall *et al.* 1996; Johnson and Meinhof 1997; Pauwels 1998).

Mode 5: auto/biographical and documentary

The documentary mode incorporates oral and life history work and also what Stanley (1993) terms 'auto/biography' (including both autobiography and biography). I look at these in turn, each of which can be enormously revealing about the lived experience of masculinity and male subjectivities, both in the present and in the past.

I start with oral history, in which the voice of the past is captured through interviewing a number of respondents and focusing on a particular event or topic. An example would be Paul Thompson's (1975) excellent reconstruction of life in the Edwardian era. To illustrate the strengths of oral history, Tosh (2000) quotes from a project on mining in South Wales and which is a vivid reminder of long-past working and living conditions. The respondent, already an old man when interviewed in the 1970s, describes the lodging house he lived in as a young man when he first started working underground in the early years of the twentieth century:

> There were no bathrooms. All you had was an old zinc tub and the landlady would have a couple of buckets of water on the fire. If there were five or six of you together, first of all five of you would bath the top half of the body. Everybody bathed the top half of the body in a rota. Then you stepped back into the bath and washed the bottom part of your body.
>
> (Tosh 2000: 195–6)

Good introductions on how to carry out oral and life history research are those by, for example, Henige (1982) and Thompson (1988), as well as the *Oral History Journal*. Many studies have much to tell us about masculinity-as-lived as, for example, Sutherland (1937), Chambliss (1972) and Jackson (1972) on the lives of professional thieves; Humphries (1981) on working class youth in the period 1889–1939; and Thomson (1994) on the experiences of Anzac troops in the 1915 Gallipoli campaign. However, I also have in mind a number of less academic texts which, nevertheless, make a valuable contribution to understanding the experience and enactment of masculinities in time and place. Among these are Knight (1985) on men and freemasonry; Tony Parker (1990) on male 'lifer' murderers; Siebert (1996) on mafia culture; and Holden (1998) on First World War shell shock. Much has been written about the experience of war (for example, Clayton and Craig 1999). Typical of this genre is the work of John Golley, a former Typhoon fighter-bomber pilot, who interviewed combatants and in his highly readable books built up a detailed picture of the lifestyles of aircrew during the Battle of Britain (for example, Golley 2000, 2001).

By life history work I mean the in-depth study of an individual's 'life course', a methodology which is particularly associated with the University of Chicago in the 1920s and 1930s as a way of mapping the cultural ecology of the city, from the lives of 'hobos' (Anderson 1923), gang members (Thrasher 1926) and streetwise, petty thieves (Shaw 1930) to the lives of the suburban middle class. A key figure in the revival of interest in life history work is Plummer (1983, 1995). Through his 'sociology of story' he draws attention to the social nature of making and consuming life stories, demonstrating how sociocultural agencies shape lives experienced as 'personal'. Indeed, acts often assumed as idiosyncratic and individual can be deconstructed as the product of area, time, place, sexuality, race, gender, class, age and disability (Thurston and Beynon 1995). Life stories reveal the cultural origins of male subjectivities and how what is considered 'manly' is, in fact, learned, expressed and sustained in time and place. Thurston (1996), for example, examines the construction of a masculinity based on violence and crime and the linguistic and interactional devices used by criminal men to compose and deliver their life stories. In doing so he changes the emphasis from the traditional men-as-prisoners to prisoners-as-men. He charts the 'trajectories' of men's lives in terms of a number of 'lifespheres' ranging from family, schooling, un/employment, relationships, drug and alcohol problems, criminality and so forth. While the life story is a way of accomplishing identity it is, of course, a representation in which the tellers distort, embellish, exaggerate, conceal, even lie, but these divergences from 'the truth' can themselves be significant in a number of ways. Thurston asks, too, which stories get told and which ignored? He illustrates with a detailed analysis of 'Nigel's story' and his account of a hyper-masculinity based on violence, the sexual exploitation of women, heavy drinking and criminality, in his view all originating from his bad relationship with his father. In his ongoing work Thurston has developed 'male story telling' as the basis for interventory programmes in the prison and probation services, arguing that the stories reveal how the tellers make sense of themselves at 'critical moments' in their lives and criminal careers.

Finally, I turn to autobiography and then to biography. In the United Kingdom Seidler (1989) was among the first to argue that the rationalism upon which social theory is based can be a limitation and called for a new kind of critical and reflexive auto/biographical writing about masculinity. A number have followed in his footsteps, most notably David Jackson (1990), whose autobiography is justly regarded as one of the most compelling texts about masculinity-as-experienced that has yet to be published. An interesting recent study drawing upon autobiographical data is that by Broaddus (2000), who demonstrates how 1960s American Black Panther autobiographies were a means to construct a forceful and positive black masculine identity to counter the prevailing deficiency model of the black American male. When it comes to biographical studies of masculinity *per se*, then Roper and Tosh (1991), Dawson (1994) and Rutherford's (1997) *Forever England* (with biographical studies of Rupert Brooke, T.E. Shaw and Enoch Powell) are essential reading. An example of the biographical being used to throw light on a particular individual's enactment of masculinity is Parker's (1996) short study of Bobby Moore, the 'Roy-of-the-Rovers' captain of the 1966 World Cup-winning England football side. Parker shows how, at the time of his premature death (at 50) from cancer in 1993, Moore was iconized as the 'golden boy from a golden time' and his image as a loyal, chivalrous, gentlemanly sportsman was contrasted strongly with the alcohol and drug-abusing megastars of the 1980s and early 1990s. Moore had come to symbolize not only the greatest achievement of English soccer, but also a time when football belonged to the fans, not business people and television companies, when it was still hooligan free, and when players had lifelong loyalty to their local club. Even more than this, Moore had come to stand for a golden age for England itself. He died the same year that the toddler James Bulger was murdered in Bootle and many felt Britain was degenerating into a new barbarism, epitomized by drug-ridden estates and porn videos. But, as Parker (1996) shows, Bobby Moore's ideal 'sporting masculinity' was contradicted by some aspects of his private life and nostalgia obscured the fact that the 1960s was also the decade of the Krays and London gangland killings, the Moors' murders and the horror of the slagheap slip that resulted in the unnecessary loss of children's lives at Aberfan in South Wales.

Mode 6: ethnographic

Connell (1998) looks back at the 1990s as the decade when research into masculinity looked at its construction and expression in a particular milieu or moment, for example Klein (1993) on the culture of bodybuilding or McElhinny (1994) on the gendering of police work. He pays tribute to what he terms this 'ethnographic moment' because the results not only introduced new lines of research, but also contradicted the simplifications of role theory. Among other things, masculinities emerged as diverse, enacted differently across settings and even within the same setting (for example, Barrett 1996; Messerschmidt 1997). The potential of ethnography to study how masculinity is 'brought off' in a variety of cultural settings needs to be exploited more, as in the important book entitled *Dislocating Masculinity: Comparative Ethnographies*, edited by Cornwall and Lindisfarne (1994) to which I am greatly indebted. They advance the case for ethnography as the most effective way of exploring the enactment of a range of masculinities in a variety of settings; and of investigating

> to what extent the familiar oppositions ('male–female', 'men–women' and 'masculinity–femininity') are everywhere belied by a much more complex social reality . . . [including] the enactment of hegemonic and subordinate masculinities in a single setting.
>
> (Cornwall and Lindisfarne 1994: 2, 10)

A good example of the studies included therein is one already mentioned, namely that by McElhinny (1994) of female police officers and the strategies they employed to demonstrate their competence in a highly masculine environment. While they adopted a masculine role and persona, becoming hard and unemotional and engaging in the physical violence the job demanded, they subverted the 'association of objectivity with masculinity by seeing themselves as objective, but not as masculine' (McElhinny 1994: 169).

Del Castillo (2000) investigated the projection of masculinity by unemployed men in Mexico City whose wives supported them by working as bar girls. As a consequence they had to overcome both their dependency on women and the fact that their wives earned their living by using their sexuality to attract and entertain other men. Another interesting study is by Swart (2000), who reported on hardline Afrikaner masculinity in post-apartheid South Africa. Once powerful, these men (followers of the disgraced former leader, Eugene Terre Blanche) have, in little over a decade, been socially marginalized. The importance of such an ethnographic approach is that it combines politics, history, racism, militarism and paramilitarism, sport, celebrity and other factors in the formation of a range of masculinities in the political and cultural cauldron which is post-apartheid South Africa. Other masculinities in post-apartheid South Africa include 'the exemplary' (for example, sporting heroes), 'the marginalized' (members of ethnic groups) and 'the dishonourable' (homosexual).

I want to conclude this section by referring briefly to four ethnographic studies I have undertaken since the mid-1980s and, in the process, stress the potential of ethnography to facilitate the generation of **grounded theory** to 'explain', in this case, specific, setting-related masculinities in schools, hospitals and prisons.

Victoria Road Comprehensive School (Beynon 1985, 1989)

This study examines how masculinity was defined in Lower School, described by its headmaster as 'a school for men'. I observed pupils 'sussing-out' teachers and typing them (as 'good', 'bad', 'woman', and so on) on the basis of how they responded to the provocations and, also, documented the basis upon which teachers judged and typed pupils (as 'good', 'disruptive', 'abnormal', and so on). The central role played in this by actual and threatened ('symbolic') violence was investigated. The 'mirror image' templates operated by the dominant pupils and teachers ensured that in the definition of manliness enshrined in the social order of the school, the outright winners were 'manly' pupils' ('rough diamonds') and 'hard' (but consistently fair) teachers, who got on well together; the outright losers were 'unmanly' pupils and 'soft' and 'poncey' teachers, including women teachers.

Vaughan Ward, Hilltop Hospital (Beynon 1987)

A few years later I undertook an ethnographic study of Hilltop Hospital, South Wales. The fieldwork focused on Vaughan Ward, in which the patients were elderly men, mostly former miners, dockers and steel workers. Masculinity, in our consumerist society, is presented as the sole preserve of young and middle-aged men and it is tacitly assumed that as men age they relinquish not only their sexuality, but something of their masculinity as well, thus becoming 'lesser men', even 'non-men'. However, it was quite evident from the outset of the fieldwork that these old and ill, mostly bed-bound men, retained a strong masculine identity. It was, given the circumstances, mostly displayed verbally through, for example, repartee with nurses, often based on sexual innuendo, public displays of being able to cope with pain and extreme discomfort, loud condemnation of 'unmanly behaviour', male camaraderie and supportive comments ('buck-ups'), male 'sporting chat', standing up to 'ignorant' doctors and arguing for patient rights, stories of proud achievements during their working lives, comparing themselves favourably to the 'soft' younger generation of today, accounts of personal feats of bravery (especially in the Second World War), sporting achievements and sexual exploits, boasting about wealth and achievement, and validatory accounts of well-spent lives as fathers and husbands as opposed to the 'goings on' in present-day 'immoral' society.

Green Acres Junior School (Beynon 1993)

The study documented how computers were being introduced to a junior school in South Wales. The teacher in charge of computing, Mr Micro, signalled it clearly as an essentially male activity. I recorded how girls were repeatedly harassed and brushed off the 'male domain' of computers by groups of boys I termed 'computer bullies' ('Hannah, it's not a toaster, it's a computer!'), who constructed a macho identity based on their domination of keyboards and expertise. Computing became a ready resource for boys to construct and express a strong, masculine identity based on 'superior' technological knowledge and keyboard expertise.

The Young Prisoner's Unit, Cityton Prison (Beynon 2001)

This study is ongoing and examines a masculinity based on pride in being a 'professional' and 'successful' criminal. It documents the young men's backgrounds and 'criminal careers', life in prison and its culture, and the daily enactment of 'prison masculinity' by both the young prisoners and the officers. In particular, the study explores 'mitigation strategies', the devices by which many prisoners 'explained away' their crimes. For example, many invoked the figure of Robin Hood to 'explain' their criminality in that they perceived themselves, like him, to be victims of 'unjust justice', thus justifying 'stealing from the rich to benefit the poor', and so on.

Conclusion: the need to research contemporary masculinities

In this book I have attempted to demonstrate how men experience and live masculinity in various ways: the evidence for the diversity of men's lives and the diversity of masculinity is all around us. The link between men's lived experiences and masculinities needs to be more extensively investigated. Far more needs to be known about how men live their lives, both now and in the past, what is going on (and has gone on) inside their heads, and what guides their presentation of masculinity. There is ample scope for students to devise their own research projects utilizing one or more of the six modes outlined above. In the mean time I shall end as I began – by repeating David Morgan's (1992) suggestion that the initial study of masculinity can be embarked upon very near to home indeed, perhaps as a prelude to more field-orientated research using life history, oral history or ethnography. I'll lead by example. My son left home a few years ago and his bedroom bookshelves now contain a mixture of books he has left behind and books of mine that have overflowed from other parts of the house. They are a mixture, therefore, of old sociology studies, past and recent novels, sporting autobiographies, a few biographies. A quick glance immediately throws up a treasure trove of resources that has much to say about masculinity, both now and in the past. Here is what the start of just one shelf contained in order of appearance:

R.L. Keiser's (1979) *The Vice Lords: Warriors of the Street*; Brian Jackson and Dennis Marsden's (1962) *Education and the Working Class*; Brian Jackson's (1968) *Working Class Community*; Michael Young and Peter Willmott's (1957) *Family and Kinship in East London*; Richard Hilary's (1942) Second World War classic, *The Last Enemy*; Andy McNab (1993) *Bravo Two Zero*; Bret Easton Ellis's (1991) *American Psycho*; Daniel Defoe's (1720) *Robinson Crusoe*; Irvine Welsh's (1993) *Trainspotting*; Mark Twain's (1876) *Tom Sawyer*; an extensive collection of sporting autobiographies; David McCullough's (1992) monumental biography of President Harry Truman; and piles of pop audio tapes (from Dire Straits to recent artists and groups I do not recognize) and a collection of videos (from old black and white films recorded off television to recent blockbusters). So:

> Go to the bookshelf and take down a book. Any book, don't hesitate for too long. Start reading. What does it tell you about men and masculinity?
>
> (Morgan 1992: 48)

Further reading

Beynon, J. (1985) *Initial Encounters in a Secondary School*. Lewes: Falmer.

Burt, R. (1995) *The Male Dancer: Bodies, Spectacle and Sexuality*. London: Routledge.

Clayton, T. and Craig, P. (1999) *Finest Hour*. London: Hodder and Stoughton.

Jackson, D. (1990) *Unmasking Masculinity: A Critical Autobiography*. London: Unwin Hyman.

Knights, B. (1999) *Writing Masculinities: Male Narratives in Twentieth Century Fiction*. London: Macmillan.

Parker, T. (1990) *Life after Life: Interviews with Twelve Murderers*. London: Secker and Warburg.

Schoene-Harwood, B. (2000) *Writing Men: Literary Masculinities from Frankenstein to the New Man*. Edinburgh: Edinburgh University Press.

Turner, B. and Rennell, T. (1995) *When Daddy Came Home: How Family Life Changed Forever in 1945*. London: Pimlico.

GLOSSARY

Against the grain: a way of reading which resists the dominant ideology of the text. Texts are read in deconstructive ways 'from the margins' to reverse the ideology and thus expose it as ideology. For example, much nineteenth century colonial adventure literature, reread through the lens of feminism, reveals extreme misogyny and, through postcolonial spectacles, extreme racism and bigotry.

Angry masculinity: refers to the figure of the rebellious young male anti-heroes in British novels in the latter part of the 1950s who objected to the values of the British middle class.

Arnoldian masculinity: a masculinity based on Christianity and promoted by the reforming educationist Dr Thomas Arnold (1795–1842), who was appointed headmaster of Rugby School in 1828. A feature of Muscular Christianity was the promotion of physical fitness through a regime of physical exercise and participation in team sports. A picture of Rugby School in Arnold's time is provided in *Tom Brown's Schooldays* (1856), a novel by Thomas Hughes (1822–96).

Beveridge Report: influential 1944 report, chaired by Sir William Beveridge (1879–1963), which pointed the way forward for the postwar reconstruction of Britain, particularly in social reform, education, housing, welfare and health.

Black masculinities: a controversial term referring, in particular, to a hegemonic stereotype of cool and stylish hyper-masculinity, primarily associated with, and promoted by, black sports' stars and pop celebrities. Clatterbaugh (1998: 26) comments that it cannot be assumed 'that all who partake of black masculinity are black, or that all black persons, if they are masculine, are 'black masculine'.

Boy code: the term used by Pollack (Pollack and Shuster 2000) to describe the narrow regime of behaviour into which boys in the United States are inculcated and by which, he argues, they are damaged.

Breadwinner: the traditional role of the man as wage-earner and head of his family which was at the heart of patriarchy. Breadwinning was the hallmark of the respectable working class man, being central to his sense of masculinity.

Bricolage masculinity: a term to capture the more mobile and fluid versions of masculinity currently on offer and which allow some individuals to 'channel hop' across these as the occasion demands (for example, from work to leisure-pleasure domains) and in which fashion and 'image management' are clearly primary elements.

British race: the racist notion, widely accepted in the nineteenth and into the twentieth centuries, that British imperial ascendancy was, in fact, attributable to Anglo-Saxon racial superiority.

Celebrity culture: term to describe our image and media-saturated society, dominated by style-setting, iconized individuals. (Also used: 'celebrity dads', 'celebrity industries', 'celebrity lads')

Clarendon Commission: the 1864 report that examined the philosophy, purpose and curriculum of the leading British public schools as 'factories for gentlemen'.

Commercial masculinity: the commercial appropriation and exploitation of masculinity that took place throughout the 1980s in advertising, fashion, menswear, magazines, film and television, along with the representational and promotional strategies behind this market-led enterprise. (Also used: 'commercial man', 'commercial narratives of gender')

Commodification of masculinity: the commercial devices whereby masculinity, in all its varieties, is packaged and promoted in advertising, fashion and the media. Masculinity was, thus, rendered a 'product' to be bought and sold much like any other. (Also used: 'commodified masculinities'; 'men's market')

Consumerism: the reification of 'desires' over 'needs' in a culture in which personal worth is increasingly defined in terms of fashionable appearance, possessions and overall 'style'. (Also used: 'consumerist society'; 'me-culture'; 'product fetishism'; 'spectatorial consumer subjectivity')

Creative advertising: the way in which advertising from the 1960s on used extensive market research to identify and open up niche markets and develop innovative ways and images, in order to promote fresh brands in a range of media in an increasingly competitive consumerist environment.

Crisis in masculinity: contemporary masculinity is held to be in crisis because the central tenets upon which previous masculinity was based (patriarchy, bread-winning, tasks demanding strength) have been eroded. (Also used: 'crises in masculinities')

Cultural borrowings: term used by Cornwall and Lindisfarne (1994) to indicate the way in which different versions of masculinity can cross over and influence each other so that hybridization occurs.

Deep structure of masculinity: the idea that there is an elemental masculinity common to all men, whatever their social or geographical positioning. It is difficult, however, to identify what these might consist of without resorting to crude biologism.

Discourse: designates the forms of representation, conventions and habits of language use producing specific culturally and historically located meanings. In recent times the term has been particularly associated with the work of the French philosopher Michel Foucault (1926–84) which drew attention to how things are written about, spoken about and thought about in a given society at a given time, who has the power to impose these meanings, and the sources of that power.

Discourse analysis: in modern cultural theory the term is used to indicate any coherent body of statements that produces a self-confirming account of reality by defining an object and generating concepts with which to analyse it. The analysis of 'discursive practices', 'discursive strategies' and 'discursive regimes' reveal how meanings are constructed, how they operate and from where they originate. (Also used: 'discursive construction'; 'discursive themes'; 'discursive unsexing')

Dramaturgy: the American sociologist Ervin Goffman's (1922–82) influential way of analysing everyday life as a form of theatre and how people as 'actors' take on 'roles', follow 'scripts' and even engage in self-presentational 'performances', using 'props'. (Also used: 'dramaturgical accomplishment')

Ecriture masculine: term associated most recently with Knights (1999) and Schoene-Harwood (2000), who examine the historical development of literary representations of masculinity, particularly contemporary re-imaging of masculinity beyond the confines of traditional gender formations and which subverts patriarchal masculinity. Complements 'ecriture feminine', or the inscription of the feminine body and female difference in language and text.

End of masculinity: MacInnes' (1998) argument that traditional notions of masculinity are dying and that this is to be welcomed as it is liberating for both men and women.

Eugenics: the highly controversial 'science' of improving humankind through selective breeding associated with Francis Galton (1822–1911). Viewed with extreme suspicion since its espousal by the Nazis, eugenistic ideas still shape attitudes to, for example, immigration and the rights of mentally ill people and of handicapped people to procreate.

Fabian Society: an influential socialist society founded in 1884 by Sydney (1859–1947) and Beatrice (1858–1943) Webb. Fabianism provided a way of implementing socialist ideas by concentrating on practical reforms and shunning grandiose theoretical speculation.

Family capitalism: a phase of capitalism dominated by entrepreneurial local capitalists and characteristic of the nineteenth century and which has now been replaced by corporate capitalism operating on a global scale.

Fascist masculinity: an ideology driven masculinity based on extreme nationalism and militarism, the glorification of violence and the pursuit of dominance, and ideologies of racial supremacy (documented in Theweleit 1987; Mosse 1996), which is likely to surface in periods of political and economic turmoil (as in the Germany of the 1920s and 1930s).

Fatherless America: Blenkenhorn's (1995) term to indicate the rising numbers of fathers in the United States who absent themselves from their progeny and even lose all contact with them.

Feminism and the feminist movement: the origins of the 'first wave' feminism is generally set in the late eighteenth century and owes much to the writings of Mary Wollstonecraft Godwin (1759–97). The movement grew in strength and organization throughout the second half of the nineteenth century in Britain and the United States, focusing on female suffrage. 'Second wave' feminism occurred in the late 1960s and 1970s in association with the contemporary Civil Rights movement and the New Left student protest movement. Feminists argued that formal political equality had not brought social and cultural equality and inaugurated a wide-ranging critique of patriarchy. Contemporary 'third wave' feminism remains united in opposition to male domination and continues the quest for equal rights in all areas of society. Feminism of employment: term to indicate, first, how in all advanced economies male participation rates in the labour force have been falling and female ones rising during the 1980s and 1990s, and, second, how technological advance and more sophisticated labour-saving machinery have transformed the nature of work, enabling women to do jobs formerly demanding brute male strength.

Feminization of employment: term to indicate, first, how in all advanced economies female participation rates in the labour market have been rising during the 1980s and 1990s and, second, how technological advance and more sophisticated labour-saving machinery have transformed the nature of work, enabling women to undertake jobs formerly demanding brute male strength.

Fordism: term coined in 1930 by the Italian Marxist Antonio Gramsci (1891–1937) to refer to the manner in which Henry Ford (1863–1947), the American car manufacturer, pioneered the mechanization and automation of production and applied scientific management techniques to work practices. Fordism has subsequently come to be associated with the mass production of standardized items by largely unskilled or semi-skilled workers.

Freikorps: military units (surviving from the First World War) which espoused extreme militarism and nationalism and who were a leading force behind the resurgence of Fascism in Germany in the 1920s and 1930s (detailed in Thewelweit 1987).

Gay movement: a concerted attempt on a number of fronts since the 1960s by gay men and their supporters to attack injustice and homophobic discrimination against homosexuals. (Also used: 'gay iconography'; 'gay masculinity')

Gender: the social construction of male and female identities and distinguishable from the biological distinction between men and women. (Also used: 'gender ideologies'; 'gender map')

Gentleman-bachelor: a stock figure in Victorian romance and detective literature, epitomized most famously by Sir Arthur Conan Doyle's (1859–1930) Sherlock Holmes.

Global masculinities: the term used by Connell (1998) to describe the differential impact of globalization on the formation and enactment of masculinities, given that men everywhere are now affected in one way or another by the interaction of the 'global-on-the-local' and the 'local-on-the-global' (Beynon 2000).

Goffmanesque presentation: associated with the work of the American sociologist Ervin Goffman (1922–82), who analysed the strategies and signals 'people-as-actors' employ in their self-presentations and 'performances' (Goffman 1971). (See 'Dramaturgy')

Grounded theory: associated with Glaser and Strauss (1967) referring to the process whereby theory is generated out of empirical data rather than imposed upon it. Such micro-level theorizing is substantiated by and firmly 'grounded in' this ethnographic data.

Hegemonic masculinity: a form of masculinity that gains ascendancy at a time or in a place and to which other forms are subordinate. One of the first uses of 'hegemony' was by Antonio Gramsci (1891–1937) to indicate the predominance of one social class over others and it has now been applied to the analysis of masculinities, particularly by Connell (1995) and Mac an Ghail (1994, 1996). (Also used: 'hegemonic colonial masculinity'; 'hegemonic masculine values'; 'hegemonic representations')

Homosociality: a term used by Eve Kosofsky Sedgwick (1985) to depict comradeship, close friendship and intimacy between men that is distinguishable from homosexuality. (Also used: 'homosexual–homosocial gaze'; 'homosocial friendships')

Hybridized masculinity: expressions of masculinity which are the outcome of cultural cross-overs and borrowings from other versions of masculinity. (Also used: 'bricolage masculinity'; 'hybrid scripts')

Hyper-masculinity: an exaggerated display of the overtly 'masculine', both in appearance and behaviour conveyed by, for example, shows of physicality and 'hardness' in the form of highly developed muscularity, tattoes, shaven heads, demeanour and speech.

Ideology: refers to a system of ideas that succeeds in hiding any contradictions for the person by whom the ideology is lived. An ideology, then, is simultaneously a way of looking at, interpreting and living the world. Other definitions differ on whether an ideology is necessarily a form of false consciousness, whether it can give a 'true' insight into reality, or whether it represents and furthers the interests of a particular class. The French Marxist Louis Althusser (1918–90) argues that ideology is always a distortion of reality. (Also used: 'gender ideologies'; 'manhood ideologies')

'Image-ing' masculinity: the commercialization of masculinity through a wide range of advertising and media techniques employing carefully crafted images. (Also used: 'image industries'; 'imaged masculinity'; 'image management')

Imperial man: a patriotic servant of Queen, country and Empire in the nineteenth century, the attributes of whom were adventurousness and fearlessness, stoicism, emotional reticence and coolness under pressure, a strong sense of fair play and justice, physical fitness and the capacity to take the lead as the occasion demanded.

Kitchen sink literature: a term applied to British literature (particularly drama) of the latter half of the 1950s because of its emphasis upon working class life and experience.

Laddism: essentially a commercial project associated with (in particular) the 1990s magazine *Loaded*, in which young men were extolled to engage in heavy drinking, drug-taking and riotous behaviour. (Also used: 'Jack-the-lad'; 'lad culture'; 'laddist personas'; 'ladette'; 'lad mags'; 'old lad'; 'lad phenomenon'; 'telly lads')

Life scripts: the idea that life trajectories are largely 'scripted' by age, class, belief system, geographical and cultural location and that, consequentially, the scope for individual agency is comparatively limited.

Literary masculinities: how masculinity in all its variety is represented in literature and the narrative and stylistic devices used to do this, issues discussed in both Knights (1999) and Schoene-Harwood (2000).

Machismo: a highly masculinist culture based on violence (or the threat of violence) and domination and particularly associated with the Hispanic nations. (Also used: 'macho masculinity'; 'macho men')

Male backlash: term coined by Faludi (1991) to express the fear that the advances made by feminism since the 1960s might be subjected to a male fightback and reversed.

Male certainties: benefits previously accruing from 'being a man' and attributed solely on the basis of being male. (Also used: 'male domain'; 'maleness'; 'male roles'; 'male toys')

Male liberation: general term for movements established by men largely in response to feminism and particularly prevalent in the United States, most of which are pro-feminist and which seek to escape the narrow strictures imposed by patriarchy upon both women and men themselves.

Male subjectivities: how masculinity has been internalized by individual men and how this perception guides their presentations of 'the masculine'.

Masculine essence: the idea that in spite of the wide variety in the expression of masculinity there is, nevertheless, a fundamental aspect which is common to all, but which stops short of identifying what this might be. (See also: 'deep structure of masculinity')

Masculinism: the culture of 'being a man', traditionally based on physical power, aggression and competition. (Also used: 'masculinist narratives'; 'masculinist imaginings')

Masculinities: plural term now widely used in academe and indicative of the wide variations in masculinity, in how it is understood, enacted, experienced and lived. (Also used: 'masculine essence'; 'masculine ideals'; 'masculine masquerade'; 'masculine rights'; 'masculine scripts'; 'masculine shift'; middle class masculinity; 'mythic masculinity'; 'sporting masculinity'; 'telemasculinity'; 'working class masculinity')

Masculinity-as-a-text: places emphasis upon masculinity as something diverse and culturally constructed and enacted ('authored' and 'performed') in time and place, rather than rigidly fixed by biology.

Men-as-victims: highly controversial idea voiced by a number of writers (for example, Coward 1999; Faludi 1999) that feminist advances and the spread of equity policies have now resulted in men being disadvantaged in a number of areas (for example, in respect to aspects of the law pertaining to divorce settlements and child custody arrangements). Faludi (1999) particularly refers to men's entrapment by consumerism.

Men-in-the-mirror: term used by Edwards (1997) to describe the promotion since the 1980s of narcissistic versions of masculinity based on fashion and appearance.

Men's movements: attempts by groups of men world-wide to address masculinity, some adopting a pro-feminist stance, others masculinist ones (Clatterbaugh 1990). The many forms include the Promise Keepers (religious revivalists, studied by Messner 1997); the 'mythopoeticism' of Bly (1991); anti-sexist, pro-feminist groups in both the United States and Britain (Seidler 1989, 1991); the Canadian White Ribbon Campaign of men against male violence towards women; the far right Militia Movement (widely held responsible for the Oklahoma City bombing); and militant fundamentalists and misogynists like the Afghan Taliban.

Moral panic: a concern, often comparatively trivial, which becomes magnified out of all proportion, particularly by the media.

Muscular Christianity: a training for manhood and masculinity associated with British public schools in the nineteenth century and based on strenuous physical exercise and the inculcation of strong Christian beliefs.

Narrative analysis: the use of methods (derived from linguistics) to investigate how narrative techniques operate to allow the reader to generate meanings. Narratology denotes the branch of literary study devoted to the study of narratives and forms of narration.

New lad: a resurrection as a commercial project in the 1990s (and particularly associated with the magazine *Loaded*) of the historical figure of 'Jack-the-lad', namely that of a riotous young man enjoying life to the full. (Also used: 'ladette'; 'lad phenomenon')

New man: a term often used in at least two separate senses. In the first, originating in the 1970s, the new man is a pro-feminist (the ideology-led 'nurturer' tradition), attempting to put his 'sharing and caring' beliefs into practice in his daily life. In the second sense, originating in the 1980s, he is a hedonist, seeking out the latest fashions and taking a great interest in grooming and appearance (the consumerism-led 'narcissist' tradition). The argument in this book is that these two have now become inextricably linked in a vague, generalized 'new man-ism'. (Also used: 'old man')

New man-ism: a widely held notion that, while acknowledging that men and the male role have now changed, is unclear how and so indiscriminately scrambles together elements derived from both the 'nurturer' and 'narcissist' strands.

New masculinists: a term associated with groups of men, particularly in the United States, who are seeking to regain many of the 'rights' previously enjoyed by men and which have been largely lost (see Clatterbaugh 1990; Bly 1991, 1997).

New masculinity: a vague term usually defined in terms of its differences to the now outmoded patriarchal masculinity ('old masculinity') of the recent past.

New times: a term used by Hebdige (1989) and others reflecting a belief that postmodernity has ushered in genuinely transformatory possibilities in politics, culture, lifestyles and civil rights facilitated by the advent of technology with a global reach.

Obsessive moral masculinization: term used by Gilmore (1990) to encapsulate the diverse and damaging pressures placed on boys in the latter half of the nineteenth and early twentieth centuries to become 'manly men' to participate in the Imperial mission. This is echoed in contemporary writers like Pollack (2000), who regard the 'boy code' into which American boys are socialized as a behavioural and emotional straitjacket.

Old patriarchs: term used by McDowell and Court (1994) and McDowell (1997) to describe the 'old school tie' middle and senior managers of the immediate post-Second World War decades (see Roper 1991). (Also used: 'old industrial man')

Ornamental culture: Faludi's (1999) term for consumerism, which she now sees as having objectified and commodified masculinity and the male body and so trapped men in a similar manner to the way in which it has long trapped women and objectified the female body. (Also used: 'ornamental entrapment'; 'ornamentalization of men'; 'ornamental imprisonment')

Pathological masculinity: a damaging masculinity associated with individual men who cannot live with failure, threats to their sense of masculinity, or cope with setbacks to their self-image. This often results in them resorting to violence with catastrophic consequences.

Patriarchy: the social system by which men enjoyed economic ascendancy and power over women who were, as a result, confined to the private world of the home (see, for example, Walby 1986, 1990). (Also used: 'patriarchal masculinity')

Physical culture: a strict regime of training using exercises and weights devised and promoted by the professional 'strongman' and publishing entrepreneur, Eugene Sandow (1867–1925).

Playboy: a soft porn magazine, the brain child of the American editor and publisher Hugh Hefner, which first appeared in December 1953, featuring the then unknown Marilyn Monroe posing nude. A unlikely mixture of 'girly' photographs, practical advice on sexual problems, men's 'buddy talk' and articles of a high literary standard by leading writers of the day combined to make the magazine both notorious and successful. Hefner soon expanded his empire to include nightclubs, staffed by his scantily clad 'bunnies'. Over the past half-century many have tried to imitate the *Playboy* formula, most notably *Penthouse*, which first appeared in the early 1960s. Successful, narcissistic 'Playboy man', half sexual predator, half intellectual, was a highly seductive, scandalous and liberating alter ego for many men trapped in the grey world of a Britain still struggling to recover from the ravages of the Second World War.

Politics of looking: the way in which the commercialization of masculinity in the 1980s resulted in men being invited to look at and admire other men's appearance and bodies in ways previously reserved for 'male-on-female looking'. (Also used: 'politics of identity')

Popular Imperialism: term used by Dawson (1994) to describe the enthusiasm towards the Imperial mission shown by the British public in the latter half of the nineteenth century.

Post-Fordism: the more flexible phase of production that has replaced the mass production characteristic of Fordism and, instead, is based upon niche marketing and short production runs.

Postmodernism and **postmodernity:** the phase of capitalism based on high technology, short-run production and niche marketing, which has replaced the previous, mass production phase of modernity and reflects the way in which capital now operates on a global scale in an emerging global economy. (Also used: 'postmodern times')

Queer theory: a development of the 1990s drawing upon the earlier work of gay studies, gay activists and lesbian theory and constitutuing an eclectic critique of essentializing intellectual and socio-sexual assumptions. Queer theory sets out to defamiliarize texts, attitudes and identities commonsensically assumed to have fixed meanings and which endorse heterosexuality as the norm.

Redundant male: a term first coined by the British novelist and journalist Fay Weldon in 1996 to convey the idea that men are now no longer essential to women, either as economic providers or partners in child-rearing, or even biologically, given the development of new reproductive technologies.

Re-masculinization: measures taken, either actually and/or discursively, to revitalize and improve a nation's 'stock' of men and a nation's 'masculine reputation', particularly after a humiliating setback or defeat (like, for example, the 'filmic re-fighting' of the Vietnam War in American film in the 1980s (see Jeffords 1989).

Rite of passage: associated with Van Gennep (1960) who documents the initiation ceremonies into manhood of a number of native cultures. The meaning has now been widened to include the challenges and stages of induction that novices have to pass through successfully in order to prove their aptitude for particular tasks, to be accepted into an organization or institution or to be accorded a particular status.

Scout movement: founded in Britain by Robert Baden-Powell (1857–1941). The objective was to train boys to be healthy in body and pure in mind and able to participate in homosocial activities with other boys.

Self-help discourses: Charles Smiles' (1812–1904) *Self-Help* (published in 1859) proclaimed the doctrine that people should take more responsibility for their own individual destinies and not depend on others. This was resurrected by the New Right in Britain in the late 1970s and informed Conservative Party policies under Margaret Thatcher.

Semiotics: the systematic study of signs and sign systems and what they signify, the dual origins of which lie in the work of the Swiss linguist Ferdinand de Saussure (1857–1913) and the American philosopher Charles Peirce (1839–1914).

Social facts: associated with the sociologist Emile Durkheim (1858–1917), who regarded them as the very fabric of society. For example, he argued that a rate of so many suicides per thousand of population cannot be reduced to individual cases without losing the essential meaning of a rate. A rate per thousand is a collective phenomenon and constitutes, in Durkheim's terms, a social fact.

Style press: term to describe the emergence in the 1980s of 'style manual' magazines aimed primarily at fashion-conscious, 'style literate', metropolitan young men. (Also used: 'style leaders'; 'style magazines')

Subordinate variants: Cornwall and Lindisfarne's (1994) term for varieties of non-hegemonic and marginalized masculinities.

Suffragettes: the term applied to women who were members of the Suffragist Movement and who agitated for votes for women. By 1860 their demands were gathering momentum and, in the hands of leaders like Sylvia Pankhurst and local activists like Selina Cooper, they finally achieved their goal of votes for women in the early twentieth century.

Symbolic interactionism: a branch of sociology which explores people's meanings, their definitions of the situation and the changes to these over time.

Underclass: controversial term particularly associated with the work of the American sociologist Charles Murray (1990, 1994). Murray bases his thesis on such measures as rates of dropout from the labour force, illegitimacy, family breakdown and rates of crime, both against persons and property.

Voyageurs: wise, mature and trusted older men who act as mentors and surrogate father figures to the young heroes in Victorian boys' literature.

White negro: controversial term used by Back (1994) to describe how white youth in his South London study appropriated aspects of black youth subculture as part of their own self-presentation.

Womanism: term employed by Coward (1999) to describe what she calls 'feminism's vulgate', or the easy blaming of men by women for all of society's ills. Womanism is presented as unprincipled, unlike feminism and the feminist critique.

Yob: the archetypal figure of riotous young man, up to no good and creating mayhem in urban settings, along with his alter ego, the 'lager lout'. (Also used: 'yobocracy')

Young pretenders: term used by McDowell and Court (1994) and McDowell (1997) to describe the new generation of business studies and economics graduates who flooded into middle and senior management positions in British business life in the 1980s and 1990s, ousting the 'old patriarchs' in the process.

Yuppie: a 1980s term to epitomize the young, upwardly mobile urban professional, associated with the deregulation of the Stock Market, the growth in financial services and the growth of the 'image' industries like promotion, public relations, television and advertising. (Also used: 'yuppiedom')

REFERENCES

Aitkenhead, D. (1999) Moisturiser men, *Guardian*, 6 September.

Alexander, J. (1997) Half a million men can't be wrong, *You*, 12 October.

Allan, S. (1999) *News Culture*. Buckingham: Open University Press.

Allsop, K. (1964) *The Angry Decade*. London: Peter Owen.

Anderson, P. (1961 [1923]) *The Hobo*. Chicago: University of Chicago Press.

Archer, J. (1994) Violence between men, in J. Archer (ed.) *Male Violence*. London: Routledge.

Back, L. (1994) The 'white negro' revisited: race and masculinities in South London, in A. Campbell and N. Lindisfarne (eds) *Dislocating Masculinity: Comparative Ethnographies*. London: Routledge.

Baddiel, C. (1999) Come on, you lads, it's cool to grow up, *The Times Weekend Supplement, Saturday*, 6 November.

Baden-Powell, R. (1963 [1908]) *Scouting for Boys*. London: Pearson.

Ballantyne, R.M. (2000 [1858]) *The Coral Island: A Tale of the Pacific Ocean*. London: Penguin.

Bandura, A. (1977) *Social Learning Theory*. Englewood Cliffs, NJ: Prentice-Hall.

Barrett, F.J. (1996) The organizational construction of hegemonic masculinity: the case of the United States Navy. *Gender, Work and Organization*, 3(3): 129–42.

Barrie, J.M. (1904) *Peter Pan*. London: Collins.

Belsey, C. (1980) *Critical Practice*. London: Methuen.

Benwell, B. (2000) Ironic discourse: masculine talk in men's lifestyle magazines, in Posting the Male conference abstracts, John Moores University, Liverpool, August.

Berger, M., Wallis, B. and Watson, S. (eds) (1995) *Constructing Masculinity*. New York: Routledge.

Bergvall, V.L., Ring, J.M. and Freed, R.F. (1996) *Rethinking Language and Gender Research: Theory and Practice*. London: Longman.

Bernard, J. (1981) The good provider role: its rise and fall, *American Psychologist*, 36(1): 1–12.

Beynon, J. (1985) *Initial Encounters in a Secondary School*. Lewes: Falmer.

Beynon, J. (1987) Zombies in dressing gowns, in N.P. McKeganey and S.J. Cunningham-Burley (eds) *Enter the Sociologist*. Aldershot: Avebury.

Beynon, J. (1989) A school for men: an ethnographic case study of routine violence in schooling, in J. Archer and K. Browne (eds) *Human Aggression: Naturalistic Approaches*. London: Routledge.

Beynon, J. (1993) Computers, dominant boys and invisible girls, in J. Beynon and H. Mackay (eds) *Computers into Classrooms: More Questions than Answers*. Lewes: Falmer.

Beynon, J. (1996) *Young Men, Masculinity and Crime: An ESRC Report*. Swindon: Economic and Social Research Council.

Beynon, J. (2000) General introduction, in J. Beynon and D. Dunkerley (eds) *Globalization: The Reader*. London: Athlone.

Beynon, J. (2001) Robin Hood is alive and well in 'Cityton' Prison, in H. Phillips (ed.) *Robin Hood: Interdisciplinary Studies*. Manchester: Manchester University Press.

Beynon, J. and Dunkerley, D. (1999) *Perspectives on Globalization*. Moscow: Rubrica.

Beynon, J. and Dunkerley, D. (eds) (2000) *Globalisation: The Reader*. London: Athlone.

Blake, A. (1996) *Body Language: The Meaning of Modern Sport*. London: Lawrence and Wishart.

Blenkenhorn, D. (1995) *Fatherless America: Confronting our most Urgent Social Problem*. New York: Basic Books.

Bly, R. (1991) *Iron John*. Rockport, MA: Element.

Bly, R. (1997) *Sibling Society*. London: Penguin.

Bordo, S. (1993) *Unbearable Weight: Feminism, Western Culture and the Body*. Berkeley, CA: University of California Press.

Bott, E. (1957) *Family and Social Network*. London: Tavistock.

Bourke, J. (1996) *Dismembering the Male: Men's Bodies, Britain and the Great War*. London: Reaktion.

Bowker, L.H. (1998) *Masculinities and Violence*. London: Sage.

Boyd, K. (1991) 'Knowing your place': the tensions of manliness in boys' story papers, 1918–1939, in M. Roper and J. Tosh (eds) *Manful Assertions: Masculinities in Britain since 1800*. London: Routledge.

Brannon, R. (1976) The male sex role: our culture's blueprint of manhood, in D.S. David and R. Brannon, *The Forty-Nine Per Cent Majority: The Male Sex Role*. Reading, MA: Addison Wesley.

Brittan, A. (1989) *Masculinity and Power*. Oxford: Blackwell.

Broaddus, D. (2000) Representing masculinity in 1960's Black Panther autobiographical writing, in Posting the Male conference abstracts, John Moores University, Liverpool, August.

Brod, H. (ed.) (1987) *The Making of Masculinities: The New Men's Studies*. Boston, MA: Allen and Unwin.

Brod, H. and Kaufman, M. (eds) (1994) *Theorizing Masculinities*. London: Sage.

Brook, S. (2000) The 'angry young man', class and masculinity, in Posting the Male conference abstracts, John Moores University, Liverpool, August.

Brooker, P. and Widdowson, P.A. (1986) Literature for England, in R. Colls and P. Dodd (eds) *Englishness: Politics and Culture, 1880–1920*. London: Croom Helm.

Brown, C. (1987) Great Expectations: masculinity and modernity, in M. Green (ed.) *Broadening the Context*. London: John Murray.

Browne, N. and Ross, C. (1995) 'Girls' stuff, boys' stuff': young children talking and playing, in J. Holland, M. Blair and S. Sheldon (eds) *Debates and Issues in Feminist Research and Pedagogy*. Clevedon: Multilingual Matters.

Brownmiller, S. (1975) *Against our Will: Men, Women and Rape*. New York: Simon and Schuster.

Buchan, J. (1999 [1915]) *The Thirty Nine Steps*. Oxford: Oxford University Press.

Buchbinder, D. (1994) *Masculinities and Identities*. Melbourne: Melbourne University Press.

Budd, M.A. (1997) *The Sculpture Machine: Physical Culture and Body Politics in the Age of Empire*. London: Macmillan.

Burchill, J. (1999) Way back when men were men, *Guardian*, 4 January.

Burgmann, M. (1980) Revolution and machismo, in E. Windschuttle (ed.) *Women, Class and History*. Sydney: Fontana.

Burke, J. (2000) Mothers are to blame for macho mountaineers, *Observer*, 7 April.

Burt, R. (1995) *The Male Dancer: Bodies, Spectacle and Sexuality*. London: Routledge.

Burt, R. (1998) *Alien Bodies: Representations of Modernity, Race and Nation in Early Modern Dance*. London: Routledge.

Burt, R. (2000) The performance of masculinities at the Judson Dance Theatre, in Posting the Male conference abstracts, John Moores University, Liverpool, August.

Burton, C. (1991) *The Promise and the Price*. Sydney: Allen & Unwin.

Butler, J. (1990) *Gender Trouble, Feminism and the Subversion of Identity*. New York and London: Routledge.

Butler, S. (1995 [1903]) *The Way of All Flesh*. Harmondsworth: Penguin.

Calcutt, A. (2000) *Brit Cult: An A–Z of British Pop Culture*. London: Prion.

Campbell, B. (1993) *Goliath: Britain's Dangerous Places*. London: Penguin.

Canaan, J. (1996) 'One thing leads to another': drinking, fighting and working class masculinities, in M. Mac an Ghaill (ed.) *Understanding Masculinities: Social Relations and Cultural Arenas*. Buckingham: Open University Press.

Cantarella, E. (1987) *Pandora's Daughters: The Role and Status of Women in Greek and Roman Antiquity*. Baltimore, MD: Johns Hopkins University Press.

Carrigan, T., Connell, R.W. and Lee, J. (1983) Towards a new sociology of masculinity, *Theory and Society*, 14(5): 551–604.

Castiglione, B. (1928 [1528]) *The Book of the Courtier* (translated by Sir Thomas Hoby). London: J.M. Dent.

Chambliss, B. (1972) *Box Man: A Professional Thief's Journal*. New York: Harper and Row.

Chandos, J. (1984) *Boys Together*. London: Yale University Press.

Chapman, R. (1988) The great pretender: variations on the 'new man' theme, in R. Chapman and J. Rutherford (eds) *Male Order: Unwrapping Masculinity*. London: Lawrence and Wishart.

Chibnall, S. and Murphy, R. (eds) (1999) *British Crime Cinema*. London: Routledge.

Chodorow, N. (1978) *The Reproduction of Mothering*. Berkeley, CA: University of California Press.

Christian, H. (1994) *The Making of Anti-Sexist Men*. London: Routledge.

Clare, A. (2000) *On Men: Masculinity in Crisis*. London: Chatto and Windus.

Clatterbaugh, K. (1990) *Contemporary Perspectives on Masculinity: Men, Women and Politics in Modern Society*. Boulder, CO: Westview.

Clatterbaugh, K. (1998) What is problematic about masculinities? *Men and Masculinities*, 1(1): 24–45.

Clayton, T. and Craig, P. (1999) *Finest Hour.* London: Hodder and Stoughton.

Coakley, J. (1998) *Sport in Society: Issues and Controversies*. New York: McGraw-Hill.

Cockburn, C. (1983) *Brothers*. London: Pluto.

Cockburn, C. (1991) *In the Way of Women: Men's Resistance to Sex Equality in Organisations*. London: Macmillan.

Coghill, N. (1960) *Modern Translation of Chaucer's Canterbury Tales*. Harmondsworth: Penguin.

Cohan, S. (1997) *Masked Men, Masculinity and Movies in the Fifties*. Bloomington, IN: Indiana University Press.

Cohan, S. and Hark, I.R. (eds) (1993) *Screening the Male: Exploring Masculinities in Hollywood Cinema*. London: Routledge.

Cohen, D. (1996) The financial independence of women, *Guardian Weekend*, 4 May.

Cohen, P. (1988) The perversions of inheritance: studies in the making of multi-racist Britain, in P. Cohen and H.S. Bains (eds) *Multi-Racist Britain*. London: Macmillan.

Coleman, W. (1990) Doing masculinity: doing theory, in J. Hearn and D. Morgan (eds) *Men, Masculinities and Social Theory*. London: Unwin Hyman.

Collier, R. (1995) *Masculinity, Law and the Family*. London: Routledge.

Collinson, D.L. (1988) Engineering humour: masculinity, joking and conflict in shopfloor relations, *Organisation Studies*, 9(2): 181–9.

Collinson, D.L. (1992) *Managing the Shopfloor: Subjectivity, Masculinity and Workplace Culture*. Berlin: Walter de Gruyter.

Collinson, D.L. and Hearn, J. (1994) 'Men' at 'work': multiple masculinities and multiple workplaces, in M. Mac an Ghaill (ed.) *Understanding Masculinities*. Buckingham: Open University Press.

Collinson, D.L. and Hearn, J. (eds) (1996) Naming men as men: implications for work, organisation and management, *Gender, Work and Organisation*, 1(1): 2–22.

Colls, R. and Dodd, P. (1986) (eds) *Englishness: Politics and Culture, 1880–1920*. London: Croom Helm.

Connell, R.W. (1987) *Gender and Power*. Cambridge: Polity.

Connell, R.W. (1995) *Masculinities*. Cambridge: Polity.

Connell, R.W. (1998) Masculinities and globalization. *Men and Masculinities*, 1(1): 3–23.

Connell, R.W. (2000) *The Men and the Boys*. Cambridge: Polity.

Cook, E. (1999) On cosmetics for men, *The Independent on Sunday*, 4 July.

Cornwall, A. and Lindisfarne, N. (1994) *Dislocating Masculinity: Comparative Ethnographies*. London: Routledge.

Corrigan, P. (1979) *Schooling the Smash Street Kids*. London: Macmillan.

Coward, R. (1999) *Sacred Cows*. London: HarperCollins.

Craig, S. (ed.) (1992) *Men, Masculinity and the Media*. Newbury Park, CA: Sage.

Crang, M. (1998) *Cultural Geography*. London: Routledge.

Daley, J. (2000) The racism, sexism and violence of rap culture. *Daily Telegraph*, 22 August.

Dalton, M. (1959) *Men Who Manage*. New York: John Wiley.

Daly, M. and Wilson, M. (1988) *Homicide*. New York: Aldine de Gruyter.

Davies, R. (2000) Enduring McEwan, in Posting the Male conference abstracts, John Moores University, Liverpool, August.

Dawson, G. (1994) *Soldier Heroes: British Adventure, Empire and the Imagining of Masculinities*. London: Routledge.

Defoe, D. (1963 [1720]) *Robinson Crusoe*. London: Dent.

Del Castillo, A. (2000) The crafting and performance of Mexican manhoods, in Posting the Male conference abstracts, John Moores University, Liverpool, August.

Dennis, N. and Erdos, G. (1992) *Fatherless Families*. London: Institute of Economic Affairs.

Dickens, C. (1999 [1861]) *Great Expectations*. Oxford: Oxford University Press.

Disraeli, B. (1971 [1847]) *Tancred or The New Crusade*. London: Greenwood.

Donald, R.R. (1992) Masculinity and machismo in Hollywood's war films, in S. Craig (ed.) *Men, Masculinity and the Media*. London: Sage.

Donaldson, M. (1993) What is hegemonic masculinity?, *Theory and Society*, 22: 643–57.

Doyle, J.A. (1989) *The Male Experience*. Dubuque, IL: Wm. C. Brown.

Durkheim, E. (1964) *The Rules of Sociological Method*. Glencoe, NY: Free Press.

Dyer, R. (1993) Rock, the last guy you'd have figured?, in P. Kirkham and J. Thumin (eds) *You Tarzan: Masculinity, Movies and Men*. London: Lawrence and Wishart.

Dyer, R. (1997) *White*. London: Routledge.

Easthope, A. (1986) *'What a Man's Gotta Do': The Masculine Myth in Popular Culture*. London: Paladin.

Edley, N. and Wetherell, M.S. (1995) *Men in Perspective: Practice, Power and Identity*. Hemel Hempstead: Harvester Wheatsheaf.

Edley, N. and Wetherell, M. (1996) Masculinity, power and identity, in M. Mac an Ghaill (ed.) *Understanding Masculinities*. Buckingham: Open University Press.

Edwards, T. (1994) *Erotics and Politics*. London: Routledge.

Edwards, T. (1997) *Men in the Mirror: Men's Fashions, Masculinity and Consumer Society*. London: Cassell.

Edwards, T. (2000) Sex, booze and fags: new men, new lads and the masculinity of men's style magazines. Address to the Posting the Male conference, John Moores University, Liverpool, August.

Ehrenreich, B. (1983) *The Hearts of Men: American Dreams and the Flight from Commitment*. New York: Anchor-Doubleday.

Ehrenreich, B. (1987) Foreword to K. Theweleit's *Male Fantasies*. Cambridge: Polity.

Ellis, B.E. (1991) *American Psycho*. London: Picador.

Elyot, T. (1907 [1531]) *The Governor*. London: J.M. Dent.

Falk, G. (1990) *Murder: An Analysis of its Forms, Conditions and Causes*. London: McFarland.

Faludi, S. (1991) *Backlash: The Undeclared War Against Women*. New York: Crown.

Faludi, S. (1999) *Stiffed: The Betrayal of the Modern Man*. London: Chatto and Windus.

Ferrebe, A. (2000) 1945–1960 as the origin of the anxieties of the modern English-man, in Posting the Male conference abstracts, John Moores University, Liverpool, August.

Fiske, J. (1987) *Television Culture*. London: Methuen.

Fletcher, A. (1995) *Gender, Sex and Subordination in England, 1500–1800*. New Haven, CT: Yale University Press.

Forrest, D. (1994) 'We're here, we're queer and we're not going shopping': changing gay male identities in contemporary Britain, in A. Cornwall and N. Lindisfarne (eds) *Dislocating Masculinity: Comparative Ethnographies*. London: Routledge.

Foucault, M. (1972) *The Archaeology of Knowledge*. London: Tavistock.

Foucault, M. (1977) *Discipline and Punish: The Birth of the Prison*. Harmonds-worth: Penguin.

Franklin, C.W. (1984) *The Changing Definition of Masculinity*. New York: Plenum.

Freely, M. (1999) He's 14 and his 12 year-old girlfriend is pregnant, *Guardian*, 8 September.

Frosh, S. (1987) *The Politics of Psychoanalysis: An Introduction*. London: Macmillan.

Frye, N. (1976) *The Secular Scripture*, Cambridge, MA: Harvard University Press.

Fussell, P. (1975) *The Great War and Modern Memory*. Oxford: Oxford University Press.

Gaillie, D., Marsh, C. and Vogler, C. (eds) (1994) *Social Change and the Experience of Unemployment*. Oxford: Oxford University Press.

Gardner, J. (1986) *Women in Roman Law and Society*. Bloomington, IN: Indiana University Press.

Gee, J.P., Hull, G. and Lankshear, C. (1996) *The New Work Order: Behind the Language of the New Capitalism*. Sydney: Allen and Unwin.

Gerrish, A. (1999) Unpublished research for MS3D5: Men, Masculinity and Culture, University of Glamorgan, Wales, UK.

Gibson, J. (1999) Hot off the press, *Media Guardian*, 11 January.

Gilmore, D. (1990) *Manhood in the Making: Cultural Concepts of Masculinity*. New Haven, CT: Yale University Press.

Gilroy, P. and Lawrence, E. (1988) Two tone Britain: white and black youth and the politics of anti-racism, in P. Cohen and H. Bains (eds) *Multi-Racist Britain*. London: Macmillan Education.

Girouard, M. (1981) *The Return to Camelot: Chivalry and the English Gentleman.* New Haven, CT: Yale University Press.

Glaser, B. and Strauss, A. (1967) *The Discovery of Grounded Theory.* Chicago: Aldine.

Goffman, E. (1971) *The Presentation of Self in Everyday Life.* Harmondsworth: Penguin.

Golding, W. (1954) *The Lord of the Flies.* London: Faber and Faber.

Golley, J. (2000) *The Day of the Typhoon.* London: Airlife.

Golley, J. (2001) *Hurricanes over Murmansk.* London: Airlife.

Goode, E. and Ben-Yehuda, N. (1994) *Moral Panics: The Social Construction of Deviance.* Oxford: Blackwell.

Goodwin, C. and Rushe, D. (1999) Drool Britannia, *Sunday Times,* 1 August.

Gosse, Sir Edmund (1989 [1907]) *Father and Son.* Harmondsworth: Penguin.

Gray, J. (1992) *Men are from Mars, Women are from Venus.* New York: Harper-Collins.

Green, M. (1960) *A Mirror for Anglo-Saxons.* London: Chatto and Windus.

Green, M. (1991) *Seven Types of Adventure Tale: An Etiology of a Major Genre.* University Park, PA: Pennsylvania State University Press.

Greer, G. (1999) *The Whole Woman.* London: Doubleday.

Gregorio-Godeo, E. de (2000) Representations of masculinity in contemporary women's magazines, in Posting the Male conference abstracts, John Moores University, Liverpool, August.

Gregory, A. (2000) Re-visiting the 70s: music, culture and society, in Posting the Male conference abstracts, John Moores University, Liverpool, August.

Gristwood, S. (1999) Fury of fists, *Guardian,* 14 September.

Haggard, H.R. (1885) *King Solomon's Mines.* London: Cassell.

Haggard, H.R. (1999 [1887]) *Allan Quartermain.* London: Pulp.

Hall, C. (1989) The economy of intellectual prestige, *Cultural Critique,* 12: 178–81.

Hall, P. (1998) *Cities in Civilization.* London: Weidenfeld and Nicolson.

Hanke, R. (1992) Redesigning men: hegemonic masculinity in transition, in S. Craig (ed.) *Men, Masculinity and the Media.* Newbury Park, CA: Sage.

Hannabuss, S. (1983) Islands as metaphors, *Universities Quarterly,* 38(1): 70–82.

Hantover, J.P. (1978) The Boy Scouts and the validation of masculinity, *Journal of Social Issues,* 34: 184–95.

Hardy, T. (2000 [1874]) *Far from the Madding Crowd.* Harmondsworth: Penguin.

Hargreaves, D.H. (1967) *Social Relations in a Secondary School.* London: Routledge and Kegan Paul.

Hargreaves, D. (1987) *Sport, Power and Culture.* Cambridge: Polity.

Hargreaves, M. (2000) Bleeding hysterics: melancholic masculinity and hyperbolic rage in Javier de Frutos' choreography, in Posting the Male conference abstracts, John Moores University, Liverpool, August.

Harris, I.M. (1995) *Messages Men Hear: Constructing Masculinities.* London: Taylor & Francis.

Harris, M. (1997) *Odd Man Out.* London: Pavilion.

Hartley, J. (1996) *Popular Reality: Journalism, Modernity, Popular Culture*. London: Arnold.

Healey, M. (1994) The mark of a man, *Critical Quarterly*, 36(1): 86–93.

Hearn, J. (1987) *The Gender of Oppression: Men, Masculinity and the Critique of Marxism*. Brighton: Wheatsheaf.

Hearn, J. (1990) Man's violence and 'child abuse', in *Violence Against Children Study Group: Taking Child Abuse Seriously*. London: Unwin Hyman.

Hearn, J. and Parkin, W. (1993) Organisations, multiple oppressions and post-modernism, in J. Hassard and M. Parker (eds) *Postmodernism and Organisations*. London: Sage.

Hebdige, D. (1989) After the masses, in S. Hall and M. Jacques (eds) *New Times*. London: Lawrence and Wishart.

Henige, D. (1982) *Oral Historiography*. London: Longman.

Henwood, F. and Miles, I. (1987) The experience of unemployment and the sexual division of labour, in D. Fryer and P. Ullah (eds) *Unemployed People: Social and Psychological Perspectives*. Milton Keynes: Open University Press.

Heywood, J. (1997) The object of desire is the object of contempt: representations of masculinity, in S. Johnson and U.H. Meinhof (eds) *Language and Masculinity*. Oxford: Blackwell.

Hilary, R. (1997 [1942]) *The Last Enemy*. London: Pimlico.

Hill, D. (1997) *The Future of Men*. London: Weidenfeld and Nicolson.

Hilton, I. (1999) The forgotten victims, *Guardian*, 14 September.

Hoch, P. (1979) *White Hero, Black Beast: Racism, Sexism and the Mask of Masculinity*. London: Pluto.

Hoggart, R. (1957) *The Uses of Literacy*. Harmondsworth: Penguin.

Holden, W. (1998) *Shell Shock: The Psychological Impact of War*. London: Macmillan.

Holmes, J. (1995) *Women, Men and Politeness*. London: Longman.

Holt, R. (1989) *Sport and the British: A Modern History*. Oxford: Oxford University Press.

Hornby, N. (1992) *Fever Pitch*. London: Gollancz.

Hornby, N. (1995) *High Fidelity*. London: Gollancz.

Horrocks, R. (1994) *Masculinity in Crisis: Myths, Fantasies and Realities*. London: Macmillan.

Household, G. (1999 [1939]) *Rogue Male*. London: Phoenix.

Howard, C.H.D. (1967) *Splendid Isolation*. London: Macmillan.

Hughes, T. (1999 [1856]) *Tom Brown's Schooldays*. Oxford: Oxford University Press.

Humphries, S. (1981) *Hooligans or Rebels? An Oral History of Working Class Childhood and Youth, 1889–1939*. Oxford: Basil Blackwell.

Hunt, L. (1998) *British Low Culture: From Safari Suits to Sexploitation*. London: Routledge.

Ishiguro, K. (1989) *Remains of the Day*. London: Faber.

Jackson, B. (1968) *Working Class Community*. Harmondsworth: Penguin.

Jackson, B. (1972) *Outside the Law: A Thief's Primer*. New Jersey: Transaction Books.

Jackson, B. and Marsden, D. (1962) *Education and the Working Class*. London: Routledge and Kegan Paul.

Jackson, D. (1990) *Unmasking Masculinity: A Critical Autobigraphy*. London: Unwin Hyman.

Jackson, D. (2000) Cary Grant and the construction of male identity, in Posting the Male conference abstracts, John Moores University, Liverpool, August.

Jackson, K. (1999) Why should a John be a Joan? *The Times Higher Educational Supplement*, 8 October.

James, A. (2001) Drugs, guns and fights – all in a night's work, *The Times Higher Educational Supplement*, 23 February.

Jarvie, J. (2001) Teenage boys queue up for surgery, *Sunday Telegraph*, 7 January.

Jeffords, S. (1989) *The Remasculinization of America: Gender and the Vietnam War*. Bloomington, IN: Indiana University Press.

Jenkins, D. (2000) It's a man's world, *Daily Telegraph*, 10 December.

Jensen, J., Hagen, E. and Reddy, C. (eds) (1988) *The Feminization of the Labour Force: Paradoxes and Promises*. Cambridge: Polity.

Johansson, T. (1998) *The Sculptured Body: Gym Culture, Hard Bodies and Gender Identities*. Vaxjo, Sweden: University of Vaxjo Centre for Cultural Research.

Johnson, B.S. (1973) *All Bull*. London: Quartet.

Johnson, C.M. and Robinson, M.T. (1992) *Homicide Report*. Washington, DC: Government of the District of Columbia.

Johnson, S. and Meinhof, V.H. (1997) *Language and Masculinity*. Oxford: Blackwell.

Kanitkar, H. (1994) 'Real, true boys': moulding the cadets of imperialism, in A. Cornwall and N. Lindisfarne (eds) *Dislocating Masculinity: Comparative Ethnographies*. London: Routledge.

Katz, A. (2000) Contribution to *The Ill-Adapted Male*, BBC Radio 4 programme transcript, 28 December.

Katz, J. (1988) *The Seduction of Crime: Moral and Sensual Attractions of Doing Evil*. New York: Basic Books.

Keiser, R.L. (1979) *The Vice Lords: Warriors of the Streets*. Chicago: Holt, Rinehart and Winston.

Kelvin, P. and Jarrett, J.E. (1985) *Unemployment: Its Social Psychological Effects*. Cambridge: Cambridge University Press.

Kersten, J. (1995) Constructing the enemy: xenophobia and masculinities, in *Bundesminusterium fur Wissenschaft, Forschung und Kunst (Hg.)*: Fremdenfeindlichkeit Wien, 159–77.

Kestner, J.A. (1995) *Masculinities in Victorian Paintings*. Aldershot: Scolar.

Kimmel, M.S. (ed.) (1987) *Changing Men: New Directions in Research on Men and Masculinity*. Newbury Park, CA: Sage.

Kimmel, M.S. (1994) Masculinity as homophobia: fear, shame and silence in the construction of gender identity, in H. Brod and M. Kaufman (eds) *Theorizing Masculinities*. Thousand Oaks, CA: Sage.

Kimmel, M.S. and Messner, M.A. (eds) (1992) *Men's Lives*. New York: Macmillan.

Kipling, R. (1966) *Collected Poems*. Oxford: Oxford University Press.

Kirkham, P. and Thumin, J. (1993) *You Tarzan: Masculinity, Movies and Men*. London: Lawrence and Wishart.

Klein, A.M. (1993) *Little Big Men: Bodybuilding Subculture and Gender Construction*. Albany, NY: State University of New York Press.

Knight, S. (1985) *The Brotherhood*. London: Grafton (Collins).

Knights, B. (1999) *Writing Masculinities: Male Narratives in Twentieth Century Fiction*. London: Macmillan.

Landesman, C. (1997) Boyzone, *Media Guardian*, 1 December.

Laqueur, T.W. (1990) *Making Sex: Body and Gender from the Greeks to Freud*. Cambridge, MA: Harvard University Press.

Lawrence, T.E. (1962 [1926]) *The Seven Pillars of Wisdom*. Harmondsworth: Penguin.

Lemann, N. (2000) The battle over boys: will feminists or their foes win the teenage soul? *New Yorker*, 10 July.

Letort, D. (2000) Representations of masculinity in Film Noir, in Posting the Male conference abstracts, John Moores University, Liverpool, August.

Lightfoot, L. (2000) Black culture holding back boys, *Daily Telegraph*, 21 August.

Lippert, J. (1977) Sexuality as consumption, in J. Snodgrass (ed.) *For Men Against Sexism*. Albion, CA: Times Change Press.

Lloyd, M. and Thacker, A. (2000) Masculinity and class in *The Full Monty* and *Brassed Off*, Posting the Male conference abstracts, John Moores University, Liverpool, August.

Low, G.C-L. (1993) Histories, narratives and images of imperialism, in E. Carter, J. Donald and J. Squires (eds) *Space and Place: Theories of Identity and Location*. London: Lawrence and Wishart.

Lowerson, J. (1993) *Sport and the English Middle Classes, 1870–1914*. Manchester: Manchester University Press.

Lyndon, N. (1993) *No More Sex War: The Failures of Feminism*. London: Mandarin.

Mac an Ghaill, M. (1988) *Young, Gifted and Black*. Milton Keynes: Open University Press.

Mac an Ghaill, M. (1994) *The Making of Men: Masculinities, Sexualities and Schooling*. Buckingham: Open University Press.

Mac an Ghaill, M. (ed.) (1996) *Understanding Masculinities: Social Relations and Cultural Arenas*. Buckingham: Open University Press.

McCracken, E. (1993) *Decoding Women's Magazines*. London: Macmillan.

McCullough, D. (1992) *Truman*. New York: Simon and Schuster.

Macdonald, R. (1993) *Sons of the Empire: The Frontier and the Boy Scout Movement, 1890–1914*. Toronto: University of Toronto Press.

McDowell, L. (1997) *Capital Culture: Gender at Work in the City*. Oxford: Blackwell.

McDowell, L. and Court, G. (1994) Performing work: bodily representations in merchant banks, *Environment and Planning: Society and Space*, 12: 727–50.

McElhinny, B. (1994) An economy of affect: objectivity, masculinity and the gendering of police work, in A. Cornwall and N. Lindisfarne (eds) *Dislocating Masculinity: Comparative Ethnographies*. London: Routledge.

McEwan, I. (1998) *Enduring Love*. London: Vintage.

Macherey, P.A. (1978) *Theory of Literary Production*. London: Routledge.

MacInnes, J. (1998) *The End of Masculinity*. Buckingham: Open University Press.

McKay, J., Messner, M.A. and Sabo, D. (2000) *Masculinities, Gender Relations and Sport*. Thousand Oaks, CA: Sage.

McKee, L. and Bell, C. (1986) His unemployment, her problem: the domestic and marital consequences of male unemployment, in S. Allen, A. Watson, K. Purcell and S. Woods (eds) *The Experience of being Unemployed*. London: Macmillan.

MacKenzie, J.W. (1987) The imperial pioneer and hunter and the British masculine stereotype in late Victorian and Edwardian times, in J.A. Mangan and J. Walvin (eds) *Manliness and Morality: Middle Class Masculinity in Britain and America, 1800–1940*. Manchester: Manchester University Press.

MacKinnon, K. (1998) *Uneasy Pleasures: The Male as Erotic Object*. London: Cygnus Arts.

McMahon, A. (1993) Male readings of feminist theory, *Theory and Society*, 22(5): 675–696.

McNab, A. (1993) *Bravo Two Zero*. London: Bantam.

McNab, A. (1995) *Immediate Action*. London: Bantam.

Magor, D. (1999) Unpublished research for MS3D5: Men, Masculinity and Culture, University of Glamorgan, Wales, UK.

Mahawatte, R. (2000) Superheroes in post-silver age comics, in Posting the Male conference abstract, John Moores University, Liverpool, August.

Mangan, J.A. (1981) *Athleticism in the Victorian and Edwardian Public School*. Cambridge: Cambridge University Press.

Mangan, J.A. and Walvin, J. (eds) (1987) *Manliness and Morality: Middle Class Masculinities in Britain and America, 1800–1940*. Manchester: Manchester University Press.

Mangan, M. (1997) Shakespeare's First Action Heroes: critical masculinities in culture both popular and unpopular, unpublished paper.

Margolis, J. (1995) Last orders for the 'new lad' fad, *Sunday Times*, 23 April.

Marsden, D. and Duff, E. (1975) *Workless: Some Unemployed Men and their Families*. Harmondsworth: Penguin.

Martin, N. (2000) Fears over here of rap's violence and obscenity, *Daily Telegraph*, 21 August.

Mason, P. (1982) *The English Gentleman: The Rise and Fall of an Ideal*. New York: Morrow.

Mellen, J. (1978) *Big Bad Wolves: Masculinity in American Film*. London: Elm Tree Books.

Men's Health Forum (1999) *Men's Health Forum Report*. London.

Messerschmidt, J.W. (1986) *Capitalism, Patriarchy and Crime*. Lanham, MD: Rowman and Littlefield.

Messerschmidt, J.W. (1993) *Masculinities and Crime*. Lanham, MD: Rowman and Littlefield.

Messerschmidt, J.W. (1997) *Crime as Structured Action: Gender, Race, Class and Crime in the Making*. Thousand Oaks, CA: Sage.

Messner, M.A. (1997) *The Politics of Masculinities: Men in Movements*. Thousand Oaks, CA: Sage.

Miedzian, M. (1992) *Boys Will Be Boys*. London: Virago.

Mills, S. (ed.) (1995) *Language and Gender: Interdisciplinary Perspectives*. London: Longman.

Moir, A. and Moir, B. (1998) *Why Men Don't Iron: The Real Science of Gender Studies*. London: HarperCollins.

Moller, D. and Hemelrigk, S. (1999) When Dad walks away, *Reader's Digest*, June.

Money, T. (1997) *Manly and Muscular Diversions: Public Schools and the Nineteenth Century Sporting Revival*. London: Duckworth.

Moore, R. and Gillette, D. (1990) *King, Warrior, Magician and Lover: Rediscovering the Archetypes of the Mature Masculine*. New York: Harper.

Moore, S. (1996) *God's Gym*. London: Routledge.

Morgan, D.H.G. (1992) *Discovering Men*. London: Routledge.

Mori Poll (1999) Bringing up children, *Market and Opinion Research International*, 3 June.

Morrison, B. (1993) *And When Did You Last See Your Father?* London: Granta.

Mort, F. (1988) 'Boys Own?' Masculinity, style and popular culture, in R. Chapman and J. Rutherford (eds) *Male Order: Unwrapping Masculinity*. London: Lawrence and Wishart.

Mort, F. (1996) *Cultures of Consumption: Masculinities and Social Space in Late Twentieth Century Britain*. London: Routledge.

Mosse, G.I. (1996) *The Image of Man: The Creation of Modern Masculinity*. Oxford: Oxford University Press.

Murray, C. (1990) *The Emerging British Underclass*. London: Institute of Economic Affairs.

Murray, C. (1994) *Underclass: The Crisis Deepens*. London: Institute of Economic Affairs.

Newbolt, H. (1953) *Collected Poems*. London: Faber.

Newburn, T. and Stanko, E.A. (eds) (1994) *Just Boys Doing Business? Men, Masculinities and Crime*. London: Routledge.

Newell, W.R. (ed.) (2000) *What is a Man? Three Thousand Years of Wisdom on the Art of Manly Virtue*. London: HarperCollins.

Newson, J. and Newson, E. (1963) *Patterns of Infant Care in an Urban Community*. London: Allen and Unwin.

Nixon, S. (1996) *Hard Looks: Masculinities, Spectatorship and Contemporary Consumption*. London: UCL Press.

Ochs, E. (1992) Indexing gender, in A. Duranti and C. Goodwin (eds) *Rethinking Context: Language as an Interactive Phenomenon*. Cambridge: Cambridge University Press.

Orwell, G. (1950) *The Road to Wigan Pier*. Harmondsworth: Penguin.

Orwell, G. (1957 [1939]) Boys' weeklies, in *Selected Essays*. Harmondsworth: Penguin.

Osgerby, B. (1998) *Youth in Britain since 1945*. Oxford: Blackwell.

Owen, W. (1996) *The Pity of War: Poetry*. London: Phoenix.

Parham, J. (2000) The 'new man' in televised sport, in Posting the Male conference abstracts, John Moores University, Liverpool, August.

Parker, A. (1996) Sporting masculinities: gender relations and the body, in M. Mac an Ghaill (ed.) *Understanding Masculinities*. Buckingham: Open University Press.

Parker, T. (1990) *Life after Life: Interviews with Twelve Murderers*. London: Secker and Warburg.

Parkinson, M. (2000) The king of the people's game, *Daily Telegraph*, 28 February.

Parsons, T. (1999) *Man and Boy*. London: HarperCollins.

Patrick, M. (2000) Compositing African-American masculinities in videos, in Posting the Male conference abstracts, John Moores University, Liverpool, August.

Pauwels, A. (1998) *Women Changing Language*. London: Longman.

Pederzini, B. (2000) An analysis of male self-representation in contemporary television shows, in Posting the Male conference abstracts, John Moores University, Liverpool, August.

Penman, I. (2000) Over-loaded, in *Frank Magazine* (in association with the *Observer*), June.

Pfeil, F. (1995) *White Guys: Studies in Postmodern Domination and Difference*. London: Verso.

Phillips, A. (1999) On hugs and wails and highly involved males, *Guardian*, 17 March.

Phillips, R. (1997) *Mapping Men and Empire: A Geography of Adventure*. London: Routledge.

Plain, G. (2000) Keynote address on the novelist Ian Rankin to the Posting the Male conference, John Moores University, Liverpool, August.

Pleck, J.H. and Sawyer, J. (eds) (1974) *Men and Masculinity*. Englewood Cliffs, NJ: Prentice-Hall.

Pleck, J.H. and Thompson, E.H. (1987) The structure of male norms, in M.S. Kimmel (ed.) *Changing Men*. Newbury Park, CA: Sage.

Plummer, K. (1983) *Documents of Life*. London: Allen & Unwin.

Plummer, K. (1995) *Telling Sexual Stories: Power, Change and Social Worlds*. London: Routledge.

Podmore, D. and Spencer, A. (eds) (1987) *In a Man's World*. London: Tavistock.

Polk, K. (1994) Masculinity, honour and confessional homicide, in T. Newburn and E.A. Stanko (eds) *Just Boys Doing Business? Men, Masculinities and Crime*. London: Routledge.

Polk, K. and Ranson, D. (1991) Patterns of homicide in Victoria, in D. Chappell, P. Grabosky and H. Strang (eds) *Australian Violence: Contemporary Perspectives*. Canberra: Australia Institute of Criminology.

Pollack, W.S. with Shuster, T. (2000) *Real Boys' Voices*. New York: Random House.

Ponting, I. (2000) Obituary: Sir Stanley Matthews, *The Independent*, 25 February.

Powell, A. (1999) Whatever happened to real men? *Guardian*, 21 August.

Pringle, R. (1989) *Secretaries Talk*. London: Verso.

Raven, C. (1999) All men are bastards, *Guardian*, 9 February.

Ridley, M. (1999) Violence: let it all out or keep it buttoned up? *Daily Telegraph*, 13 September.

Ridley, Y. and Goodchild, S. (1999) Bare knuckle is all the rage, *Independent on Sunday*, 19 September.

Robinson, S. (2000) Putting the stud back into gender studies, *The Times Higher Education Supplement*, 15 December.

Roebuck, C. (2000) Dancing against the grain: alternative visions of masculinity in contemporary Western theatre dance, in Posting the Male conference abstracts, John Moores University, Liverpool, August.

Roper, M. (1991) Yesterday's model: product fetishism and the British company man, 1945–1985, in M. Roper and J. Tosh (eds) *Manful Assertions: Masculinities in Britain since 1800*. London: Routledge.

Roper, M. and Tosh, J. (eds) (1991) *Manful Assertions: Masculinities in Britain since 1800*. London: Routledge.

Ross, J. (1999) *The Nineties*. London: Ebury.

Rowe, D. (1999) *Sport, Culture and the Media*. Buckingham: Open University Press.

Rutherford, J. (1997) *Forever England: Reflections on Masculinity and Empire*. London: Lawrence and Wishart.

Rutherford, J. (2000) Keynote address to Posting the Male conference, John Moores University, Liverpool, reported in *The Times Higher Education Supplement*, 25 August.

Ryle, S. (2000) Boys will be boys in the bathroom, *Observer*, 9 April.

Sandow, E. (1894) *On Physical Training: A Study in the Perfect Type of Human Form*. London: Gale and Polden.

Sandow, E. (1904) *Body Building: Man in the Making*. London: Gale and Polden.

Schacht, S. (1996) Misogyny on and off the pitch: the gendered world of male rugby players, *Gender and Society*, 10(5): 550–65.

Schoene-Harwood, B. (2000) *Writing Men: Literary Masculinities from Frankenstein to the New Man*. Edinburgh: Edinburgh University Press.

Scully, D. (1990) *Understanding Sexual Violence*. London: HarperCollins.

Seaman, L.C.B. (1973) *Victorian England: Aspects of English and Imperial History, 1837–1901*. London: Methuen.

Sedgwick, E.K. (1985) *Between Men: English Literature and Male Homosocial Desire*. New York: Columbia University Press.

Segal, L. (1988) Looking back in anger: men in the fifties, in R. Chapman and J. Rutherford (eds) *Male Order: Unwrapping Masculinity*. London: Lawrence and Wishart.

Segal, L. (2000a) Opening address to Posting the Male conference, John Moores University, Liverpool, August.

Segal, L. (2000b) Contribution to *The Ill-Adapted Male*, BBC Radio 4 programme transcript, 28 December.

Seidler, V.J. (1989) *Rediscovering Masculinity*. London: Routledge.

Seidler, V.J. (1991) *Recreating Sexual Politics*. London: Routledge.

Shail, R. (2000) Changing constructions of masculinity in 1960's British cinema, in Posting the Male conference abstracts, John Moores University, Liverpool, August.

Shaw, C.R. (1930) *The Jack Roller: A Delinquent Boy's Own Story*. Chicago: University of Chicago Press.

Shepherd, J. (1990) Violent crime in Bristol, *British Journal of Criminology*, 30(3): 289–305.

Shields, R. (1992) *Lifestyle Shopping: The Subject of Consumption*. London: Routledge.

Siebert, R. (1996) *Secrets of Life and Death*. London: Verso.

Silverman, R.A. and Kennedy, L.W. (1987) Relational distance and homicide: the role of the stranger, *Journal of Criminal Law and Criminology*, 78: 272–308.

Simon, W. (1996) *Postmodern Sexualities*. London: Routledge.

Skovmand, M. (1987) The mystique of the bachelor gentleman in late Victorian masculine romance, in M. Green (ed.) *Broadening the Context*. London: John Murray.

Smiles, S. (1996 [1859]) *Self-Help*. London: Institute of Economic Affairs.

Snodgrass, J. (ed.) (1977) *For Men Against Sexism*. New York: Times Change Press.

Sommers, C.H. (2000) *The War Against Boys*. New York: Simon and Schuster.

Southwell, T. (1998) *Getting Away with It: The Inside Story of 'Loaded'*. London: Ebury.

Spicer, A. (1999) The emergence of the British tough guy: Stanley Baker, masculinity in the crime thriller, in S. Chibnall and R. Murphy (eds) *British Crime Cinema*. London: Routledge.

Stanko, E.A. (1994) Challenging the problem of men's individual violence, in T. Newburn and E.A. Stanko (eds) *Just Boys Doing Business?* London: Routledge.

Stanley, L. (1993) On autobiography in sociology, *Sociology*, 27(1): 41–52.

Stevenson, R.L. (1992 [1886]) *The Strange Case of Dr. Jekyll and Mr. Hyde*. Harmondsworth: Penguin.

Striff, E. (2000) Middle management, masculinity and the movies, in Posting the Male conference abstracts, John Moores University, Liverpool, August.

Sullivan, A. (2000) Mainlining manhood, *Guardian*, 8 April.

Sutherland, E.H. (1967 [1937]) *The Professional Thief*. Chicago: Phoenix.

Swart, S. (2000) 'Hard right' Afrikaner masculine identity in post-apartheid South Africa, in Posting the Male conference abstracts, John Moores University, Liverpool, August.

Swift, G. (1996) *Last Orders*. London: Picador.

Talmon, M. (2000) New masculinities in film and television in the 1990's, in Posting the Male conference abstracts, John Moores University, Liverpool, August.

Taubin, A. (2000) *Taxi Driver*. London: British Film Institute.

Thewelweit, K. (1987) *Male Fantasies* (volumes 1 and 2). Cambridge: Polity.

Thomas, D. (1993) *Not Guilty: In Defence of Modern Man*. London: Weidenfeld and Nicolson.

Thompson, A. (1999) 'In hot water': extract from a biography of Charles Todd, *Daily Telegraph*, 4 September.

Thompson, P. (1975) *The Edwardians: The Remaking of British Society*. Oxford: Oxford University Press.

Thompson, P. (1988) *The Voice of the Past: Oral History*, 2nd edn. Oxford: Oxford University Press.

Thomson, A. (1994) *Anzac Memories: Living with the Legend*. Oxford: Oxford University Press.

Thomson, A. (1999) *The Singing Line*. London, Chatto and Windus.

Thrasher, F. (1963 [1926]) *The Gang*. Chicago: University of Chicago Press.

Thurston, R. (1996) Are you sitting comfortably? Men's storytelling, masculinities, prison culture and violence, in M. Mac an Ghaill (ed.) *Understanding Masculinities*. Buckingham: Open University Press.

Thurston, R. and Beynon, J. (1995) Men's own stories, lives and violence: research as practice, in R.E. Dobash, R.P. Dobash and L. Noaks (eds) *Gender and Crime*. Cardiff: University of Wales Press.

Tillner, G. (1997) Masculinity and xenophobia: the identity of dominance, conference paper, UNESCO Male roles and masculinities in the perspective of a culture of peace conference, Oslo, September.

Tolson, A. (1977) *The Limits of Masculinity*. London: Tavistock.

Tosh, J. (1991) Domesticity and manliness in the Victorian middle class: the family of Edward White Benson, in M. Roper and J. Tosh (eds) *Manful Assertions: Masculinities in Britain since 1800*. London: Routledge.

Tosh, J. (2000) *The Pursuit of History*, 3rd edn. London: Longman.

Townsend, R. (1997) *Manhood at Harvard*. New York: Norton.

Toynbee, P. (1987) The incredible, shrinking 'new man', *Guardian,* 6 April.

Toynbee, P. (1998) The myth of powerful women, *Guardian*, 6 May.

Turner, B. and Rennell, T. (1995) *When Daddy Came Home: How Family Life Changed Forever in 1945*. London: Pimlico.

Twain, M. (1964 [1876]) *Tom Sawyer*. London: Dent.

Vale de Almeida, M. (1996) *The Hegemonic Male: Masculinity in a Portuguese Town*. Oxford: Berghahn.

Van Gennep, A. (1960) *The Rites of Passage*. Chicago: University of Chicago Press.

Viner, K. (1999) Manhunting, *Guardian Weekend*, 4 September.

Walby, S. (1986) *Patriarchy at Work*. Cambridge: Polity.

Walby, S. (1990) *Theorizing Patriarchy*. Oxford: Blackwell.

Walker, C.R. and Guest, R.H. (1952) *The Man on the Assembly Line*. Cambridge, MA: Harvard University Press.

Wacquant, L.J.D. (1995) Why men desire muscles, *Body and Society*, 1(1): 163–79.

Weber, M. (1930) *The Protestant Ethic and the Spirit of Capitalism*. London: Allen & Unwin.

Weeks, J. (1995) *Invented Moralities*. Cambridge: Polity.

Weldon, F. (1998*) Analysis*, BBC Radio 4 transcript, March.

Weldon, S. (1998) Interview with Rosalind Coward, in R. Coward, *Sacred Cows: Is Feminism Relevant to the New Millennium?* London: HarperCollins.

Welsh, I. (1993) *Trainspotting*. London: Minerva.

Westwood, S. (1990) Racism, black masculinity and the politics of space, in J. Hearn and D.H. Morgan (eds) *Man, Masculinity and Social Theory*. London: Unwin Hyman.

Whyte, W.F. (1955) *Street Corner Society*. Chicago: University of Chicago Press.

Whyte, W.H. (1956) *The Organization Man*. New York: Simon and Schuster.

Williams, H. (1911) Four famous authors for boys, in *Empire Annual for Boys*. London: Empire Press.

Willis, P. (1977) *Learning to Labour*. Farnborough: Saxon House.

Willis, P. (1984) Youth unemployment: thinking the unthinkable, *Youth and Policy*, 2(4): 17–36.

Willott, S. and Griffin, C. (1996) Men, masculinity and the challenge of long-term unemployment, in M. Mac an Ghaill (ed.) *Understanding Masculinities*. Buckingham: Open University Press.

Wolf, N. (1990) *The Beauty Myth*. London: Vintage.

Wollaston, S. (1997) With 'xtremely' healthy circulation, *Media Guardian*, 24 February.

Yeandle, S. (1995) Change in the gender composition of the workforce, conference paper, European Sociological Association conference, Budapest, September.

York, P. (1982) *The Official Sloane Ranger Handbook*. London: Ebury.

York, P. and Jennings, C. (1995) *Peter York's Eighties,* London: BBC Publications.

Young, M. and Willmott, P. (1957) *Family and Kinship in East London*. London: Routledge and Kegan Paul.

INDEX

Page references in bold type indicate a glossary entry

CULTURES OF POPULAR MUSIC

Andy Bennett

- What is the relationship between youth culture and popular music?
- How have they evolved since the second world war?
- What can we learn from a global perspective?

In this lively and accessible text, Andy Bennett presents a comprehensive cultural, social and historical overview of post-war popular music genres, from rock 'n' roll and psychedelic pop, through punk and heavy metal, to rap, rave and techno. Providing a chapter by chapter account, Bennett also examines the style-based youth cultures to which such genres have given rise. Drawing on key research in sociology, media studies and cultural studies, the book considers the cultural significance of respective post-war popular music genres for young audiences, with reference to issues such as space and place, ethnicity, gender, creativity, education and leisure. A key feature of the book is its departure from conventional Anglo-American perspectives. In addition to British and US examples, the book refers to studies conducted in Germany, Holland, Sweden, Israel, Australia, New Zealand, Mexico, Japan, Russia and Hungary, presenting the cultural relationship between youth culture and popular music as a truly global phenomenon.

Contents
Introduction – Post-war youth and rock 'n' roll – Sixties rock, politics and the counter-culture – Heavy metal – Punk and punk rock – Reggae and Rasta culture – Rap music and hip hop culture – Bhangra and contemporary Asian dance music – Contemporary dance music and club culture – Youth and music-making – Whose generation? Youth, music and nostalgia – Glossary – References – Index.

c.192pp   0 335 20250 0 (Paperback)   0 335 20251 9 (Hardback)

COMPASSION, MORALITY AND THE MEDIA

Keith Tester

- Why do the reports and representations of suffering and misery move us?
- What are we likely to do about it and why?
- Why do people take part in telethon appeals?

Most of us have watched television or read newspapers and been moved to compassion by the suffering and misery that we see. We know that many people suffer thanks to war, famine or environmental catastrophe. But what do the reports and representations of the suffering and misery of others actually mean to media users? *Compasssion, Morality and the Media* seeks to answer this question and offers an engaging narrative through which it becomes possible to think about the role of journalists as moral agents. The author explores the tensions between the intentions of journalists, the horizons of the audience and the priorities of media institutions. This is a book which deals with important issues that have been relatively neglected in the academic study of the media. It is accesssible and relevant and opens up a new terrain for research and teaching on the media as a moral force. Students taking undergraduate courses on the media and others with a wider interest in media morality will find it to be compelling reading.

Contents
Introduction – Parameters for a debate – Compassion fatigue and the ethics of the journalistic field – The compassion of the audience – Lifting the lid on compassion – Telethons, investments and gifts – Conclusion – Glossary – References – Index.

160pp   0 335 20513 5 (Paperback)   0 335 20514 3 (Hardback)